ABOUT THE AUTHOR

Clarence Duff, PhD, currently lectures in psychology in the Department of Liberal Arts and Science at Humber College and is also professor of counselling and psychology at Canada Christian College and School of Graduate Theological Studies. He received his bachelor of science (BSc) degree in psychology and master of arts (MA) degree in professional counselling from Liberty University. He received his master of science (MS) and PhD degrees in educational psychology from Capella University. He is a member of the American Psychological Association and the Ontario Association of Consultants, Counsellors, Psychometrics and Psychotherapists. Dr. Duff's writing career began in the mid 1980s as a developer and writer of Bible study lessons for his church. His desire to take his writing to new levels occurred after completing his MA thesis at Liberty University. To date he has written several published works.

In addition to his relentless passion for learning and academics, Dr. Duff's life-long goal is in leading people to an understanding of their inner potential and capacity. He strongly believes that most people are only vaguely aware of what they are capable of. One of his research interests is in the areas of thinking styles and perception. His workshops and seminars are geared toward effective thinking for psychological wellness. In addition to bringing awareness in thinking for change, Dr. Duff, because of his theological background and strong Christian conviction, also has a strong interest in integrating psychological findings with biblical truths.

Dr. Duff lives with his wife, Anne, and four children in Brampton, Ontario.

Clarence Duff, Ph.D.

Discovering
THE EAGLE
Within

A Guide to
Understanding Your
Inner World of
Potential and Thoughts

DISCOVERING THE EAGLE WITHIN
Copyright © 2013 by Clarence Duff, PhD

Scripture taken from the New King James Version. Copyright © 1982 by Thomas Nelson, Inc. Used by permission. All rights reserved.

Printed in Canada

ISBN: 978-1-77069-769-0

Word Alive Press
131 Cordite Road, Winnipeg, MB R3W 1S1
www.wordalivepress.ca

Cataloguing in Publication information available from Library and Archives Canada.

Dr.

Dedication

*This book is lovingly dedicated to my wife, Anne,
and children, Stephanie, Christopher, Brittney and Nicholette.*

To: My friend Sister Pearlina.
May you live to enjoy the
fruits of your hands.
Happy 62nd Birthday
(Ps. 91.)
April 29th 2013.

Missionary Walters
with all my
love

TABLE OF CONTENTS

PREFACE

My inspiration to write this book came out of my attempt to integrate psychological findings on how the human mind works with theological teachings about the image of God, in which humans were created. It became clear to me that when God created humans he invested in us mental capacities that, when used correctly, can move our lives forward productively. It follows that, while the image of God in us has been marred by sin, our God-given mental capacities can still be used in productive ways. This means we still possess the capacity for change, growth, and greatness. I wrote this book to help people improve on the way they think and approach life. I want them to understand that they not only possess a mind capable of greatness but also have been invested with God-given capacities for such.

Discovering the Eagle Within is not just another book that attempts to motivate individuals toward thinking positively or changing habits. Neither is it about how to concentrate your thoughts to attract things into your life metaphysically. As the reader will notice, while the book is grounded in Christian theology, it is not about quoting Scriptures to indoctrinate the reader. Rather, it delves into how God has created us and expects us to function as productive human beings in a broken and confused world. It takes the reader on a personal journey of self-discovery, self-reconstruction, and self-repositioning.

Although the book is about meaningful change, it is not just about a shift in perspective or a shift from negative to positive thinking. Because most of who we are and what we are capable of is neither automatically displayed on the screen of our consciousness nor given to us in a manual upon our arrival into the world, we live out our lives ignorant of our true potentials, possibilities, and capacities. This book is written to take readers on one of the most fascinating and transformational journeys of self-discovery ever.

Discovering the Eagle Within draws from my own and others' personal experiences and is also solidly based on credible information synthesized from a range of topics in the psychological sciences. It sets forth how to overcome challenges, set goals, steer your life forward in particular directions, and change your mind from believing "I can't" to an astounding "Yes, I can." It takes you into the very heart of the world of thought and thinking and shows you how to bridge the gap between where you are and where you desire to be and from who you are to what you can become.

From the first page to the final thoughts, *Discovering the Eagle Within* takes you on a journey of self-discovery, challenging you at every turn while at the same time showing you how to extend the limits of your mind. After you have read this book, you will never be the same.

This book is written for everyone, from the lay person, high school and post-secondary students to professionals working with people and parents who have the responsibility to help shape their children's thinking. Because this book is about change and becoming, it cuts across the dimensions of the human experience, age, occupation, culture, education, and socioeconomic status.

I invite you on a journey of understanding the capacity and potential of your thinking.

chapter one

An INCREDIBLE Design

There is nothing more awesome, more fascinating,
and more wonderful than knowing that we were created
with incredible possibilities and potential.

Regardless of one's position or perspective regarding the origin of the human race, one thing is certain, and to this everyone must attest: human beings are far more fascinating, complex, and intelligent than any other creature on the earth. Although it is true that humans share some biological and physical characteristics with animals, the human potential far surpasses the limits of all other earthly creatures. It has been found, for example, that about 98 percent of human and chimpanzee deoxyribonucleic acid (DNA) is similar. This means there is a whole lot of biological similarity between humans and chimps. It is not difficult to see why some believe that we may have evolved from them. But how do we explain such similarity?

It's simple. Man's body was formed from the same material as the animals were. In this case, we must expect that there would be some very close biological similarities between us and them. This is the reason why we are just as dependent on the nutrients and produce of the earth as they are. This is not rocket science.

However, although the human brain has similarities to the brains of some animals, it differs profoundly in many ways. Let's examine three of these differences: capacity, complexity, and potentiality.

No one can deny that the human brain is far more powerful than the brains of animals. For example, unlike animals, our brains are wired to learn, develop, and change over the course of a lifetime. Our brains have infinite capacity for learning and memory. They also have the capacity to reorganize themselves in response to learning and experience. This means that even at an advanced age we are still capable of learning and change. This is called neuroplasticity, which is discussed in more detail later in this chapter.

In addition to capacity, the complexity of the brain is puzzling to scientists. They continue to be amazed at how the brain, with its hundreds of millions of neural networks, carries out its myriad of fascinating tasks with astonishing efficiency. Parts of the brain are responsible for planning, thinking, feeling, seeing, hearing, movement, perceiving, and a host of other things, and there is precise coordination between interconnected neural networks and brain regions.

Scientists now believe that the human brain may be more complex than the known universe itself. This is because the number of neural connections that can be made is inconceivable. Scientists believe they may outnumber the stars in the known universe. This is astounding! However, it makes perfect sense when we understand that we were created to have dominion in the world.

The next difference is potentiality. No one really knows what the human mind is capable of. Because the brain can extrapolate, visualize, imagine, and conceptualize, there's just no telling the extent of its potential and possibilities. Given time, it can accomplish whatever it can visualize. Its full potential, therefore, cannot be imagined, measured, or calculated by anything known to us presently. No instrument or scale has been developed that can measure its capabilities. The more scientists study the human mind, the more mystery it unfolds and the more interesting it becomes. In fact, the more they study the mind, the more they realize how little they know about it.

In addition to the three primary areas of difference between humans and animals, there are also differences in several other areas. First, unlike animals, we can think and transform our thoughts into reality. We can formulate plans, devise strategies, and develop motives for our actions. While a dog is drawn into a mating experience by pheromones, a man may have several reasons apart from biology for being attracted to a female.

Second, we can feel guilty for failing in our responsibilities and justified for actions we deem to be right or good.

Third, there is a part of us that appears to reach out and even yearn for a sort of intangible experience beyond what can be encountered through our physical senses. These experiences include such things as understanding meaning, purpose, and interconnectedness, which appear to be unique to humans.

Fourth, we can reason, extrapolate, and determine the best course of action based on careful consideration of alternatives and their possible consequences.

Finally, we have a variety of emotions, all of which are connected to our thought life at some level. Can you imagine a big angry dog coming at you and then deciding at the last moment not to hurt you because it just remembered that if it hurt you it would be put down (killed)?

Humans are moved by more than mere biological drives. The spirit within each of us, in combination with our neurological/biological design, is responsible for our amazing capacities and incredible potential. Therefore we should not be distracted by our biological similarities to animals; we should be more concerned about the capability and potential of the design itself. Coming to grips with who we really are and what we are capable of doing is a necessary first step toward understanding our incredible design and our purpose for being.

The human brain and mind are by far the most fascinating objects of study. For example, we now know that although the human mind is directly associated with the brain, there are characteristics of the mind that cannot be fully explain simply by brain processes. Yet one cannot speak of the mind without reference to brain processes. This is because the mind is intimately connected to the brain in ways that transcend our present understanding. They are inseparable. Whatever affects the brain affects the mind, and whatever affects the mind in turn affects the brain. For example, one cannot generate a thought that does not activate a brain process. One cannot feel an emotion that does not affect thought.

In addition, the brain's capacity for learning and permanent memory is unlimited. This means if you should live to be 100,000 years old, you would not be able to exhaust your brain's learning or memory capacity.

Although we do not yet understand all there is to know about the universe, no one can deny that our scientific knowledge of it is greater than it was 100 years ago and will be greater 100 years from now. Humans have the unique capacity to understand the universe and phenomena in it. It is built into our unique design.

It is important to note that many of the assumptions regarding human limitations in the past have been demolished. There is no doubt that humans have limitations. However, what people classify as limitations are merely problems of the present that have not yet been solved. Given time and the acquisition of new knowledge, the human mind can devise ways to solve long-standing problems. For example, not many years ago it was deemed impossible to verbally communicate with someone miles away, to fly like a bird in the sky, to see people beyond your immediate field of vision, to have an entire library on top of your desk, or to situate thousands of residents in a very small space. Today, as we chart new paths and develop new ways of doing things through rapid advancements in science and technology, what were seen as impossibilities in the past are now not only accomplishments but milestones to move pass. In fact, the accomplishments and scientific strides we made in the past ten years are now seen as ancient technology as we map new scientific paths. Of all the creatures on earth, only humans possess minds capable of studying their own nature and complexities.

Let the reader be advised that in some cases throughout this book the terms *brain* and *mind* will be used interchangeably. In other cases, where distinction needs to be made regarding specific functions of the mind as distinguished from brain processes, the term *mind* will be use in context.

Probably one of the greatest discoveries that have been made in brain science in modern times is neuroplasticity or brain plasticity. Previously it was believed that the neural pathways in the brain become fixed as we get older. However, over the last three decades many studies by psychologists and other brain scientists have revealed that the brain never stops changing and adjusting in response to learning and new experiences.

Norman Doidge, an eminent Canadian psychiatrist and researcher, has called neuroplasticity one of the most extraordinary and fascinating discoveries of the twentieth century (Doidge 2007). Ours brains have a lifelong ability to rearrange or reorganize neural pathways in response to learning or new experiences. In other words, as we think, learn, and acquire new skills and knowledge, the brain must continue to make functional changes to represent such new skills and knowledge. The discovery of the ability of the brain to change with thinking, learning, acting, and experience has not only shed new light on the capacity of our minds but has also challenged us to rethink what we have long thought of as human limitations. Our limitations really are just in our heads.

What makes social, intellectual, and even spiritual change across a lifespan possible? Neuroplasticity is the very reason why people can learn and change, even in old age. Without the brain's ability to rearrange itself, conversion on any level would not be possible. We are redeemable simply because we possess the capacity for change in mind and behaviour. However, as will be observed throughout this book, we change not merely when our thoughts change but when our thinking changes.

When you think a simple thought you activate chemical actions in your brain. For example, when you think sad thoughts your mind either triggers or inhibits the release of certain chemicals in the brain. Even the amount of chemical released sometimes depends on what you are thinking about. The more you think about something, the more it changes you, not only on the inside but also in your behaviour. Interestingly, the Bible teaches that the more we think about something and practice it, the more we are changed by it. The Bible also teaches that mental attitude can be cultivated and nurtured, leading to more durable behaviour (Proverbs 23:7; Philippians 4:8; Galatians 5:22-23).

Bear in mind that none of this can happen without corresponding changes in the neural operation of the brain. This means that neural processes are affected by change in thoughts and thinking, and vice versa.

Scientists now know that the brain can actually repair itself after some types of brain damage. Dr. Norman Doidge, in his book *The Brain That Changes Itself,* discussed a number of cases reported by scientists where the brain healed itself after various types of events, including strokes, without surgery or medication. He explained that one of the most fascinating discoveries of the twentieth century in neuroscience is that thinking, learning, and behaviour can turn our genes on and off, leading to changes in our brain structure. Later in this text we will explore the positive and negative implications of this phenomenal human capability.

To illustrate the idea of neuroplasticity, imagine making an impression with one of your feet in sand. In order for the impression of your foot to appear, changes must occur in the sand. The shape of the sand changes as your foot presses into it. Likewise, the neural circuitries in your brain must reorganize in response to every new experience and learning that is impressed upon them.

No matter how long you live, you will never exhaust the brain's ability to reorganize itself with new experiences and learning. Furthermore, the idea of brain plasticity helps us understand that human ability and potential is not determined solely by our genetic endowment. It suggests that human beings are meant to develop and change with thinking, learning, and new experiences. This has great significance to, and in fact undergirds, all our discussions in this text. Bear in mind that the central purpose of this book is discovering that we were created for greatness.

Uniquely Wired for Change and Greatness

Understanding the nature, complexity, and creative abilities of the human brain alerts us not only to the intricacy of its design but also to its awesome potential and possibilities. Each person's brain is genetically and uniquely wired in ways that allow him or her specific talents and abilities as well as unique ways of perceiving, thinking, and responding to the world. Although our genetic inheritance does set some limits on what we can do, because of brain plasticity and learning our genetic inheritance does not have the last say. For example, while learning mathematics comes quite easily for some individuals because of brain plasticity, others can work hard to achieve the same level of competence. Some are born with their brains wired in ways that allow them to easily coordinate their motor skills. Others may be wired for extraordinary scientific work with little talent in certain motor skills. The secret in steering our lives in certain direction and achieving success lies in discovering how our particular brain works and building on those abilities it allows us. When you discover how your brain works and what particular strengths are wired into it, you will go through life feeling less frustration and achieving much more success.

It is important to note that the unique wiring of our brain, although giving us certain latitude in our abilities, is only the beginning of the story. These natural capacities must be cultivated and developed so that their utility can reach beyond and above the basic limits set by neural connections. A person may have been born with special motor coordination, but unless he or she develops this ability it will never reach its full potential and be maximized. In other words, nature needs nurture, and nurture needs nature. They were meant to work together. Think of how many people work in jobs and pursue careers that are incompatible with how their brains work. Think also of those who live in confusion because they are not sure what particular path in life to take and those living in frustration because they have chosen the wrong career or no career at all.

The Mind and Its Capabilities

Knowledge of how the mind works and how to order our thinking is life-changing. The nature of the human mind has fascinated philosophers, scientists and scholars throughout the centuries. Today, although research has uncovered new knowledge and shed new light on the mind-brain phenomenon, we are still light years from fully understanding the nature, complexity and capacity of the human mind. This is quite understandable, given that the brain is the most complex object of study in the known universe. In fact, we should not be surprised if we never reach a full understanding of all the complexities of the human brain.

Although an extensive discussion on the science and philosophy of mind is beyond the scope of this text, to understand our inner potential and embark on the journey of self-discovery it is necessary to peek into the inner workings of the most complex entity in the universe—our brains.

The capabilities of the mind are those powers the Creator invested in our mental world through which we are able to consciously and intentionally move our lives forward and purposefully effect changes in ourselves and our environment. These abilities include thinking, reasoning, determining, feeling, remembering, imagining, extrapolating and being self-aware. With these domains of abilities we humans can accomplished just about anything we put our minds to. For example, birds are extremely skillful in building nests, but no matter how many times a bird's nest gets destroyed by wind or other means, it rebuilds it in the same fashion with the same type of material. This is true of other animals as well. There is clearly no significant indication of learning, change, or improvement resulting from past experience. The beaver builds dams by cutting down trees across the narrowest part of a stream and then piling up sticks, mud, rocks and other debris to block the flow of water. This activity is repeatedly by dam-building beavers everywhere in much the same way over time with no particular change in its pattern.

This is, however, not so with humans. We improve on the works of our hands or the works of others based on experience and future expectations. We can change the way we do things in the present by reflecting on the failures of the past. We can also change things in the present in expectation or anticipation of how the future might be. We can extrapolate, using known information to make projections. From a single thought, each person can formulate ideas and plans of grandeur. With imagination people can construct images and move across the three dimensions of time—past, present and future. We can reflect on how a past experience could have been different given known variables. Each of us can construct a possible future scenario in our mind and mentally work out precise details of how it can be accomplished, modifying variables to fit with circumstances. In other words, we can imagine how things can appear and be in a possible future. We can even go further and construct how we desire the future to be. This will be discussed in more detail later.

Our volitional ability gives us our willpower, the power to freely choose between alternatives. We can determine our path and destiny at any given time by a single choice. In fact, it is fair to say that we are active participants in the creation of our future and destiny by the choices we make each moment of our lives. Later in this text we will discuss the nature of destiny and the rethinking of it.

Not only can we use our willpower to choose freely, we can also use it to overcome counterproductive impulses to achieve challenging goals. Our volitional ability sets us apart from all other earthly creatures in that with it we are not limited to any one situational restraint. When faced with two or more alternatives, we can chose freely any of them, even one we know is not good for us.

Through our capacity to feel we can experience the things around us. We can experience our desires, joys, expectations, thoughts and so on. Not only can we experience these things, we can give meaning to them. For example, feelings generated from contemplating a certain action may detour us from carrying out the action or motivate us toward actually doing it. Our feelings and the meaning we give to them play important roles in how we evaluate our own selves and the degree of worth we place on us. People who feel favourable or good about themselves are said to have high self-esteem; people who feel unfavourable and negative about themselves are said to have low self-worth. Your self-esteem, the level of it from day to day, how it is affected by external events, can greatly influence how you think, feel and behave.

In addition to our conscious life, those experiences we are moment by moment aware of, our mind possesses capacities below the threshold of awareness. This domain we call the unconscious. According to Sigmund Freud, this domain occupies a larger portion of our mind and has significant influence over our day-to-day life. While this writer does not hold to all of Freud's theories, it is important to note that some of his thoughts on the unconscious, especially those relating to the effects of early experiences on present functioning, have shed much light on our understanding of the inner workings of the mind. Further, current studies on dreams are unraveling tremendous information about the abilities of the unconscious part of our mind. Below the level of awareness our minds can work out solutions to problems and generate insights and make these accessible to our consciousness while we were not even thinking about them on the conscious level. This just goes to show the abilities that our brains possess. To this we will return later.

There is so much about our capabilities that we are not aware of. Such unknown aspects of our selves either are hidden from us because of lack of self-reflection or reside below the level of self-reflection and can only be revealed in small bits under unusual or extreme situations. Do you remember when your own behaviour, response or thoughts surprised you, causing you to say, "That's just not like me" or "How could I have done such a thing?" or "I can't believe I did that" or "I must have been out of my mind"? But it was you and not someone else. It was merely the part of you that's hidden from your self-reflection, drawn out in response to some unusual situation.

Your inner nature and capabilities are a fascinating part of your creation. Many of us live out our lives in ignorance of who we really are and how our lives can be different, how we can plan toward and accomplish our goals, chart our future with a high degree of confidence, build better relationships and actually know why we are here.

Dynamic Neurological Support

We were created with the capacity to succeed. Everything about us, from our biological and neurological construction to our psychological abilities and spiritual capacity, confirms that we were built to accomplish greatness. If a car is built according to particular specifications it will drive. In the same way, we have been designed to succeed at whatever we do. If this is so, why do so many of us lead unsuccessful and frustrated lives?

While it is true that God created humans to be great and to succeed at the work of our hands, our ability has been compromised due to the fall. Consequently, no human being is born perfect. We all inherit a broken personhood that negatively affects everything we do. Without divine intervention we would never understand what we are capable of accomplishing. We would not know how we are designed or how far we can reach. With this in mind, the central message in this text is not about perfection but about the pursuit of excellence and self-discovery.

Let us now examine the case of a car more closely. Everything about its design, from its wheels, steering wheel, engine, transmission, gas pedal and brakes to all the other associated components, is designed to support what the car has been designed to do—that is, to drive. In addition, its oil, coolant and other types of fluid play critical supporting roles in the car's overall performance and functionality. Therefore, for the car to operate and function well at its full capacity, these components must be activated at some point and to some degree.

Likewise, humans are created with neurological capacities and processes that must be activated if we are to be successful in what we do. Modern neuroscience, social neuroscience, biology and psychology have converged on many points of interest and uncovered incredible links between neurological processes and social behaviour. They have given us tremendous insight into how these processes lend crucial support to everything we do, from thinking and feeling to motivation and actions. We now know that for every thought, feeling experience, level of motivation, desire, and even conscious overt behaviour there is supporting neurological activations and release of chemicals in particular regions of the brain. Some of these brain chemicals are called hormones and neurotransmitters, or chemical messengers. For example, we cannot have the feeling of being in love without the release of supporting brain chemicals from particular brain structures. We cannot feel motivated or driven to do something without the release of particular supporting brain chemicals.

To sit down and plan an activity or an evening's meal requires supporting activation of regions in your frontal lobe (located in the frontal area of your brain). In much the same way that you cannot begin driving a car before turning on the engine, you cannot succeed at anything or operate at a high level of your potential unless you engage the supporting dynamics of your brain. Your brain with its processes and structures is built to support your social, intellectual, moral, emotional, volitional and even spiritual experiences. Although many neurological processes are activated without your conscious control, others are generated as a result of your own initiative, motivation and volition.

The brain not only supports us by releasing those neurochemicals that are needed for particular thoughts and behaviour, it also has the ability to generate an unlimited assortment of images and display them on the screen of our minds. This is called imagination and is a mental capacity and neurological support system for intention and behaviour.

Imagination is one of the brain capacities that falls within human control. Long before you buy a car, your motivation for driving one is fueled by the images you generate of yourself driving one. Long before an individual becomes a doctor, a lawyer, a nurse, a pilot or a teacher, she sees herself operating in the field. Before you decide to go out with a particular date, propose or say yes to a potential spouse, you have images of you in the future with him or her.

As we delve into, uncover and understand the mysterious dynamics of our brain it will become clear that our neurological design is far from being an accident of nature. Everything about it shows evidence of divine imprints. Note that it is only when neurological processes are not working properly that we are affected negatively. If the correct levels of particular neurotransmitters or hormones are not activated or do not flow as they should or are inhibited from carrying out their proper functions, then we become ill or severely hampered in our natural abilities to function successfully in our lives.

In a sense, the brain can also be said to reversely support unproductive behaviours. For example, if you continue to think negatively or develop an unproductive pattern of behaviour, the brain begins adjusting itself to that condition. To adjust itself it might inhibit or significantly increase the flow of certain brain chemicals in order to accommodate your new pattern of thinking.

If you continue to think depressive thoughts, over time a depressive pattern of thinking emerges, indicating that the brain has shifted in its neural operation to accommodate this new pattern. To accomplish this, the brain has to inhibit the flow of certain neurotransmitters necessary for the generation of a positive mood.

No one needs to hit us on the head to negatively affect these processes; our own way of thinking and perceiving can negatively affect the very processes that are design to positively support or volitional, social, intellectual, spiritual, and moral behaviour and development.

Conclusion

It does not seem that we are accidents of nature. There is something great about us. Our brains and the capacities they allow suggest that something remarkable is wired into us. In addition, we are separated from other species not by our biological nature but by the operation of our minds. This means the primary difference between humans and animals is particularly rooted in the way our brains are wired and the unique way in which our minds can work. This means the foundation for greatness is built into each of us and can be accessed and released through the careful exercise of our own thinking. Unlike the animals, who are limited to their environment, with our minds we can transcend what is, visualize how things can be and take ourselves to what can be.

chapter two

Personal Agency:
YOUR GOD-GIVEN CAPACITY FOR
Change

Your sense of destiny provides you with the navigational
and positioning tools to channel and order your life; the time and resources
to manage life's circumstances, and the purpose whereby you can give
appropriate meaning to your complex and changing experiences.

What is destiny? How do we know when we are living in or have arrived at our destiny? Do we have one or multiple destinies? Furthermore, what role does divine intervention play in determining our destiny? This chapter has two purposes. The first is to unveil the myths and mysteries surrounding the concept of destiny and help you understand what it is and how it is connected to your unique creation. The second purpose is to position your mind for the rest of the book. The importance of this topic cannot be overstated. A discussion of our unique design, our thinking ability and other inner capabilities will be meaningless without understanding the nature of destiny and what part we play in shaping it.

How would you define destiny in your own words? Some people understand destiny to be a fixed sequence of events that is bound to happen no matter what they do. For others, it is something that may or may not occur, determined by chance or luck, over which they have absolutely no control. There are also those who believe that their destiny is determined by the circumstances surrounding their birth, such as the place, the time, and the positions of planetary objects. For these individuals, their destiny is written in the stars and therefore lies outside their personal control. In order to know what life holds for them, what career is best suited to them, what type of life partner to select or the right moment to invest, they consult astrological charts or their horoscope. There are also many church folks who believe their destiny lies outside their human control because God has predestined the events and circumstances of their lives.

Understanding the nature of destiny will change the way you think, not only about yourself and life in general, but also about God's role in human experience and particularly your human responsibility for your own life. In this chapter, I invite you on a journey of rethinking destiny.

Destiny: A Life by Design or by Default?

To begin our exploration of destiny it is important to tackle a central issue, that is, whether or not destiny is by design or default. This writer takes the position that destiny is by design and not by default. When something is in a state of default it is thus because no action has been taken to create any change.

When you purchase an alarm system for your home it usually comes with a default code that unless changed remains the same. Computer systems as well as other type of electronic devices come with factory default codes and programs that the users can change, allowing them to customize their device to fit a particular use. In a similar way, we can either live lives set by our past experiences and people's expectations or take control and positively customize our lives. People who do nothing to change things in their lives are living a life by default. This means that whatever happens, good or bad, is dictated by circumstances, not by deliberate and careful thinking and planning.

For example, you think you are a failure because you have experienced many failures in your life. Consequently, you feel that making a choice to engaging in a new task will only end in failure, so you refuse to do so. By refusing to make a choice to engage in a new task, you have in fact made a choice to keep yourself in a default state. Could you have made another choice? If you had made a different choice you would have placed yourself on a different path.

On the other hand, people who take positive actions to move their lives forward are living a life by design. They are making intentional choices that will move them toward particular paths. Their future is shaped by their choices, not by default.

Implications of Beliefs about Destiny

What you believe about your destiny will bear significant implications on your life. When one believes that his or her destiny is set or predetermined and that nothing he or she can do will change it, life becomes void of personal vision and dreams, self-determination, self-directedness and intrinsic motivation. The same is true for those who believe that destiny is controlled by chance or luck. For those who believe that their destiny is written in the stars, there will be constant consulting of horoscopes and palm readers. No real effort will be put into achieving any particular goal, because such beliefs set boundaries against directional thinking. Those who believe that God has predestined their future and order the events of their lives will become unproductive and be led to see God merely as a crutch. They will develop no plans and try to solve no problems on their own. Everything good or bad that occurs in their lives will be attributed to God. If they fail to maintain their car and it breaks down on the highway, they will believe it is somehow the will of God being worked out for a higher purpose. If they fail to be responsible in their job, arriving late and working carelessly, and end up being fired or laid off, they will attribute this to God's will for them. If they fail to pursue a career, seek a well-paying job or properly manage their finances and end up living from paycheck to paycheck and unable to afford the things they desire in life, they will claim they are living a life by faith.

It makes you wonder, though. Isn't faith supposed to give God permission to work in our lives? If your faith is not producing positive effects in your life, then it should be reviewed carefully.

Does this mean that God cannot and does not preordain certain paths for us? While God does not preordain all aspects of our lives, he chooses certain processes and ordains certain paths that we must take in order for certain aspects of his will to be done in the earth and in our lives. This in no way means he is in the business of taking control over every aspect of our lives or that we should make no choices about our own lives. He would not have given us a mind if he intended to think for us.

People who hold these beliefs about destiny tend to accept negative circumstances in their life as fate, outcomes and events that could not be avoided. More times than not, pulling themselves up from these undesired circumstances, encouraging and refocusing themselves toward change, is hard, if not impossible. They see themselves as victims of circumstances, puppets of nature, or simply pawns in the plans of God, rather than personal agents of change. This kind of mentality fits well with some Greek traditions and tales that teach the futility of trying to avoid an inescapable fate or destiny. Finding out that we have personal agency over our lives may be one of the greatest discoveries of all times.

Destiny: Your Converging Life Zone

The term *destiny* has been used to describe an end point or an inescapable fate that is firmly established or determined for one. When people use the terms *fate* and *destiny* in the traditional sense, they usually refer to something that befalls a person over which the person had no control and could not have avoided. These events are believed to be predetermined by some ultimate or divine agency.

In this text, destiny is viewed by no means as something beyond human control but as something very much contingent on human agency. We are the agents that determine and establish our destiny.

In the traditional definition, destiny is also viewed as a point of completion, a point you reach and need not go any farther. In this sense, you have arrived at your destination. In this text destiny is conceptualized not as a dead end but as a converging life zone.

This means destiny is more than a static arrival point. Human beings are not designed to be stagnant and inert. Everything about us is active and dynamic. Destiny is conceptualized as a life task or life path in which all the significant dynamics of one's life exert their fullest influence. This life task or life path is what I call your *converging life zone*.

The idea of *converging* in this context means an area or zone in which several factors come together and exert the most influence. The concept of a *life zone* simply means the current course of one's life in which all the converging factors are working to produce very strong effects. These factors are discussed later in this chapter. Your destiny is the converging life zone around which these factors revolve, exerting their greatest influence.

From this it is clear that our destiny is not something written in the stars or carved in eternity from which we can not escape. Rather, our destiny is determined by factors operating in our own lives. This therefore makes us active and responsible agents in the creation and discovery of our destiny.

To conceptualized destiny as a life path or life task, and particularly a converging life zone, is to believe that it is something that falls within human control. A path can be discovered as well as created. So too can a task. One can intentionally design a task as well as discover a new or particular purpose for it. When one discovers his destiny he discovers not only a converging life zone but the primary function or purpose of being.

Let's explain this with an example. The primary purpose or function of a knife is cutting. It is designed with a particular shape, a type of handle that allows the user to hold and use it effectively, and a specific length and thickness that makes it the ideal instrument for cutting certain things. However, it can also be used for tasks outside its primary function. Under certain situations a knife may be used to undo or tighten a screw, open a cover or flatten a soft object. But none of these is the primary purpose or function of a knife.

In the same way that a knife is constructed for a specific purpose, each human being is equipped with certain skills and groups of abilities that when brought together allow him or her a certain primary purpose of being. Does purpose of being mean that some people are born specifically to become medical doctors, dentists, psychologists, scientists, lawyers, cooks or crooks? Absolutely not! Special skills and abilities, inborn and acquired dispositional factors work together to channel a person down certain life paths toward a converging life zone. In this sense, not one but several life tasks may fit well with a person's way of being.

Bear in mind that although the primary purpose of a knife is to cut, it might not be designed to cut only one particular thing. The user can use her knife successfully to cut a group of items without compromising the use of the instrument. This is because the design of the knife fits well with a particular group of tasks, which may include cutting bread, peeling fruits or cutting other soft objects. Like a knife that can be used successfully to cut several different items, each of us has specific ways about us, particular skills and experiences, that can fit us perfectly for a particular grouping of life tasks.

On the other hand, using a knife inconsistent with its normal use, such as tightening or undoing a screw, will eventually compromise its ability to function in its proper capacity. In other words, it can become damaged or blunted. In the same way, individuals operating outside the consolidated dynamics of their capacity will have difficulty feeling fulfilled and purposeful in what they are doing.

Furthermore, although a person may be good at several life tasks, the converging effects of the factors in his or her life will allow more focus and fuel more energy toward one of these tasks. A person may be a skilled and accomplished writer as well as a superb and masterful researcher, but a careful observation will show that these two endeavours may converge to produce a dominant life task.

You cannot have discovered your converging life zone or be on your life path or operating in your life task, whichever term you like best, and not feel good about yourself or feel that at least part of your life is being fulfilled in some way. Living in your converging life zone should be the most enjoyable, the most exciting and the most fulfilling experience next to having a spiritual connection and relationship with God and a relationship with your family. This is because all or most of the significant dynamics of your life are converging here. This may be the reason why so many people living and operating outside their life zones are so frustrated, unfulfilled and unhappy with what they are doing and with the course of their lives.

Given our understanding of personal destiny, several things become clear. First, once created or discovered, destiny becomes a priority of life and the full focus of one's being. It becomes the centre of gravity toward which everything in your life is drawn or attracted. People who have no passion, zeal or burning desire have not yet discovered or established their destiny. Once you have discovered your life path, your life becomes focus and channeled towards a purpose.

Second, destiny is your life path with a purpose; it is your authorization for living. Only when you are living in your destiny is your purpose for being realized. It is here that you know and feel that your life is meaningful and has significance and value.

While we can embrace the truth that we are people of value because we were created by design and did not arrive here by some evolutionary accident, we must also come to the understanding that as people of value and worth we must manifest such within the context of our lives. When we are operating outside of our life zones, we not only feel unfulfilled but are unable to put our finger on what our purpose for being really is. When the elements of our lives are not converging, we will not be able to answer the question "Why am I here?"

Third, as you change and develop the boundaries of your converging life zone become extended and refined. This is what I call the *elasticity* of destiny. This is because your destiny is influenced by changing factors operating in your life. Just as a knife can become sharper, extending its effectiveness, so can a person develop himself or herself. From our discussion so far it is clear that destiny is not merely an end point but a dynamic process that engulfs one's entire life.

Let's now review the factors responsible for creating our converging life zone. Consider setting out to New York City from Toronto and ending up in Montreal. Would you say you have arrived at your destination? In the same way, then, destiny is not an arrival at some arbitrary or random position in life. The path to the arrival at a specific life task or destiny is a guided journey that usually follows an intentional path. Consequently, such a path is influenced by several factors.

Factors Influencing Destiny

Your destiny is influenced by many factors operating in your life. To believe that we have absolutely no input or influence on our destiny is simply nonsense. Such belief deprives us of volition and strips us of personal agency. It is not possible to have a personal sense of identity, volition, the ability to think and reason, to extrapolate and visualize, and not have some degree of personal agency over the direction our lives take. Remember, everything about the design of a knife, from its shape and size to its blade and handle, determines how it is used. Everything about us, from our thoughts and thinking ability to our volition and reason, points to personal agency.

The first task given to humans after their creation was that of personal agency. This is clearly seen in the instruction to care for the garden, name the creatures, and reproduction. If the Bible is clear on the subject, why are so many confused about it?

The following diagram is an illustration of the concept of destiny as a converging life zone. We will discuss a few of these factors in turn.

Figure 2.1. Converging Factors Influencing Destiny

Dispositional Influences

Let us begin by exploring what is meant by dispositional factors. These are inner components that exert strong influence on the direction and choices of a person's life course. These include but are not limited to the following:

- Personal interest
- Motivation
- Locus of control
- Personality type
- Personal preferences
- Personal values
- Beliefs
- Sense of self
- Attitudes

Most of the choices we make in life rest heavily on dispositional influences. Whether we are conscious of their influences or not, they channel the direction we take and choices we make. For example, why did you buy the kind of car you drive? Why did you select the partner you live with? Why did you select the career you now have, are pursuing or intend to pursue? A careful reflection on the reasons behind these choices will reveal profound dispositional influences. While these influences do not by themselves create your destiny, they nonetheless influence a great portion of it.

Let us examine some of these dispositional factors. Let's begin our discussion with an exploration of *personal interest.* Even though your personal interest itself is influenced by other factors in your life, such as past experiences and personality type, once it is developed your interest influences the balancing of your lifestyle. Your interest helps you define what you want out of life and the general direction you are inclined to go in.

We are the most happiest when we are engaging in activities and pursuing goals we find interesting. I often observed that students tend to do better in subjects they find interesting. If you have a strong interest in being around and with people you will probably pursue a hobby or a career that brings you into close contact with them. If you have a strong interest in the outdoors, you might select a hobby or career that brings you into contact with outdoor activities. It is important to catalogue your interests from lowest to highest in terms of degree of appeal to see which one has the most influence on the choices you make and the course of your life.

Your interest tells you a lot about who you are and your particular zone of fascination, curiosity and attraction. For example, if you are pursuing a career or endeavour that holds no attraction or fascination, you are probably frustrated and bored out of your mind. In fact, it would be difficult for you to exert the degree of motivation and enthusiasm needed to bring you optimal success in such pursuit.

The next dispositional factor that bears influence on your life zone is *motivation*. Your motivation can be derived from external or internal sources. Motivation derived from internal sources is defined as the inner drive or intrinsic push that channels you toward a specific goal. Your intrinsic motivation is your inner transmission. Once engaged, it moves you forward. It is your private spark that when ignited sets your trail ablaze. People have different levels of motivation for different things. The level of your motivation for something depends on the degree of interest you have in that thing.

Motivation is also dependant on the presence of a need or goal. Here is how it works. First, you sense that a need exist. Second, you attach a specific measure of importance to the need. Third, the measure of importance you attach to the goal or need generates your desire to achieve or attain it. Your desire here is your sense of longing, appetite or craving for something that brings satisfaction.

Fourth, once your desire is generated, it leads to a motivational arousal. The level of motivation aroused is a response to the measure of importance attached to the need and the degree of desire you have for its attainment. Notice here that your motivation is directly proportional to the measure of importance you attach to your need or goal. As the importance of the need and desire increases, so does your motivation toward it. Motivation does not exist without the desire for something or the importance attached to it. Conversely, if the importance you attach to your goal or need is low so is your desire and motivation toward achieving it. It is your level of desire that provides the fuel that will ignite the spark of your motivation into the fire necessary to stay on course and overcome difficulties and challenges that would have otherwise stopped you from attaining your goals. If the thing or things you are pursuing hold little or no importance to you, it will be difficult for you to feel motivated to achieve them. As a result, the moment you are faced with challenges you will quickly give up.

The level of motivation one feels does not necessarily lies outside the range of conscious control. You can motivate yourself by attaching measures of importance to the things you desire to pursue or accomplish.

The next dispositional influence we need to discuss is *locus of control*. In social psychology this refers to the extent that a person believes he or she has personal agency or control over the events that affect his or her life. The concept goes back to 1960s with Julian Rotter's study of how people's attitudes influence the outcomes of their lives. The term *locus*, according to *Webster's Dictionary*, means "place" or "locality." Locus of control tells us whether or not a person believes he or she has some measure of control over external situations that impact his or her life.

We live in a world in which events and experiences around us are constantly changing. These include experiences with people, encounters with life situations, and so on. Do you feel that you are been carried along by these experiences by forces beyond your control? If so, your locus of control is said to be external. This means your destiny lies outside your control and will be determined by the circumstances in your life. Consequently, where you end up in life is not by your choice but by forces outside your power.

On the other hand, if you feel that you are at the helm of your ship and have at least some control over the direction of your life regardless of how external events are changing, then your locus of control resides within you. This means that, although things are not aligned in your life as you would like them to be, you nonetheless believe you can make choices to turn your life in the direction you want.

People with strong internal control do not attribute their success or failure to luck or chance. They are aware of the effort they need to exert for success. They are aware that if they fail at something, trying harder or re-evaluating and changing their approach can turn things around successfully. It does not matter what people say or think about you; neither does it matter how many failures you had in your past. It is your view, interpretation and response to these that exert the ultimate effects on you.

As noted earlier, realizing that you have personal agency over your life may be one of the most exciting discoveries of your life. How would you feel after being told that you have failed your driving test after weeks and months of practicing? Would you say, "That's it, I will never try again"? Would you say, "I am just not good at this driving thing; it is just not for me"? Would you say, "I just have bad luck; I will never be able to drive"? Would you say, "Maybe it is God's will for me not to drive"? If you would answer yes to any of these questions, then you would be resigned to the failure. As a result, you would hold your head down and forget about ever trying again.

Or would you decide to pick yourself up, practice some more and book another driving test?

People with internal locus of control will do the latter. This is because they believe that if they work at the area they failed in, the possibility of succeeding the next time around increases significantly.

Why do some people give up and resign themselves to failure when the challenges seem bigger than what they perceive they can handle? Remember that God does not specialize in or get glory from our failures. More than anything, he wants all his people to live successful, productive and meaningful lives. Attributing our failures to the will of God is bad theology.

Influences from Past and Current Experiences

Our destiny or converging life zone is not only influenced by dispositional factors. Our past and current experiences also give shape to the path in life we take and the things we have strong leaning to do or avoid. More times than not we overlook or underestimate the subtle yet powerful influence our past experiences impose on the choices we make and the life zone in which we live.

Your past experiences can impose influence on your destiny in several ways. They can shape your interest, underscore your motivations, define your values and colour your outlook on life. They can also give rise to thought patterns and ways of thinking, feeling and perceiving in general. They can shape you positively or negatively, each of which will bear profound influence on the path in life you take.

Have you ever asked yourself why you feel or think the way you do about certain things, people or events in your life, why certain things affect you the way they do? Why are you uncomfortable around certain types of people and not so around others? Why do you prefer certain kinds of jobs above others? Why do you like certain colours and can't stand others? Why do you select certain type of individuals to be your friends and not others? Why do you feel inhibited by certain things and open for others? Or maybe you thought that preferences just happen by chance and that your past experiences had absolutely no influence on them.

How you define yourself, the beliefs you have about yourself, what you think you can or cannot do have a great deal to do with your past experiences and how you interpret them. The type of parents you had and the parenting style they employed left a profound impression on your sense of self. The challenges you had while growing up and the people who were part of your peer group left lasting influence on your sense of self. Further, the words parents and others used to describe you may also have added to your self-definition, and as you got older you used those same words in defining who you are.

A young man told me that there was no way, given his experiences in the past, that he could be any better off than he was. At the time he was suffering from emotional and relational challenges. He believed his past was the ultimate defining factor of what he had become and would ever be. I asked him two questions. The first was "Can you imagine what you can be like in five years?" The second was "If your life was a book and the first few chapters were written by others, and you had the opportunity to write the last few chapters and the conclusion, would the final content of your book be any different from the content of the previous chapters?"

His response to the first question was that if he had anything to do with it, in five years he would be a completely different person. His response to the second question was that the content of the rest of his book would read nothing like what was written in the previous chapters. Notice how his responses to the two questions differed significantly from his perception of the controlling and defining effects of his past experiences. Notice how the voice from his future sounded different from the voice from his past. He initially felt that his life was defined and shaped by his past experiences. He also felt that fate had dealt him a wicked blow from which he could not recovery. However, when he was challenged to think of himself under different conditions his inner capacity for personal agency emerged, and that too with a different voice.

How many people do you suppose are living out their lives without knowing that they possess the capacity for personal agency? Think of the many students who have labeled themselves as C and D students simply because these grades have characterized their past test-taking experiences. How many of us failed to raise ourselves from the failures and clutches of the past simply because we have defined ourselves within the context of these experiences? We conclude that the path on which we find ourselves is a result of fate, luck or the will of a divine power from which we cannot escape.

It would be unfair to say that past experiences exert only negative influence on us in the present. For many people past experiences exert positive influence on the present. It tells them where they are the most strongest and where they have weaknesses, what their values are, what things and people they find most interesting or most uninteresting, which paths they should avoid or pursue, and so on. Past experiences can even work as prototypes for future endeavours and challenges.

Residing within each of us are dormant and concealed abilities for greatness that can only be activated by particular experiences or situations. In other words, the challenges and trying events that bear down on us can either trigger some internal strength we didn't know we possessed or help us recognize things about ourselves that under ordinary circumstances would never have been manifested. Our greatest strengths and most profound abilities usually do not emerge when things are normal, stable or customary. Therefore, instead of falling apart when we have challenging experiences, one of the most productive things we can do is ask ourselves what abilities and strengths are being manifested or need to be brought out. Recognizing and embracing these emerging elements of who we are inside will aid in channeling us toward our destiny.

Influence of Choice

The ability to choose is an inherent capacity of being human. Choice provides control or personal agency over life's alternatives. The choices we make set us on paths towards particular ends.

Regardless of the skills, dispositions and possibilities we possess, it is our choices that finally determine where we end up. Where we end up might be exactly where we need to be in order to fulfill our primary function or true purpose, or it could be a messed-up reality that is incompatible with our natural abilities, talents, dispositions and the greatness we are capable of accomplishing. The moment-by-moment decisions we make each day add up to affect the sum total of our lives. Most people go through life unaware of this profound yet simple truth.

Examine your day. Look back on the decisions you made, beginning from when you got up. You will find that each decision you made affected how your day turned out. Is it not clear then that the path you are on now is a result of choices you made in the past or failed to make?

It is important to clarify that not everything that befalls us is a result of bad choices we make. The choices others make can also affect us. There are variables in life over which we have absolutely no control. A man decides to get drunk before driving his car on the highway. At the same time another person is on his usual path going to work with no idea that a drunken driver is on a collision course with him. This is an example of a life variable that cannot be controlled with prior choice. However, God can divinely intervene to save a life.

Influence of Skill Sets

By definition, a skill is the ability to do something. A skill set, then, is a person's specific combination of skills that allow the person to perform a specific task with a high degree of competence and efficiency. The following list is an example of a group of skills or skill set that you would expect a leader to possess:

- Planning
- Leading people
- Managing people
- Communicating effectively
- Motivating others
- Decision-making
- Modeling
- Visioning

Some people (if not all) are born with certain genetic predispositions that make them able to do certain things easier than others. Some of these predispositions can also lead to the development of skill sets. Others can develop these from early exposures and experiences.

Let's look closer at the list. It illustrates the idea that a range of skills can work together to make a person an effective and competent leader. If you identify a person as a good leader, you do so because you see that he or she possesses a combination of certain attributes.

Believe it or not, everyone has at least one skill set. Think of the things you excel at doing with a high degree of efficiency. Now list all the particular units of skill that were used to bring about such excellent performance. These are your skill set.

People fail to excel at the things they do because of several reasons: they lack motivation, they lack preparation, or they lack the skill set necessary to do well at the task.

A person's skill set for a particular task does bear strong influence on their converging life zone or destiny. Can you think of a life task or of operating in your destiny without thinking of those skills that combine to make your performance stand out and give you a sense of satisfaction and mastery?

Merely knowing or recognizing that you have a combination of skills is not enough. These will not work at their highest level for you until you bring them together so they work toward a central purpose.

Influence from Externals

External means those things in your immediate environment that influence what you do and how well you do it. Not everyone is intrinsically motivated. Some people derive their motivation to do things from outside themselves. While intrinsic motivation is usually preferable, external sources of motivation can and do exert strong influence on what people do and the paths they take in life. This is easily seen in the strong influence exerted on a person's choice by peers, friends, family, the media and people considered important. The incentives and compliments one receives from external sources can also play significant roles in moving the person toward certain tasks in life.

Although we will take this up in greater detail later, it is important to know how much influence friends and peers have on one's converging life zone. Such influence can be positive or negative but usually never neutral. Such influence can take one of two forms.

The first is comparative influence. People have the tendency to evaluate themselves based on the images they see in others. Such comparisons may relate to the physical, academic, or social. The results of such comparisons then becomes the basis on which a person judges himself or herself.

The second form of peer influence is informational. People have a tendency to believe that their peers are correct in their judgment. More times than not people integrate the perceptions and beliefs others have of them into their own self-concept. Are you really like how others see you or say that you are?

Sometimes unconsciously we live out the expectations and beliefs people have of us or what they say about us. A great number of people select careers and occupations or pursue certain life paths simply because of the expectations of others or because of what they hear others say about them. The people and environment in which we are situated can influence how we think, what we believe about ourselves, and the choices we make. More times than not, the images we have of ourselves reflect the opinions of people we associate and hang out with. We see in ourselves a reflection of their beliefs and expectations about us.

Our uniqueness is often clouded by the context in which we are embedded. Consequently, the meaning and expectations we have for our lives do not reflect who we really are and can become but the expectations of others. While we cannot fully detach ourselves from all the unhealthy contexts of life, we can work to understand and limit their subtle negative influences on us and ultimately our destiny.

Influence from the Future

We cannot complete our discussion on the converging influences on our life course without touching on the role the future plays in the mix. In much the same way that the past can influence and shape our lives in the present, the future can also produce significant effects on our lives in the present.

27

The past has the power to affect the present and shape the future. This means the negative experiences a person had in the past can shape how he or she thinks in the present. This type of thinking not only affects the present but also affects how the person thinks of the future. Conversely, the future also has the power to affect changes in the present and offset the negative and defining power of the past.

It is important here to understand that the future cannot break from the past if the past is not redefined. This means the future will be created in the same image as in the past unless the past is reframed or reinterpreted.

Here's how it works: you have had several failures in the past that have led you to believe you are nothing but a failure. You now stand between the past and the future. However, the moment you imagine yourself succeeding in the future you are challenged to rethink what you believe about the failures of the past. You must now see your past failures as contextual, situational or conditional and not life defining. In other words, you must see it as occurring under specific sets of conditions and contingent on those situations. Once you acquire this level of thinking you would have successfully situated your failure within a specific historical context of the past and disconnected its defining grasp on your future.

Let's say you failed repeatedly at something in the past, but after much reflection you concluded that your failure was due to your lack of maturity, adequate knowledge, consistency, focus, skills or the resources needed to succeed. This is the type of thinking that is necessary to break from the holds of the past.

How does the future exert such cancelling effects on the past? The way we think of and situate ourselves in the future will either confirm the past or cancel its negative influence over us. The power the past has on us is proportional to how we think of and situate ourselves in the future. The way we think of ourselves in a future situation reaches back and influences the choices we make in the present. Once the choices we are making in the present reflect a positive future situation that is different from the past, the break with the past has began and a new chapter of our life has begun.

There are a number of people in our time who have had experiences in their past that would have otherwise crippled their lives, but they have overcome these by envisioning themselves in more positive situations in the future. This positive view of themselves in the future works to offset the crippling effects of their past experiences. We know many of these individuals because of their testimonies and their positive effect on and contributions to society. Their lives are living examples that tell us that the past, no matter how bad it was, does not have to shape the future or determine where we end up. Our past does not have to create our destiny or our future in its image.

Figure 2.2 illustrates the concept of the converging effect of the factors in our life. Here we see all the factors that bear significant influence on our lives in the present converging to determine our converging life zones. They consolidate to produce a dominant life effect.

Figure 2.2. Illustration of Consolidating Effect

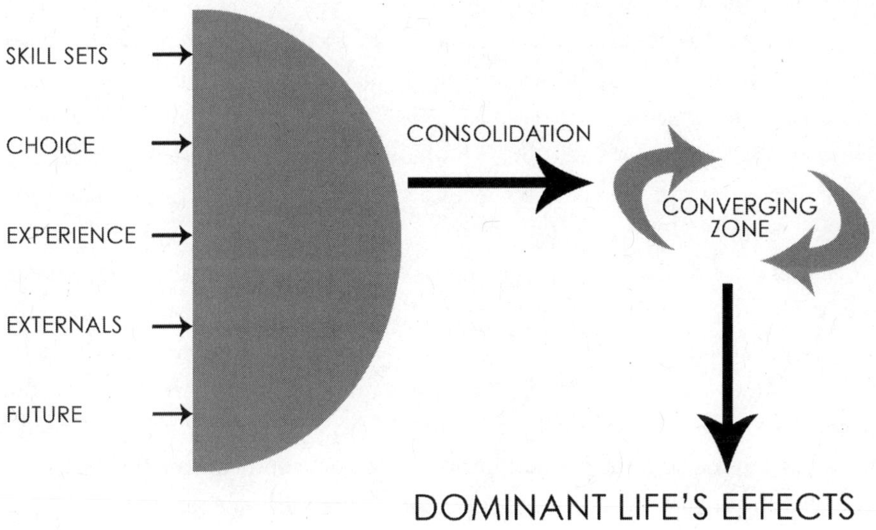

SKILL SETS →

CHOICE →

EXPERIENCE →

EXTERNALS →

FUTURE →

CONSOLIDATION

CONVERGING ZONE

DOMINANT LIFE'S EFFECTS

Do Multiple Destinies Exist?

Is there one or multiple destinies? Can a person have more than one destiny? The answer is, it depends on how one explains multiple destinies. If one defines multiple destinies as several converging points in one's life, then multiple destinies do not exist. In this text multiple destinies is defined as a destiny within a destiny, or nested destinies. This means a destiny can be multi-layered.

While a person may excel in several areas and have more than one skill set and even multiple interests, the converging factors in the person's life usually bring these together to produce an overall dominant effect. If one has several destinies at the same time, one will either overrule the other or they will work to accommodate each other, leading to lack in all.

Although we do not have multiple destinies, we can have what I call nested destinies. King David in Scripture had several areas of strengths, including skill sets that distinguished him as a mighty warrior, a caring shepherd, and a famous king. Looking back at David's early life, no one can deny that he had all the qualities and skills of a great warrior king, which he eventually became. But notice how all these qualities converged, allowing him to fulfill his destiny as the shepherd king of Israel. However, King David was not only a shepherd and warrior king but also a poet king. Which of these was his true destiny—a warrior, a king, a shepherd or a poet? Keep in mind that he was extremely successful as each one. This is a classical example of nested destiny. All of these skills worked together to make him the great king he was.

Let's take another example. Dr. Baker is an excellent researcher whose work has led to new scientific innovations in his field. He is also a competent and passionate professor who has received several awards for excellence in teaching. He is also an accomplished author who has written several academic textbooks. Dr. Baker appears to be very good at research, teaching and writing. What is Dr. Baker's destiny or life zone?

To answer this question, let us ask, What is Dr. Baker's primary passion that consolidates all three factors? We find that Dr. Baker's central purpose that cuts across all three interests is his passion to share his knowledge and educate people. He conducts research because he wants to uncover new insights into particular phenomena by which he can impact his field with new knowledge. He has a passion for teaching because he wants to share and help students construct knowledge. He writes for the very same reason he conducts research and teaches. We find that all three interest and skills (or nested destinies) converge in a life zone of educator. Everything Dr. Baker does seems to revolve around one single point and purpose, that is, educating others. While the term *educator* is often used in the limited sense for teaching, at the core it really has to do with sharing knowledge to educate others. Sharing of knowledge with others can take many forms. Consequently, Dr. Baker's destiny is to educate people through a combination of different set of skills and interests. Figure 2.3 below illustrates the concept of nested destiny. Notice that writer, researcher and teacher all revolve around the activity of educator.

Figure 2.3. *Nested Destiny*

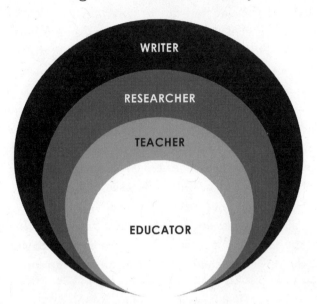

Divine Will and Human Freedom

We cannot complete our discussion on destiny without touching on the topic of divine will and human freedom. I have alluded to this topic several times in our discussion. This is of course not a new topic or a new discussion on the topic. This topic has occupied the conversations and debates of philosophers and Christian scholars for hundreds of years.

There are those who hold that all actions are predetermined by divine will, and therefore freedom of choice is impossible. On the other hand, there are others who hold that man is an absolutely free agent and therefore free from all divine restraint. The question, whether God is sovereign, meaning having absolute control, and humans free in their choice, is an absolutely important one. I tackle this question here, not to delve into any deep theological or philosophical discussion but merely to highlight the importance of human agency.

Can God be sovereign (having absolute control) while humans have freedom of will? This question can be answered with an astounding yes! Human freedom lies on the continuum of God's divine will. This means that while humans are free agents their freedom is not totally outside divine supervision and influence. For example, in a democracy we believe that all citizens are free, but such freedom does not lie outside legal supervision. While it is true that all the choices we make are in some way or other influenced by antecedent factors (preceding circumstances), our choices are based on our own volition. While the choices are of our own free will, they are not without some internal or external influence. Can you influence the choices your children make? Can you influence them to do certain things and not others? While there is no doubt that your influence bears on the choices they make, do they not make those choices freely of their own volition and are therefore responsible for them?

It is in this sense that God also gives us free volition and remains sovereign. At any given time he can bear influence on our life circumstances leading us toward a certain choice. He wanted Jonah to go to Nineveh, but Jonah with his own volition said no. God then influenced circumstances in Jonah's life that led him to face a choice between the belly of the fish or life in ministry. Jonah made the choice for ministry but not without divine influence. While the choice was under divine influence, it was nonetheless of Jonah's own free volition.

In much the same way that we can influence each other and parents can influence the choices of their children, God can influence our choices. The key to note is that while we are free agents, no human choice can escape the sovereignty of divine will. They must fall somewhere on its continuum. We can conclude by saying that while our choices can be influence by God or others, the choices we eventually make are our own responsibility and therefore should be considered free.

What would you say of a man who is charged for raping a woman and while standing before the court declares that the woman had dressed sexually provocatively, and therefore he could not resist? Would you drop the charge against him because he says he was strongly influenced by how the woman was dressed, leading to him raping her? I think not! You would let him know that he is thoroughly responsible for the choice he made. You would charge him because you believe he made a free choice. Although you do not deny that he was influenced to some degree by the circumstances, you believe he could have made the choice to not do what he did. Given the situation he made a free choice and is therefore responsible for its consequence.

The message here is although there are influences bearing down on a choice, as long as there are alternative ways of choosing the choice made is free and therefore the responsibility of the one who made it.

There is no doubt that we have free volition and so have personal agency. Why then do so many people, even Christians, continue to use God's sovereignty as an excuse not to take personal agency over their lives? They say, "Unless God tells me to do this, I will not do it" or "I am waiting on God to tell me what to do." These are the same people who end up complaining that God has forsaken them because of some sin (known or unknown) they have committed.

I wish that we would rise up and understand that there is a divine investment in us through the personal agency that has been bestowed on us. Unless we use our minds, make choices, plan our lives, set goals and work toward their achievement, our lives will remain empty and unfinished. Nothing is more unfulfilling and tragic (besides not having a relationship with Christ) than the failure to discover that one was created for greatness or to discover that one is occupied in life with things, tasks, or situations that are not compatible with your true calling.

The Power of Your Sense of Purpose

Our destiny can be said to be a function of our sense of purpose. Earlier in our discussion we conceptualized destiny as our converging life zone. In this section of the chapter we will expand on this concept with a discussion on the power of your sense of purpose. While the terms *purpose* and *destiny* can be used interchangeably, the term *sense of purpose* refers to the extent to which one has identified and is focused on a goal or destiny. If you have a sense of purpose you recognize your worth, what you need to focus on, what you need to do in life and how much effort you need to invest in reaching your goal. Your sense of purpose moves you beyond just working at something to knowing that this is what you need to focus on, this is the direction you need to take, and this is how diligent you need to work at it. It is your sense of purpose that gives birth to your destiny and keeps you focusing on it. It is not your level of education, status, money, or enthusiasm that carries you towards your goal or keeps you steadfast working at your life's task. It is your sense of purpose that provides you with the motivation and internal power needed to take your life to higher levels. You can think of your sense of purpose as your internal authority for living meaningfully and productively. The sense of purpose is so critical that we need to explore several dimensions of it.

It Is Your Seed of Potentiality

Your sense of purpose is your seed of potentiality. What you can become, how high you can reach and how effective you can become in life are encased in the single seed of your sense of purpose. Everything in life that was created to have continuity and produce offspring was created with the seed of potentiality in it. The first humans, plants, animals, birds, and so on were all created with seeds of potentiality that ensured the continuation of their particular species. God created only two people and planted in them the potential of producing families and nations.

Nothing in life can become without potential. It is potentiality that unfolds into actuality. This is one of life's most profound principles. A single seed has the potential to sprout and develop into a tree that produces more seeds that in turn produce more trees that eventually produce a forest. For the seed to sprout and grow into a tree it must be planted in an environment conducive for germination and growth. Only when the seed is planted under the right conditions can it become what it is meant to be. Conversely, if a seed is put in a jar and placed somewhere on a shelf or in some storeroom or cupboard, it will never actualize into a tree, never attain its purpose or fulfill its real destiny.

In the same way that a seed can live out an unproductive life somewhere in a jar on a shelf, individuals can stifle their potentiality by hiding behind excuses or being in environments that are not conducive for the unfolding of their potential. There is a seed of purpose in all of us. But not until we feel the sense of it can we say we are pregnant or infused with it. To be pregnant with a child is to be in an expectant state with a life inside. Only when a woman becomes aware that she is pregnant can she look forward to having the child. Only when you feel that there is something alive in you can you look forward to giving birth to it.

Although everyone can, unfortunately not many will feel that there is something alive in them to be brought forth. In other words, while everyone has a seed of purpose in them, some will live sterile lives, unable to bring it to the point where it germinates and produces.

Not many people on the earth know the full potential of the sun. We love its warm rays and often bask in its soft heat and believe that is all the sun has to offer. Notice how the sun can shine on a forest all day without burning the trees. It can do this because its rays are scattered. What do you think would happen if you brought several of those rays together into a single beam? If you use a magnifying glass and focus a few of these rays on a single spot, you will see the potential of just a few concentrated rays. The rays create heat with enough intensity to severely burn the spot or cause a fire.

Having a sense of purpose will do the same thing for you. It will bring all of your strengths to focus on a single goal and unleash your potential onto it. What you will create is a converging life zone with a powerful consolidating effect. This is what earlier we called destiny. But it is your sense of purpose, the seed of potentiality, that turns the key and brings it all together.

It Is Your Life's Assignment

Your sense of purpose positions you toward what you need to do in life. It is not possible to know what you need to do as a life task without first having a sense of purpose. Your life's assignment becomes clear to you only when you have a sense of purpose. It is here that all your strengths converged and become focused on what your life is all about and should be. If your purpose is to work as a missionary among people who live in severe poverty and illness, you will never be truly fulfilled working with a pen, papers and computers in an office on the 39th floor of one of the most luxurious buildings in the core of downtown. You will feel frustrated and empty getting up each morning and going to a job where your strengths are not converging. This is because your life's assignment is not just a job that puts food on the table and money in the bank; neither is it a mere profession that gives you certain level of status among peers. While it may include these, it is much more. It is your mission in life, what your brain has been uniquely wired for, what your experiences have shaped you for, and what your personality traits have bent you toward. Consequently, this is the assignment in life in which you will have the greatest impact and feel the most profound satisfaction.

No one can argue about what the life assignment of Dr. Martin Luther King Jr. was. Dr. King was an educated man, an ordained minister who had a love for working with underprivileged individuals. Notice that his sense of purpose brought all these strengths toward a single life assignment where he was profoundly effective.

What is your sense of purpose? What is your life assignment? If you discover or create your destiny, there you will find your life's assignment.

It Is Your Sense of Meaning

One of the distinguishing features of being human is that we tend to seek meaning in almost everything we do and experience. This is because meaning resolves confusion and brings order and purpose to bear on a perplexing event or experience. Without a sense of purpose, it doesn't matter what people possess or achieve; they are aimless and feel that their life has no order.

It is your sense of purpose that creates order and gives your life meaning. It is your reason for arriving and being here, your guide to what you do next, and your signature on the pages of life. Imagine that a person gives you a cheque written for one million dollars that has no signature on it. The cheque is worthless because no bank will honour it. In a similar sense, your life is unsigned, aimless and uncertified unless it is authorized and validated by the meaning you give to it, dated by your sense of purpose. Such a life can end up in any direction with symptoms such as frustration, emptiness and even depression.

Some may develop an extreme need to conform and for validation. People who lack a sense of purpose in their life tend to be bored with life itself and may even be easy candidates for addictive behaviours. Such is a sad waste of the tremendous power and potential that God has invested within them.

When we discover the meaning for our life we become grounded and more certain as to where we need to go and what we need to do. It is our sense of meaning that gives us direction and sparks our motivation toward creating or discovering our destiny.

Conclusion

Taking charge of our lives means coming to grips with the fact that we have personal agency and can give shape and direction to the course of our lives. Destiny is not some cosmic or divine predetermined point we reach in our lives or some state we acquire by luck but rather the converging of our various strengths into a harmonious whole that produce the greatest effect on ourselves and others.

However, the personal shaping of our destiny, as noted, is not without external, internal or divine influence. The choices we make do come under various types of influence, which can be from the past, present or future and even divinely placed in our volitional path by God himself. Regardless of the source of the influence, the choice is ours to be exercised. It is we who must evaluate the influences and select the path that brings us toward our most productive life zone.

The rest of the book not only builds on this chapter but takes you deeper and further in discovering who you are and what you can accomplish with your thinking.

chapter three

Eagle
IN A CHICKEN'S
World

*Our environment influences us to the extent that we know ourselves;
the more we come to know who we are and what we are capable of
achieving, the less power we give to the influencing variables in our lives.*

More and more we are discovering that the relationships in which we are embedded interact with our minds and influence what we do and become. In other words, the human mind does not operate in a vacuum but is influenced by factors operating in the environment in which it is embedded.

When we were young, for example, we heard things about ourselves from the people in our lives. Some of these were positive and others were negative. As we developed and got older we internalized the perceptions, beliefs, opinions and expectations of significant people in our lives. In fact. we even participated by using some of the same vocabulary to describe ourselves. Over time, we came to know ourselves as others see us.

Not only have we come to see ourselves as others see us, we also learn to be like how others are. If.they fail at a task, we think we will also fail; if they are afraid of a challenge, we think we should also be afraid. Although we cannot escape some influence from the world, it is important to know that the degree of such influence depends on the knowledge we have about our uniqueness and what we are capable of achieving.

The primary intent then of this chapter is to help you distinguish yourself from the environment in which you are embedded and to see yourself not as helpless victim of circumstances but as unique, with personal agency for change and greatness. In the last chapter you were challenged to rethink destiny and your part in shaping it. This chapter takes you further and shows you how your environment can inhibit and even condition the capacities within you, blinding your eyes to who you are and who you can become. This chapter is the first of several chapters that will explore how the environment in which we live exerts influence on us.

The World of the Chicken

Chickens are good creatures; a great deal of people love to eat chickens. It is not my intent to demean such a soft-natured and awesome bird. The chicken metaphor is employed here because chickens have certain characteristics that fit well with describing the attitude of certain people. In fact, the term *chicken* has come to be associated with such characteristics as cowardice, timidity, shyness and fearfulness. Several things about the world of the chicken can be employed as metaphors to help us conceptualize and understand the type of environment in which some people live out their lives.

To begin, chickens are birds that are easily given to domestication, living out their lives in a barnyard or in some type of controlled and protected environment. An animal or bird is said to be domesticated when it has become *tame* and *adjusted* to human conditions and control. It has become dependent on the provision provided by humans. Domestication is a type of captivity that sets boundaries around the domesticated.

A chicken farmer usually ensures that adequate barriers or fences are in place to limit how far his chickens stray, as well as for their safety. This is because chickens are easy prey for various types of predators. From my own experience with chickens as a boy growing up in the country, they do not mind being fenced or cooped up. They easily adjust themselves to their condition.

Third, chickens live out their lives in *dependence* on the provisions of their owners. It is important to note that while they depend on their owners to provide for them, chickens are not entirely helpless birds; given the appropriate conditions they can provide food for themselves. They are smart enough to realize that the ground on which they walk provides nutritious little creatures that they can eat. However, they are easily satisfied with what is provided for them in their coop.

Fourth, the chicken's life is characterized by *routines*. If they could experience boredom, there would be no need to kill them; they would all die from it. One of the defining factors of domestication is routine. It is not hard to see that a domesticated routine stifles potential and possibilities. It blocks your view of who you really are and what you can actually do. It is no wonder that chickens never learn to fly beyond their domesticated environment.

Fifth, the chicken's world is usually a grounded one. Everything occurs on the same plane each day. This is because chickens have *poor flight ability.* Could their poor flight ability be attributed to their belief that they have everything they need at hand, at their claws or at their beaks, so they don't need to go anywhere else to seek new possibilities? Because chickens rarely fly, some people don't know that they can fly. Yes, most chickens can fly. Some can even fly over high fences. Because of their poor flight ability they cannot fly very high or maintain a long duration of flight. For those chickens who like to fly over their protective fences, their owners usually clip their wings to discourage flight and to keep them fully grounded. Because of their poor flight ability, domesticated chickens do not migrate or escape their controlled life condition.

So far we have identified several conditions of the chicken's world, all of which appear to be strongly linked with domestication. These are illustrated in figure 3.1.

Figure 3.1 *Effects of Domestication*

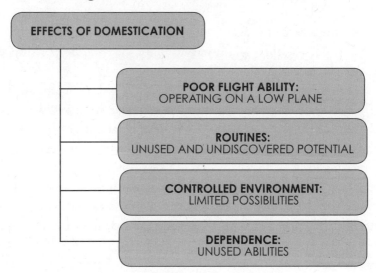

EFFECTS OF DOMESTICATION

POOR FLIGHT ABILITY:
OPERATING ON A LOW PLANE

ROUTINES:
UNUSED AND UNDISCOVERED POTENTIAL

CONTROLLED ENVIRONMENT:
LIMITED POSSIBILITIES

DEPENDENCE:
UNUSED ABILITIES

The World of the Eagle

For centuries eagles have fascinated and inspired humans all over the world as a symbol of strength, power and courage. Armies of the ancient world used the symbol of the eagle to generate courage in soldiers for battle. Many countries around the world used the symbol of the eagle on their coat of arms. Ancient civilizations such as Sumer used the eagle as their symbol of power and strength. The Roman emperors as well as Charlemagne adopted the eagle as their symbol of power and might. Napoleon also is said to have chosen the eagle over the lion as the symbol of his army. In 1782, the United States Congress selected the bald eagle as the emblem of the United States of America. Today on American currency you will see the symbol of the bald eagle with outstretched wings.

Several distinguishable characteristics stand out about the eagle. First, eagles have extremely sharp and excellent vision. Their large eyes are equipped with several times more light-sensitive cells per square millimeter of retina than humans' eyes, allowing them the ability to see small objects at a great distance. The sharpness of their vision is said to be about four times that of humans with perfect vision. An eagle can see a small animal at a great distance, some estimate up to or more than one mile.

Second, eagles perch high. Therefore they do not need to jump from branch to branch as birds on the lower planes do for fear of predators. Neither do they move their heads in a fashion that suggest imminent danger as chickens do. Even when there is no danger the chicken seems to be passionately alert, and at the slightest noise it jumps to attention with its head moving in a circular motion as if looking for the source of danger. I guess no one can blame the poor chicken. After seeing its poor brothers and sisters taken for food and never returned, its hypervigilance is understandable.

Third, eagles have large and powerful wings as well as sharp and strong talons. The bald eagle, also known as the American eagle, has a wing size that can spread to almost eight feet wide. Such powerful wings give the eagle its awesome lifting and gliding power. In addition to its powerful wings, the eagle can kill its prey by inserting its powerful talons into it. Everything about this bird, form its large and strong hooked beak, sharp vision and powerful wings to its deadly and strong talons is fitted to give the eagle greatness in the air and on the ground. Consequently, the eagle stands on top of the food chain, while chickens are situated at the lower end.

The world of the eagle stands in direct contrast to that of the chicken. For one, eagles are not domesticated birds like chickens. Generally, they are not limited by any of the domesticated conditions and restraints of the chicken. People do not breed them for food. They can't be fenced in like chickens—there is no fence in the world high enough to keep an eagle from flying over it and away. They exist on more than one plane. They can be earthbound as well as airbound. This means they have a wider scope of input than chickens do, which are restricted to the same day-to-day visual stimulation of their fenced world. A number of studies estimated that some eagles can reach soaring height of several thousand feet.

Some estimates say over ten thousand feet. Only when travelling in an aircraft can one appreciates such height.

Domesticated Chicken Syndrome

Imagine for a moment that a newly hatched eaglet is found by a chicken farmer who decides to raise it along with his chickens. Imagine further that as this eaglet grows into an adult eagle it acquires the belief that it is a chicken. As the conditions of domestication further bear upon the growing eagle it becomes much harder for it to access its true identity or utilize its capabilities. Bear in mind that the eagle has not lost its identity or memory of what it is. The eagle has lived among chickens all its developing life and does not know any other life. It has no memory but those it has made amongst the chickens and no experience but those with chickens. So naturally, accessing its inner natures and true identity will take a lot of work. Living among chickens for so long, it develops what I call the *domesticated chicken syndrome,* an acquired pattern of chicken behaviour that is incompatible with that of the eagle's true nature.

It is important to note here that a chicken cannot have this syndrome, because it is a chicken by nature and therefore behaves naturally like one. Therefore, only the eagle can have this syndrome. To behave and live like a chicken is not its true nature but a learned and acquired one. Although it is built for the open sky and heights it has learned to live behind a fence in a limited and prescribed area with clipped wings. Although it is built for autonomy and power, it has learned to be weak and dependent. Although built as a powerful predator, it has learned to be tamed and dependant on handouts for its survival. Although build for greatness and the exceptional, it has learned to be satisfied with the mundane and routine. As a result, over time it acquires the same type of domesticated characteristics as the chicken. Eventually, it learns to think and behave like a chicken.

Because of its inability to access its true nature and identity, it develops domesticated chicken syndrome. This means that while the eagle has not lost its eagle abilities, it has never learned how to access them. Simply put, it has learned to be a chicken. Until the eagle is placed in an environment that allows it to access its abilities, it will never behave like one. Its true nature and potential will forever lie dormant in the world of the chicken.

This illustrates the implications of domestication. Domestication is an effective process that can bring any animal or bird into submission by the restraint of circumstances.

We now turn to the main meat of this chapter, that is, how humans, designed for the greatest purpose, with potential beyond any other creature in the known universe, can become domesticated and tamed by circumstances.

Effects of Domestication

From the very first moment we were born, we were thrust into a world of people and circumstances. Everything about us has to do with people and circumstances, as well as our own internal world of perceptions and thoughts.

A great deal about us is shaped by our environment. Our very thoughts and feelings have not escaped some shaping and conditioning from the contexts in which we are embedded. Some of these are good and positive; they help sharpen our natural abilities and point us along the path toward our destiny. Others are not so good; they domesticate us.

Much like the eagle with domesticated chicken syndrome, some people grew up in conditions and circumstances that shaped their thinking in believing they are failures and therefore doomed to live out their lives in domesticated and restricted chicken conditions. Let us examine some of the domesticated conditions in which people are often embedded and consequently conditioned and shaped.

Poor Flight Ability: Operating on a Lower or Ground Level

Chickens have wings but poor flight ability. The eagle raised in the chicken's world may be living with clipped wings, which prevent it from flying or flying too high. The condition of poor flight ability situates chickens and the domesticated eagle in a world of lower order or ground-level-only mobility. Almost everything about the world of the chicken suggests a lower state of being when compared to that of the high flying eagle. It is the lower end of the food chain; a bird cannot go any lower. It is a world of limited vision and therefore limited possibilities. Untamed or undomesticated eagles soar high with the wind and can see the big picture. They are able to see and engage more possibilities. The same is not true for the domesticated eagle or chicken.

People who are domesticated by their circumstances are not able to rise to an altitude of greatness where they can see the big picture or a range of possibilities. They are unable to see beyond their past or immediate circumstances that have a domesticated hold on them. Their wings of potential are clipped by their perceptions of their own situations. Like chickens, which find comfort and safety in their coop and in the company of other chickens, people domesticated by their circumstances often retreat to the perceived comfort of their coop circumstances or the company of others having similar experiences. Here the cliché "misery loves company" is lived out in their lives. They constantly use what I call *the Adam syndrome.* This syndrome was passed on from Adam to the rest of humanity but has come to more closely define people who are born to soar like eagles but live out their life as barnyard chickens. This syndrome is the *excuse disease,* which has invaded and fenced almost every area of potential in some people's life. Those existing with a severe case of this disease have become pathological excuse makers. Some of their excuses have to do with not having enough time for anything to do with breaking out of domestication in pursuit of greatness. They are of the opinion that time is measured out in quantity and not much is given to them. Sometime they will say that they will get to it in time, as if they are masters of the future. Another common excuse they make is not having enough of the needed resources to accomplish what they need to do in order to break out of domestication. They are of the opinion that resources are rare jewels to which they have no access. They also often make the excuse that they don't have anyone to help them get started. They are of the opinion that people are obligated to come to their aid or invest their resources in them.

These people usually have almost an infinite repertoire of excuses from which to draw. What is surprising, though, is that while they use these and other excuses to not access their eagle identity and resources, they also use them as reasons why they have to remain in the lower state of mediocrity and continue scratching in the dirt for mere survival. In a later chapter you will learn more about the disabling power of excuses and how to overcome them.

I have met many people with the potential of eagles who unfortunately are unable to access their true nature due to domesticated chicken syndrome. They are fully equipped with flying and soaring powers and capacity to reach the maximum elevation of success, but every time they feel the powerful wind of change they fold their wings and gladly run back to the comfort of their coop among the chickens, who so gladly receive them.

Controlled Environment: Limited Possibilities

While a fence is a good thing in that it provides protection for the weak and the vulnerable, it can impede the ability of those without such vulnerabilities. Fences, coops or other forms of controlled environments are good protection for chickens because they are weak and vulnerable birds. They are easy prey for wild animals and birds of prey. Given their vulnerabilities and the many dangers they face, domesticated chickens must be protected by any means necessary. While they can defend themselves from small predators they stand no chance against others. Their beaks are small and only provide them with enough strength to peck small things off the ground. The beak of the eagle, on the other hand, is designed with a powerful hook-like feature to catch and kill prey in a swift and deadly fashion. Because it is a meat eater, its beak is strong enough to pull and rip an animal's flesh with profound and deadly efficiency. To domesticate and fence in an eagle is to tame its soaring abilities, limit the range of its visual reach, deprive it of its possibilities and take away its independence. When you fenced in an eagle, you capture it along with its potential.

While many people are not responsible for the circumstances that invaded and fenced in their lives, they are responsible for continuing to remain behind these fences and limiting circumstances. They are responsible for perceiving and believing that there is no possibility beyond their present situations. This is because learning who we are and what we are capable of is our responsibility.

The following statements highlight characteristics of people who are domesticated and fenced in by their circumstances:

- They feel that they can do nothing to change the situations in their lives.
- They don't believe they have what it takes to accomplish anything great or significant.
- They often just feel glad to have a job and settle with the way things are.
- They feel they are too old or too tired to do anything about their situation or anything else.
- They often blame others for not helping them to get started or to get ahead.
- Even though they are not satisfied with their lives, they have come to accept the way things are and have no desire to change them.
- They often point to their bad experiences in the past as reasons why things are the way they are in the present.
- They have no particular goal, plan or dream that occupies their thoughts and is their passion towards which they are presently moving.
- They often feel that life is difficult as it is, so why bother anyway.

By nature an eagle is an eagle. All it ever needs to live like one is self-knowledge. The sad news is, if it never discovers what it is and what it is capable of, it will forever live like a chicken.

You cannot discover possibilities in a fenced and restricted environment. Your vision is limited and your possibilities are few. You cannot see or know what lies beyond the fence of your circumstances. Many people throughout history and even in our own time have transcended their circumstances to soar to heights of greatness and prominence.

The story of Nelson Mandela tells us of a man who did not allow years in prison to fence in and limit his potential, abilities and possibilities. After his release from prison, Mandela delved into his life work, which was started almost forty years before. What he endured never quenched his fire or clipped his wings. In 1994 he became the first black president of South Africa.

Another great person of our time is Dr. Stephen Hawking. He gradually lost the use of his limbs and voice and is said to be almost completely paralyzed due to a disabling disease. Although severely hampered by his illness, Dr. Hawking continues to do research, write and lecture around the world. This man is a model of what it means to transcend limiting, captivating and domesticating circumstances.

Oprah Winfrey, another great person of our modern time, has inspired women and men across culture, race, religion and language everywhere. She is not just an icon but a high flying and soaring eagle. Having experienced many challenges, she refused to be fenced in by any, took to the skies like a soaring eagle and became one of the world's most famous women. Her love for people has won the hearts of millions around the world. Like a true eagle, she has demonstrated with her own life that people are built to soar and to reach their fullest potential.

Another eagle of our time is Barack Obama, the president of the United States at the writing of this book. On January 20, 2009, he was inaugurated into office as the 44th president of the United States of America. History was made on this day when the first black man assumed the greatest office in the land. The history of black people in the United States has been one of challenge and struggle. Who would have thought the day would come when the dream of Dr. Martin Luther King Jr. would come to pass? By becoming the president of the United States of America, Barack Obama demonstrated to people everywhere that anyone, regardless of skin colour or ethnicity, is born with the capacity to soar. There is no doubt that President Obama has inspired black people all over the world with his rise to the White House. Can you break free of your fenced and captivating environment? President Obama would say, "Yes, you can!"

The final eagle I wish to mention is Dr. Benjamin Carson. This man has truly inspired me as well as many others. After attending one of his presentations in

Toronto I was moved by his story of a poor and humble family life. His story begins with his mother, Sonya Carson, a domestic worker, who instilled in her sons the idea that being black and poor was no excuse to live out their lives like chickens when deep inside they were born to soar like eagles. Although she had limited reading ability she managed to get her sons to read and do writing assignments, which led to improved grades in high school. After graduating with honours from high school Ben Carson attended Yale University, where he received a degree in psychology. Then he attended Michigan Medical School, where his interests finally led him into neurosurgery. At age thirty-three he became the youngest person and first person of colour to direct the John Hopkins Hospital Division of Pediatric Neurosurgery. Dr. Ben Carson made medical history in 1987 when he became the first surgeon in the world to successfully operate on and separate twins conjoined at the back of the head. In his own testimony, he said he and his surgical team of fifty members worked for twenty-two hours and with prayer and the help of God were successful in their work. After the surgery, the twins were able to survive independently on their own. To date, Dr. Carson has performed many other incredible medical procedures. He has written several books, each of which revolves around a central theme, that is, there is an eagle in each of us waiting to be discovered.

Each of the persons highlighted had opportunities to throw their hands in the air and give up because of their life's conditions and the fenced environment in which they found themselves. What made them push ahead and fly over their fenced conditions to new possibilities? What fueled the spark of greatness in each of them? What did they feel that other do not? What did they discover about themselves that others have not?

The answer to these questions is simply that they discovered the eagle within. They discovered that you don't have to live out your life in the environment of limited possibilities. They discovered that you have personal agency over your life and that you have responsibility over the choices you make in life. They discovered that if you want to raise yourself to new heights and discover new possibilities in life you cannot continue to live behind the domesticated fences of excuses, past failures, poor beginnings, early abuse and misuse, fear of the unknown, fear of change or an inferiority complex. Rather, you must spread your wings and with the help of God and the wind of change raise yourself to the skies.

Dependence: Unused Abilities

Another condition of domestication is dependence. Domesticated dependency puts you in a subordinate position to someone else. This means you are in a needy and restricted relationship and totally reliant on the efforts of others. In this text I have distinguished between domesticated dependence, which I refer to as *subordinate dependence*, and normal dependence, which I call *mutual dependence*. In normal dependence, people exist in a mutual supportive relationship, and one person's contribution is usually reciprocated by those they are in relationship with. These two types of dependencies are fully illustrated in figure 3.2.

Figure 3.2. Continuum of Dependence

NORMAL Dependence   DOMESTICATED Dependence

EXAMPLES:
Unrestricted dependence
Interdependence
Mutual dependence
Seller-buyer context
Doctor-patient context
Negotiating power

EXAMPLES:
Restricted dependence
Subordinated dependence
Top-down controlled
Master-slave context
Master-servant context
No negotiating power

Conditions that characterize the two types of dependence are located at the two ends of the continuum. As shown, domesticated dependence involves a situation in which a person exists in a subordinate, top-down controlled, restricted, non-negotiating or master-servant relationship. Existing in such a subordinate role does more than restrict negotiating power; it provides no opportunity to use one's unique abilities. It does not facilitate the releasing and use of one's natural abilities. These abilities remain unused and dormant. This type of domesticated dependence fits well with the nature and capacity of chickens. In contrast, such contexts stifle and inhibit the true potential of an eagle.

At the other end of the continuum lies normal dependence. Everything in this world is dependent on something else to some degree for its existence or continuation. Normal dependence occurs everywhere in nature, in the physical, social and spiritual world. For example, normal dependence exists between a doctor and his or her patient. Without patients a doctor would not be needed or have any income. The patient, on the other hand, depends on the medical expertise of the doctor to take care of any medical condition he or she may have. In this relationship, neither the doctor nor the patient is in a subordinate position; each is serving the other in a mutual and beneficial way.

The seller and the buyer are also in a relationship of normal dependence. Without the seller the buyer will not have needed resources, and without the buyer the seller will end up with unwanted goods. Again, none of these individuals are in a subordinate position; each has an equal right to negotiate the prospective deal. What can the chicken negotiate? It is in a subordinate role and a one-sided relationship in which only the owner has any right. In the same way that the chicken is subordinate to its owner, individuals can become subordinate to their circumstances, living without any allowable negotiating powers or rights. They are in a continuous master-servant or restricted state of domesticated dependence.

It is hard to miss this master-servant relationship that exists between people and their circumstances. Their experiences dictate their every move and set limits on how high they reach and how far they go. One just needs to listen to the excuses people make. For example,

- If it wasn't for _____, I would be able to _____.
- If my parents hadn't been so poor, I would be better off today.
- If I hadn't had such a rough early life, I would be farther ahead today.
- If only I'd had the opportunity to ___, I would be farther ahead.
- I would, but _____.
- When I sort myself out I will _____.
- If I had enough time I would _____.

While some of these circumstances may very well be genuine, why do people continue to allow them to hold them back and to dictate how far they go, when they start or what they do? Why does a good future have to be inhibited by these excuses? Why do they continue to shape people's destiny into a domesticated coop of a life?

Routines: Undiscovered Potentials

Like dependence, there are two sides to routines. These two sides I will refer to as domesticated routines and normal routines. When someone does an activity over and over it is said to become a routine. A routine is normal, positive and good if it helps you develop commitment for something that is productive and beneficial. This means that continuing your routine produces good benefits in particular areas of your life and work. If you follow your routine and exercise daily, your health and well-being will increase. If your routine is to wake up at a certain time to catch a particular bus so you can reach work on time, this routine will help you keep your job.

Routines can also have a dark side. The dark side of routines is what is here referred to as *domesticated routine.* This type of routine can damage potential so that it is never realized or discovered. Domesticated routines lead to a life of mediocrity. The quality of your life is poor and unchallenged. You yearn for change and challenge but feel afraid that you are not ready or prepared for it and may fail if you try to embrace it.

If we go back to our example of the domesticated eagle, we find that the eagle has developed the same routine of wondering aimlessly around the farmyard day after day, just like the chickens. Over time it has developed pecking routines like the chickens, a walking routine from fence to coop, and jumping routines. It is clear that none of these routines is productive and beneficial to the eagle. The natural everyday routines that are beneficial to the chickens do not benefit the eagle in any way. In fact, these chicken routines work to block the eagle's true potential and capabilities. Furthermore, while chickens are comfortable and happy with these routines, the eagle is frustrated. The chickens have perfected these routines by nature, but the eagle by nature cannot. Because everything about it is oversized, the eagle will always feel different, odd and awkward among the chickens. Think of the eagle trying to scratch for worms with its large talons. There is no way it can gain mastery over these routines.

Why are some people frustrated over the way their lives are lived, from paycheque to paycheque and from hand to mouth? Why do they yearn for something bigger, better and greater? They have the potential for greatness but have difficulty accessing it. They feel awkward and uncomfortable among people who are satisfied with mediocrity and unproductive routines of life and even wonder how they are so easily satisfied with such things.

Like the eagle trapped in chicken routines, some individuals are inhibited by their perception of their circumstances and cannot move their lives forward. Like chickens, these individuals wander aimlessly around with unproductive habits and patterns of life, never discovering or unlocking their true potential. Their potential remains undiscovered and blocked due to routines that do not help them discover who they are and what they are capable of achieving. Here are some hints to uncover domesticated routines:

- Routines that prevent you from making positive and needed changes in your life
- Routines that block your ability to be creativity and imaginative
- Routines that keep you from looking at different possibilities
- Routines that make you feel that where you are is good enough and you do not need to improve any further

Zones of Domestication

Are you a chicken or an eagle? If you believe you are an eagle trapped in a chicken's world, how domesticated do you think you are? For some people, classifying themselves as a chicken is unthinkable. Yet these same individuals consistently demonstrate severe domesticated symptoms. They are living like chickens but refuse to believe they are domesticated.

Others who accept the fact that their lives are domesticated believe there is more they could do with themselves but admit fear of the unknown. On the other hand, there are others who are so frustrated with their condition that they have resolved to embrace change.

Examining these different ways that people tend to categorize themselves suggests the existence of a continuum of domestication. Not everyone is at the same level of domestication. Some seem to be deeper, others seem to be somewhere in the middle, and still others appear to be at a point of resolution for change. From this observation we can conclude that domestication can be conceptualized as occurring across three main zones. At one end is the *extreme zone* of domestication. In the middle is the *moderate zone* of domestication and at the other end is the *resolution zone* of domestication. This is illustrated in figure 3.3. The illustration also shows how much of a chicken or an eagle you are.

Figure 3.3. Zones of Domestication

EXTREME ZONE

- Believe they cannot change their condition
- Live in the shadow of the success of others
- Blame others for their perceived inabilities
- Blame their past for present perceived failures
- Accept life's small handouts as ideal
- Believe others have better luck than them
- Do and say things that hinder others from flying
- Extremely dependent on the efforts of others

MODERATE ZONE

- Feel there is more to them than what life is offering but usually does little to move forward
- Often feel frustrated with their mediocre life and long for something bigger and better
- Are often influenced by those living in the extreme zone
- Have ambitious goals and visions but no definable plans to reach them
- Are dependent on the efforts of others for their success

RESOLUTION ZONE

- Have growing wings and they are attempting to fly.
- Begin to discover their true nature
- Can see the mountain and believe they have soaring ability to get them to the peak
- Are less dependent on the efforts of others to determine their success

Zone of Extreme Domestication

People at the extreme zone of domestication do not feel the need to change. They believe their life is fine as it is and therefore make no attempt to change its course. Every challenge is perceived as a mountain that can never be climbed or a valley that can never be crossed. They are extremely dependent on the efforts of others. They often live in the shadows of the success of others. Their life story is often one of excuses, blame, self-doubt, lack of self-confidence, and pessimism. They are complacent and are quick to accept the small things life offers as the best they can achieve. When the subjects of growth and becoming are discussed, they will often talk about what they had dreamt of doing and becoming. Their thoughts about becoming and vision are usually a reaction to what others say about themselves. They lack originality and creativity in their thinking and conversation. If they do speak in term of vision and the future it is usually unrealistic and lacks appropriate measurability. If you ask them what their goal is for the next three or five years they will either give you an unrealistic goal or struggle to come up with one. When the conversation is over, they usually go back to their old ways of thinking and being, that is, their domesticated life. They have no motivation, imagination, passion or enthusiasm necessary to move their life to the next level. They have no long-term plans, no plan for change and no conceptualization or vision of how the future might be better than the present. They are willing to live one day at a time without the challenge of peeking into the future or daring to chart a path toward what can be. At the core they are unable to think and see too far into the future. They often question and even criticize the motives of others who have visions of greatness and often remind them that they will never get too far with their vision. They make it difficult for others in the moderate zone of domestication to grow their wings and fly. They consciously and unconsciously do everything they can to hinder the discovery and the unfolding of potential in others. They are afraid to see others grow and become when they themselves are not. In fact, some people are so domesticated that they will even create chicken environments for others. They will become the fenced situation that blocks others from discovering their true potential.

They are easily overwhelmed and become discouraged by the smallest challenge and disappointment and quickly retreat into their coop of *down in the dumps*. They constantly complain about life but feel they can do nothing to change their condition. They often speak of their condition as their fate, God's will for them, bad luck, or their lot in life. They constantly engage in what is called *self-fulfilling prophecy.* This concept describes situations in which a person makes statements of expectations or prediction about a future situation and then acts in ways that actually make this expectation or prediction come to pass.

Self-fulfilling prophecies can be negative or positive. For example, Susan says, "I know I am not going to do well on this final exam." In view of this expectation, Susan puts little effort in her studying for the final exam, therefore bringing to pass what she predicted or expected. People living in the extreme zone of domestication constantly engage in the negative side of self-fulfilling prophecy. They sabotage any thought of grandeur or any idea that suggests that they may be able to lift themselves from their coop condition. In fact, their negative, helpless and pessimistic view of life often penetrates their own zone, exerting significant influence on their close neighbours in the moderate zone.

It is important to note that not all who live in the extreme zone of domestication are critical and pessimistic. Some are very optimistic and positive. They often believe that things will change for them and that their future will be different. The problem is that they do not believe that the change has to begin with them initiating it. They believe that somehow something miraculously will happen that will change their life forever. With this mindset, they continue in the same low-paying job with no intention of improving their education or skills, hoping and expecting that their break will come by some divine intervention, miracle or luck. They look for a genie in every situation. They prefer to borrow than to initiate, to beg than to create, to reap than to plant, and to lean on others than to stand on their own. They will push and even encourage others toward success but never attempt to ignite their own spark. They may often say that they are living by faith. Faith for them is mere and meagre survival, which is oftentimes living from paycheque to paycheque and hoping for a miracle at every turn. Their view of faith never allows them to see beyond their domesticated sense of being. They often speak of the goodness and riches of God and his ability to do and provide all things, while at the same time they are unable to find the basic things of life. Such faith is toxic if it paints God as one who has all things and is able to do all things while allowing his people to live from hand to mouth in conditions that are less than ideal.

The truth is, it is not that God keeps people on these levels; rather, it is that people have the wrong concept of their personal agency in life and therefore attribute their lack of success to the action or will of God. God wants to be a divine partner, not a divine wheelchair or divine crutch. God has given us feet and the ability to walk; why would he give us a divine wheelchair when we have the ability for mobility? What he will give us is divine insight and guidance, not more feet. If God has given us feet and mobility, it is our responsibility to get up and walk. By the same token, if God has given us a mind and we can think, why do we make it the responsibility of God to think for us? All we need to do is ask him for guidance and insight as we think, but thinking is a human exercise and responsibility.

Some people by no choice of their own are thrust into conditions of domestication from which it may be impossible to rise without some help. Sometimes the sociocultural, socioeconomic and political forces that give rise to these domesticated conditions makes it extremely difficult to even turn, much more fly, out of these debilitating conditions. In these extreme situations, it becomes the responsibility of others to come to their rescue.

Zone of Moderate Domestication

People in the moderate zone of domestication feel that there is more to life than what they are experiencing. They often feel frustrated with their mediocre life and long for something bigger and better. They have a deep longing for bigger and better things but fear that if they attempt to do more they will only end up failing. They often generate visions of how the future can be but eventually surrender them to the criticism and pessimism of their close chicken neighbours living in the extreme zone. Their self-confidence is low and fragile and therefore easily damaged. They know that there is more for them than what life is offering in the present. Their wings are clipped but have some lifting power. Because their wings do not have the necessary wing spread for sustained flight and soaring, they fear the very winds of change that they often feel. They have come to the realization that they are not the same as their close domesticated neighbours living in the extreme zone, but they are nonetheless fearful to move out into unfamiliar territories. They will often initiate great projects, like going back to school, starting a business, or making some financial change, but because of the inability to reach and sustain soaring heights like a free and unclipped eagle, these endeavours usually never get off the ground and often end in failure, leaving them with more disappointments and feelings of inadequacy.

While they are not as dependent on the efforts of others as those in the extreme zone, they are still moderately dependent. They do not feel they can initiate and sustain change on their own accord. They often blame others for failed projects they initiated. This is because they believe that personal success always depends on the contributions of friends, family and community.

They long to be like their neighbours in the resolution zone but lack the flight ability to rise above the status quo. They are usually motivated by them and often try to be around them. Being caught between those in the resolution zone and those in the extreme zone sometimes leaves them in confusion and uncertainty. Some of those in the moderate zone have great dreams of grandeur, massive and attainable visions, and great ambition. However, they often fail to move themselves toward the achievement of these goals simply because they fail to settle on any one plan. They usually have a host of workable plans but are never able to settle on any particular one. Consequently, the vision continues to be no closer to fulfillment than when it was first conceived.

Soon any bird will realize that while the right wind is always great, it does not have to stand around and wait for that special wind. Their wings were made with flapping ability to raise them to heights even without any great wind. Sitting around waiting for that special plan or that heavenly miracle will never raise you to heights that reach to the mountaintops and above the clouds. No matter how ambitious the goal or how spectacular the vision, a plan must be developed to attain it. Continuously vacillating between plans does not get you to your goal—not even off the ground.

Resolution Zone of Domestication

People in this zone of domestication have begun to redefine themselves. They are feeling the wind of change and have begun to embrace it. They are no longer allowing themselves to be influenced by a domesticated mentality. Not only can they see the mountain, they realize they have the soaring ability to get there. They are less dependent on the efforts of others. They do not sit around and complain about the lack of support and contributions from family, friends or community. They believe that while they are not absolute masters of their destiny or independent of the help and contributions of others, they bear a large responsibility for how their lives turn out. They have come to realize that getting out of their domesticated condition begins with their own desire and initiative. They are developing a healthy faith in God. They believe God gives wisdom to the wise and helps those who are willing to think and take initiative for their lives and to exert energy and motivation for success.

What people living with a domesticated mentality fail to understand is that while family, friends and community can and may support their vision and initiatives, the responsibility of bringing the vision into full view is theirs alone. As I have noted on several occasions, while we live in constant dependence on others, we must distinguish between normal and domesticated dependence. Every project, every vision, and every initiative at some level will depend on the contributions of others.

Someone might ask, what if you don't have anyone to help you get started on a particular initiative? What do you do then? My response to this question is another question: If you have no one to contribute to your initiative does that mean you sit and wait until someone is ready and willing to contribute? What if no one comes? Where does that leave you? It is you alone who is responsible for your initiative. It is entirely up to you to turn it into a workable solution. You may have to modify it, redevelop the idea or fit it into the path of those who can help, but you must make it work. You can solicit the ideas of others in the reconstruction of your idea, but the ownership of the initiative belongs to you. Its failure or success is your responsibility.

Built for Challenge

Anyone who has seen an eagle or read about them will agree that these birds are built for challenges. They are built for speed, strength, vision and height. In the first chapter of this book we discussed the awesome and surpassing abilities and capacities of humans. Like eagles humans are built for challenge and greatness. Humans were created to engage the dynamics, uncertainties and complexities in every domain and frontier of life.

For example, for centuries humans have looked up at the heavenly bodies and have wondered in amazement about them. Some have even thought of them as superior to humans and worshiped them as gods and goddesses. Today, we don't need to view them in those ways anymore. Men have walked on the moon, held the dust and rocks of the moon in their hands and brought back pictures of the surface of the moon. They have sent unmanned spacecraft deep into space to explore and help them understand the nature of the universe and what's out there. Many of the aspects of the universe that once mystified humans are now merely the subject of scientific investigations.

Everything about us is about learning, becoming, growing, knowing, discovery and attaining. Our brains are designed with the ability and capacity to learn and develop. They can even grow new dendrites and make new neural connections to accommodate new learning and experiences. Given time, nothing in the universe will be too complex or difficult for the human mind to explore and understand. This means we are created for challenges.

Therefore it is not good for us if everything is easy. Great strength and endurance are built under severe pressure; muscles are developed by lifting weights; effective performance is attained after many hours of strenuous practice, and understanding of complex subjects is reached after lengthy and intense investigation and studies. Why then are some individuals afraid of challenges? Why do they give up at the slightest indication that something is difficult?

The answer is, some people like things easy. While they wish that their lives could be lifted to higher levels, they are not prepare to exert much energy or time to reach those desired levels. Some have lived so long on the help of others that they have no motivation to build their own mental muscles or chart their own paths. While they will commit themselves to small projects, they will quickly give up if such requires significant effort that may draw them out of their comfort zone or from their status quo. These people are unable to commit themselves to a task and persevere toward its attainment if it appears challenging and takes too long. Some people may consider going back to school too demanding because it requires dedication to academic requirements and a require commitment of time.

Many people live below their financial earning ability, their academic potential, social capability, and even spiritual capacity. They stay on this low plane and refuse to engage the world of challenge and opportunities because achieving such goals requires determination, commitment, endurance and tenacity. They are afraid to stretch, push or raise themselves to heights that match the potential they already possess. They have become soft, fearful, helpless, and even lazy. They respond to every challenge with overwhelming feelings of helplessness and despair.

In 2 Timothy 1:6–7, we read about young Timothy, Paul's understudy, who appears to have been struggling with fear and timidity. It seems that, because of his youth, he was doubtful of his ability to undertake the task assigned to him. The apostle Paul rebuked him and instructed him to ignite the flame of giftedness God had given to him for ministry. Paul also reminded him that God had not given him a spirit of timidity and fear, but of strength and soundness of mind.

What does this example from Scripture teach us? First, that God has invested abilities in us. Second, that he expects us to do something about their development. Third, the fear, inhibition or helplessness we feel is not of divine origin but developed from our own flawed perceptions of our circumstances. Fourth, we are responsible for the development of our ability. Therefore we should not sit around and tell ourselves that we are waiting on God to fix our situation, on a miraculous or lucky break, our ship to come to shore or someone to come to our rescue. We must arise and get to work in fanning our spark into full flame.

Conclusion

This chapter introduced you to the nature of domestication and its effects on people. Not knowing what potential you possess and what possibilities are yours will lead to a life lived out in severe limitation controlled by negative experiences of the past as well as perception of helplessness in the present. This chapter not only presented you with insights that can stimulate change in every area of your life, it challenged you to break out of domestication and become who you can be. Not knowing is always a valid excuse for not acting, but once knowledge is gained you become responsible for the actions and the change they can produce. The truth is, humans were not created to be boxed in by circumstances or to live out their lives behind bars of helplessness. Yet for the most part, that is exactly what appears to be happening to so many. In the next chapter you'll learn more about how you can limit the negative influences that bear upon your life from your situated experiences.

chapter four

SITUATED
Identity

No matter how we try, we cannot escape
the influence others have on us. We can, however,
limit the degree to which we are changed into their image.

The metaphoric example of the eagle raised among chickens who over time failed to access and develop its true identity and capacities helps us understand that who we are situated among can influence the accessing or the development of our own identity. The company we keep and the people we come to depend on in our lives exert powerful influence over our thoughts and actions to the point where it becomes difficult to separate our own sense of self from the understanding of ourselves we derive from others.

Many social psychologists believe that the image we have of ourselves is at least partly derived from the people with whom we associate. The people who formed part of our social lives at different stage of our development usually leave significant impressions on our sense of self. Accordingly, our sense of self is a construction that developed over time and includes not only our own reflections from our experiences but also other's expectations, opinions and statements used to describe us.

Understanding our embedded associations and connectedness with the people we relate to and live among and the consequences on our sense of self is critical. In this text the concept of *situated identity* refers to the understanding and view of ourselves we derive from our experience and connectedness with others. In other words, our social experiences help us locate ourselves relative to others. Once acquired, such identity provides the text through which we understand who we are and the mirror through which we see ourselves. Our ability to lift ourselves, to act and move our lives forward thus becomes greatly dependent on the type of identity we develop in our situated conditions.

The intent here is to help you understand the nature of your embedded associations with the world of people, the effects of such connectedness and how you can effectively navigate your way through the maze of negative influences and soar to the height of your God-given ability and potential. To accomplish this it is necessary to delve into two basic discussions related to our situated identity. The first of these has to do with our core social desires. The second has to do with how we see ourselves. These two topics will help you understand how your association with people and your own reflections help create the lenses through which you see yourself. After reading this chapter you should understand particularly why most people find it difficult to pull themselves away from the negative influences of the people with whom they are associated.

Our Core Social Desires

No one lives in a vacuum. Everything we do is to some degree influenced by others. No matter how we try we cannot escape some level of influence on our lives from others. Our sense of self and worth unfolds not when we are isolated but when we are interacting and connecting with others.

Social connectedness and interaction allow people the opportunity to perceive themselves and others in meaningful ways. Our concept of our own self as well as others develops within the context of our social interactions.

Think for a moment how many times each day you interact with other people, friends, co-workers, family members, intimate partners, neighbours, teachers, customers or salespersons. Besides, how many times each day do you think about other people? People are the source of our greatest joy and, unfortunately, also our deepest sorrow. We are in many ways eternally connected to others.

Our core desires are deeply entrenched in our relationships with people. How do we select our own path, change, or move forward without being influenced or affected by others in ways that are not compatible with who we are or want to be? How do we avoid changing into the image others expect us to have? Furthermore, how can we be ourselves, set goals and achieve them when people sometime make us feel weak, afraid, worthless, incompetent and even foolish?

The answers to these questions can be arrived at by understanding our core social needs and how they function in the social dynamics of our life. These include our need for affiliation, self-expression and social validation. Let us now turn our attention to these core desires by which we are brought into situations with others and through which we at least partially develop our own sense of self.

Our Desire to Belong

What do you want most in life? What would make you feel truly satisfied and happy? I believe the answer most people would give would involved a truly loving and lasting relationship or at least some form of meaningful relationship. I believe human beings everywhere have a fundamental need for affiliation. This is why there are groups, villages, towns and cities. Friendships, marriages and other forms of relationships are also results of people's need to affiliate. This is because we are not meant to be alone or to be totally self-sufficient.

In the 1950s, psychologist Abraham Maslow constructed what he referred to as a hierarchy of the five basic needs that he believed all humans must have met in order to develop and grow. Maslow believed that our first and most basic need is our physiological or body needs. His second category of needs has to do with safety. His third category is the need for affiliation or the need to belong. His fourth has to do with esteem needs and his fifth and highest deals with self-actualization needs. The fact that belonging needs fall below esteem and self-actualization needs in his model shows how fundamental and critical this need is to both. Its position below esteem and self-actualization needs means that a person desire for affiliation, family and friends runs deeper than the need for respect, confidence and achievement. Numerous scientific studies have been done on the human need to belong. Results across these studies consistently suggest the dominant effect of the need to belong on people's motivation, relationships, learning and other dynamics and endeavours of life. My own doctoral research in educational psychology explored the effects of the need to belong among older learners in an intergenerational classroom setting and found it to be profoundly transformational on people's sense of self in a learning context. The need to belong exerts strong influence on the thoughts and actions of human beings at every stage of their development. We not only crave the context of a meaningful relationship but are to a great extent dependent on it for our social identity. What we come to know about ourselves is greatly influenced not only by our relational associations and connectedness with others but with how affiliated we feel among them. This means the more affiliated we feel among people the greater their influence on us.

Although people often fight with each other, at the core, they would love to live in harmony. Although people often say "leave me alone," at the core they long for meaningful connections. Although people often divorce and walk out of relationships, at the core they wish it could have worked. We would like to have good relationships with our bosses, neighbours, spouses, siblings, co-workers, peers, teachers, students and so on. If you think this does not apply to you, consider how you would feel if you suddenly realize that no one wants you around, and I mean no one, not your spouse, siblings, parents, children, or friends, whichever applies to you. The need to belong runs so deep that people have been known to become ill and even depressed due to their perception that they are not needed among significant others. It is a feeling that you are standing on the outside looking in. The perception that you don't belong can undermine your motivation and weaken your zeal for accomplishing important things and even for life itself. Conversely, when we feel that we are needed, that we belong, that there is a place for us among others, we are motivated and inspired to move forward. Recall that in Maslow's hierarchy of needs both esteem and self-actualization needs are both undergirded by belonging needs. I have read and listened to the news about the broken lives of many celebrities. In many cases, their lives are not broken because they have lost status or out of a job and broke, but rather because their relationships are not fulfilling and satisfying. At the end of the day, you want to know there is someone you can share your success or your disappointment with. There seems to be a profound truth to the cliché "money cannot buy happiness." This is because, at the most basic level of human nature, people's need for affiliation is stronger than their need for achievements, fame and fortune.

Within the context of these meaningful relationships and connections we come to appreciate the positive way others talk to us, what they say about us, and the statements they use to describe us. Often times we internalize and integrate these perspectives of others into our own self-description and self-definition. We come to be affected or influence by them sometimes consciously and at other times unconsciously. For example, ask a young child to describe herself and listen if her description does not more times fit with those of significant people in her life. This is because our need to belong situates us in social contexts in which we derive self-understanding. What we believe we can do and how far we can aspire rest heavily on the understanding we develop about ourselves in our social associations with people. If the people we hang out with and feel a great sense of belonging among are not ambitious, aspiring, and have no desire to move their lives forward, our sense of community with them can work to acculturate us in ways that our own outlook in life is no different from theirs. On the other hand, being a part of the right company, can help us see ourselves as capable with a "yes I can" attitude.

The Negative Side of Belonging

While the need to belong is a natural part of our nature, it does not always work in healthy and productive ways for all people all the time. Sometimes the desire to belong is so great that some people will do anything to fit themselves in with others even at great cost to themselves and their future. They become what and who others expect them to be. In so doing they lose who they are and conform to the norms and expectation of others. When this happens we move down a path that is far different from that which fits with who we are and what we can be. Our own dreams, values, attitudes, beliefs and expectations become modified to fit with those whom we desire to be like. When people do this it is usually because their need for affiliation runs deeper than their need for distinctiveness and individuality, and without the balance their sense of self becomes lost within the identities and expectations of others. When a person's need for fitting in and be accepted by others surpasses the need to be one's self, the person becomes extremely adjustable even to the point of redefining who he or she is in line with the standard of others. Although we are created for relationship and community, we should guard against losing the awareness of our own self, values and ultimately our own destiny. Does this mean we should isolate ourselves from others? Absolutely not! What this means is that we must seek to balance our need for affiliation and our need for individuality and distinctiveness. The need or desire to belong should never bring us to levels where we lose who we are and become domesticated by the values, norms and attitudes of others, unless those values and norms are healthy, productive and can help us reach soaring heights. Remember, each person is created with the capacity for greatness and must therefore guard against losing complete access to it.

Being humans our nature allows us both the need for affiliation and the need for distinctiveness. Striking the balance between the two can sometime be difficult. Leaning to one side at the expense of the other can be damaging. While like the eagle, our nature craves individuality and uniqueness, it can also be tamed by domestication leading to unhealthy and damaging conformity. This been said though, it is important to note that some people have such abnormally high sense of individuality and uniqueness that their sense of self becomes inflated and skewed. Such self-absorption usually leads them down the path of narcissism and insensitivity to the needs of others. These are the type of people who think they don't need others. To them people are mere resources to get them to their mountain peak of success. What's interesting though, is when they get there they suddenly realize how lonely it is at the top without someone to share it with.

While some people see themselves as extremely independent of people, others are at the other end of the continuum of belonging. They have an extremely high need to fit in with others. Such extreme need for affiliation exists probably because it reduces the burden of personal agency and from making hard and difficult decisions. Like chickens, they love to know that others are watching their backs, looking out for them, making hard decisions and giving them direction at every turn, and ready to pull them out of a hard spot. In such a case, they collapse their needs for individuality, uniqueness, personal agency and creative rights into a state of dependent and utter helplessness. Consequently, they deprive themselves of the capacity for self-discovery and the type of fulfillment that comes from discovering and creating their own destiny. In this extreme case of belonging a person's sense of self is totally dependent on their associations with others. Their self-esteem becomes a function of their embedded connections and relationships with others.

What does the phrase "eagles fly alone" mean? In fact, have you ever seen an eagle? Not many people have seen eagles. This is because eagles usually fly high, usually live in high places, and usually fly solo. The phrase may mean different things to different people, but for most people I think it carries the connotation of not being a follower. While there is absolutely nothing wrong with being in a group with a sense of belonging, having an eagle mentality protects one from losing their individuality and the awareness of their own sense of personal agency. People with eagle mentality are aware that they are unique and that it might be necessary for them to stand alone even against group norms if such norms conflict with their own sense of self, values and beliefs. These individuals have developed the understanding that safety is not always in number. This is in direct contrast to people with chicken mentality. Usually, wherever you see one chicken you can expect to find others not too far away. You can say, for a chicken, there is safety in number. People with chicken mentality easily become deindividualized, which is the state in which a person loses his or her sense of self and values and become adapted to a group norms and behaviours.

Our Desire for Self-expression and Validation
Another core social desire humans have is the need for self-expression. Like the need to belong, the need to express ourselves also has implications that

underscore our sense of self and therefore plays a defining role in whether we feel and function like chickens or eagles. This fundamental human need has to do with our deep desire to be seen, heard and understood. If we are not allowed the opportunity to express ourselves we develop the sense of been invisible among others. Therefore, at the core of our need to express ourselves is the fear of being invisible to others.

Think of it, how do you feel about yourself when someone compliments you about something you wear or a task you complete well? On the other hand, how would you feel if after you went through all that work of painting your house or spending all that time on your hairstyle, only to realize that no one noticed what you did? In fact, have you ever put a great deal of effort in your dressing, a project or a speech and not consider how others will receive it? Probably not! Most of us cannot help thinking what others will say or think when we make some type of public presentation. Just like the need to belong, the need to be seen through the public expression of ourselves also runs deep.

People express themselves in various ways. They express themselves in their physical appearance, the way they talk and what they talk about, how they work at tasks, and how they relate to others. Everything we do that has others in view is an expression of who we are. Without self-expression we do not get feedbacks and therefore have difficulty understanding ourselves and our true impact on others, which is a measure of how effective we are. We increase and become to the extent that we express ourselves. Self-expression tells us and others how far we have come, what stage we are at, how much we have learned, the degree of effectiveness we have and what our true worth is. Without the opportunity to express ourselves we tend to feel stifled, incomplete, and unfulfilled. We are beings capable not only of self-expression but are at our best when we are expressing ourselves effectively.

The capacity to meaningfully express our internal states and experiences sets us apart from all creation. We can formulate thoughts and opinions and also experience a wide range of emotions all at the same time. However, none of this would make much sense without the opportunity and appropriate context in which they could be meaningfully expressed. Our thoughts, capacities, ideas, feelings, opinions, abilities must be brought to the surface in order to impact the world in some way and at some level. For that reason, we measure ourselves, our competence, value, and potential by what others say when they receive what we present of ourselves. If every time you wear a certain style dressing your friends told you it makes you look weird, no matter how you like it, you will lean strongly toward changing it. Why? Simply because you feel your self-expression needs the validation of others. Do you remember how you felt after sharing your aspiration or your accomplishments with someone who took the time to listen and then complimented you positively? Or, do you remember how you felt after giving that planned speech, or after presenting that project you had so tirelessly worked on through so many sleepless nights? The sense of accomplishment you felt was based not only on the fact that the project came forth from your own creativity and skills, but was also based on the confirmatory responses you got from significant others. Your true feeling was completed when others noticed the finished product in positive ways. The finish project, whether it was a college essay, a university research paper, solution for a complex business problem, or a well-cooked meal, will express your feelings, thinking process, unique perspective, and distinctive ability to organize and synthesize information. However, not until your work is noticed do you feel that sense of accomplishment and that sense of visibility. Think about it, no matter how happy you felt after completing your project and presenting it as a representation of you, until you received validation for the work from significant others, your elation was incomplete. In fact, how well you think you did will only be confirmed in your mind when you receive comments from individuals capable of such validation. On the other hand, if after putting so much work and energy in the project you receive a feedback that says your project is far from acceptable, no matter how good you felt about your project you would become dispirited. Why? Because what people have to say about your presentation or your performance, tend to override your own feelings and cuts deep into your sense of competence. This is because how we measure and judge ourselves is linked with whether we perceive that others notice us and also what they think and feel about how we express ourselves. This tells us that our desire to express ourselves can often make us vulnerable to the feedbacks we receive.

There is no doubt that validation from significant others help shape the view we have of ourselves. Such approval provides us with information about ourselves. Without such validation we would be unsure of ourselves leaving us to wonder if what we said was correct or appropriate or if what we did was good or competent. Most students judge their competence from the feedbacks and validation they receive from their teachers.

Validation is one of the most important elements in social interaction and interchange. It is a natural and essential element in social life and relationship building and maintenance. We need it from our spouses, children, parents, teachers, friends, bosses, and so on. It is one of the embedded dynamics of our social life which helps us develop our sense of self and competence. It does not mean you are a chicken or that something is wrong with you because you look for and expect validation from others.

What does self-expression and validation have to do with your thinking, identity and your ability to be like eagles? A whole lot! For one, we not only connect with and express ourselves to people, but in so doing we acquire a view of who we are as reflected in the feedbacks we receive from them. It is this reflected view of ourselves that we eventually think about and incorporate into our own self-understanding. Consequently, it is this self-understanding that will either enable or inhibit your capacity for growth and becoming. If people are so vulnerable to the feedbacks from others, how do we come to really know who we are and capable of becoming? While our sense of self is not free from our associations with others, knowing who we are must be derived from the revelation that we are unique individuals who have been created in the image of God and of such possess capacities for greatness regardless of failures or how others see us and what they say about us.

The Negative Side of Social Validation

While social validation can be healthy in that it provides us with some measure of self-knowledge, it can also be detrimental to our sense of self. It is detrimental to our identity when we believe we are competent or incompetent at a task just because others validate or invalidate us. It is detrimental to us when we believe we have a right to feel and express certain types of emotions only when someone validates them. The sense of self we develop as a result of our extreme need for validation can distort the image of who we are and what we are really capable of becoming and achieving.

I have listened to the stories of many people who were invalidated or told by significant people in their lives, including parents and teachers, that they were not good enough and therefore will not be able to pursue certain goals. Some of these individuals validated themselves and achieved their goals.

Validation or invalidation from others should be received tentatively. This means it should pass through the grid of your own sense of self.

Many people live either in dependence on the validation of others or as victims of invalidation. The sense of self developed in either of these cases will only work to prevent these individual from accessing their true capabilities. This means if their vision of a possible future situation is not validated it may not be pursued. They will never be satisfied with themselves, their ability or a completed task without the approval of others.

Our capacity to move our lives forward, make choices that takes us to new levels, visualize what the future can be and determine our own path in life rests heavily on our ability to validate our own self as well as our understanding that God has already validated us through the redeeming sacrifice of Christ. Our sense of who we are and what we are personally capable of should never rest totally on the validation of others.

While there is no doubt that certain types of feedbacks and comments others give us can work to help us understand more about ourselves, by themselves these are not meant to give us a clear image of who we are and what we are capable of becoming. A person's feedback to us only informs us about a particular instance or set of conditions in the present, not what can be in the future.

How We See Ourselves

I once asked a young man, "Are you a chicken or an eagle?"

Surprisingly, his answer to me was "I'm a chicken."

I asked him why he came to that conclusion. He said that the friends he associated with were all chickens, and he was no different from them.

I then asked him to tell me what he knew about eagles. His response was that eagles are not afraid of heights, they fly usually alone, they are not followers, and that they are very powerful birds. Chickens, on the other hand, he noted, are cowards, run at the slightest sound, are usually found in a group and cannot fly very high.

My dialogue with this young man demonstrated a profound reality: our sense of self and how we define ourselves has a great deal to do with the people among whom we are situated and have close association. If you were asked the same question, what would be your response? In classifying yourself as either a chicken or an eagle, what thoughts would be going through your mind?

Probably you would think about the things you have accomplished, the kind of friends you have, and how people have described you. Regardless of whether you identify yourself as a chicken or an eagle, your self-identity will in some ways be based on your embedded associations and connections with others. How you see yourself and the image you have of who you are play a crucial role in how you see the future and the type of image you can create in your vision of it.

Bear in mind that the image you are able to create in your vision of the future is really an extension of who you believe you are in the present and how that image can change in the future. If the image you have of yourself is entirely the image you are seeing through the lenses of others, then the image you create in your vision of the future is really not yours.

Earlier in this chapter we discussed how our core social desires bring us in close association with people. We saw that the situations created through these needs have self-defining implications. In other words, how people define themselves has a lot to do with their situated conditions and associations. In this section of the chapter we want to expand on this earlier discussion by specifically focusing on the lenses through which people see themselves.

As an example, consider the following questions. How do you see yourself? What do you tell others when you talk about yourself? Do other people see you the same way you see yourself? Is the image you have of yourself compatible with the image others have of you? Moreover, how did you arrive at the image of yourself you currently hold? Do you often struggle to reconcile the differences, if any, between the images of yourself you hold and that which others hold of you? The question of how we see ourselves is both relevant and critical to the discovering of who we are.

It is not unnatural to be influenced by how others see us. Neither is it unnatural to see ourselves as others see us. In fact, a clear view of ourselves includes input from others as well as our own view. The problem is when our view of self leans more toward the image others have of us. Let us examine several lenses through which we see ourselves.

The Lens of Social Comparison

How we see ourselves is related to how we see others. In social psychology this is referred to as *social comparison*. The theory of social comparison was first proposed in 1954 by social psychologist Leon Festinger (Festinger 1954, 117–140). According to the initial formulation of the theory, people have an internal tendency to assess their own opinion and desires by comparing themselves to others. This means individuals look to the images of others as the standard by which they should measure themselves in order to get a feel of who they are, where they are, how well they are doing, how competent they are, how good they look, and even how far they should go in life.

Think about how many people wear name-brand clothes because these garments link them with people they think are important. People want to be like others because they believe others are the standard for who they should be and how they should behave.

Measuring ourselves against others can be a healthy activity if our goal is to use such information to enhance our own growth and well-being. It is unhealthy if the goal is merely to associate us with others. Sometimes when people compare themselves with others in order to survive they lose their unique and distinctive edge and become merely uncritical followers. It can also be detrimental if the information arrived at leads us to have an inflated sense of self because the comparison shows that we are ahead of others. Not striking the right balance when we compare ourselves with others can generate feelings of inflated superiority as well as feelings of helplessness and downright incompetence.

Let's say you get 69 percent in an exam. This is your highest grade in the class so far; your previous grades ranged between 59 and 65 percent. Obviously, you are elated. However, after class you find out that your friend who sits beside you, who rarely comes to class, scored 95 percent on the same test. In fact, his lowest mark in the class is 82 percent. How would you see yourself when compared with your friend? Some people would see themselves as not very smart.

Let's extend this to another example. Let's say a friend who talks with you after class is a bit depressed because his grades have been failing. His marks range between 45 and 57 percent, and on this exam he got only 55 percent. The passing mark for each test is 60 percent. He is clearly failing the course. How would you see yourself now after your conversation with this student? Most people would feel better about themselves seeing that they did better. This tells us that how we see ourselves is to a great extent dependent on how we see others.

Indeed, our self-confidence and self-esteem rise or fall as we compare ourselves with other. In the process we develop a view of our own selves as competent, incompetent, or somewhere between. Whether this view has some truth or not, it is fragmented and unfiltered. This means the result of a social comparison should always pass through the grid of one's personal and independent knowledge of self. The results of a comparison should never be the final definition of who one is or can be.

Our potential is never limited or set within the boundary of how we perform in a single or series of events. We are always more than the discrete experiences in our lives. Who we can be and how far we can reach are never defined by how we perform, in the past or in the present, or how we compare with others.

The Lens of Others' Expectations

Whether negative or positive, people's expectations and attitude toward us can be taken as a mirror through which we conceptualize ourselves. Why have you pursued the goals you have in life? Why have you not pursued particular goals in your life? What do you believe about your current self? What do you believe you are capable of achieving or becoming?

While you are pondering the answers to these questions, think how many of these goals and beliefs are reflective of the expectations of significant people in your life. In fact, think of how much of your own behaviour is reflective of the expectations of others. The expectations of significant people in our lives can have defining effects on what we do, how well we do, how high we aspire, what we become, and how we see ourselves.

Consider the following example. When Mr. Thomas told his son, Mark, that he knew he could win the game, he established an expectation of success for his son. While Mark might have initially entered the game just for the fun of it, winning now became an expectation of his father. Such expectations will affect not only how Mark plays the game but also how he sees himself as a player. The expectations of others have a subtle and profound influence on how we behave and think and how we see ourselves.

There are several ways that people's expectations of us work to influence our view of ourselves. First, people's expectations of us can work as a self-fulfilling prophecy. This means that when people expect certain things of us they usually behave toward us in light of their expectations. For example, a mother communicates to her daughter that she expects above-average success in her piano classes, because she knows she has what it takes to become a skillful player. Now, if the mother's actions and attitude toward her daughter are supportive and in line with her expectations, what are the odds that her daughter will drop her piano lessons or be unmotivated towards them? If a father communicates that he does not expect his son to succeed at a certain task and gives his son little or no support, the son might eventually give up and come to see himself in light of his father's expectations. People have the tendency to play up to the expectations of others, consciously and unconsciously. If we know that people expect the best that we can do, we tend to behave accordingly. On the other hand, if people expect the worst from us we may not be motivated to give them anymore than they expect.

Second, people's expectations of us can act as statements of assumptions that in turn lead us to see ourselves in certain ways. For example, when Mr. Thomas established his winning expectation for Mark, the assumption was that Mark had the skills to win the game. Seeing himself through the lens of such expectations, Mark might be led to believe that he really has what it takes to win the game. He arrives at this conclusion by seeing himself through the lens of his father's expectations, which function as an unwritten statement of assumption about his ability to win.

Can you recall those students you knew in grade school or high school who were always unruly and disruptive? What were the general expectations among students and teachers of these so-called disruptive students on a day-to-day basis? Didn't they come to expect such behaviour and communicate it around the school so that these disruptive students heard it? When people are perceived in a certain way and are in fact expected to behave in such ways, it makes it easy for them to behave in such ways, even if at first such actions are unintentional.

What expectations do you know people have of you and how do you see yourself in light of those expectations? Go as far back as childhood and see if you can remember and identify some specific ones your parents had of you. Then try to describe their effects on your view of yourself now.

The Lens of Personal Experiences

We not only see ourselves through the lens of social comparison or the expectations of others; we also see ourselves through our own personal experiences.

How would you respond to the question "What do you believe about yourself?" Most likely your answer would include information about yourself derived from the experiences you have had. If you did poorly throughout high school and as a result did not pursue college or university, you probably believe you are not academically smart. If you had several failed relationships and have not held a good and stable job in several years, you may believe that you are a failure in life.

The view you have of yourself through the lens of your experiences is the same view you project in your future situations. If the view of yourself as perceived from your experiences is negative, this is the same view you are most likely to have of yourself in a future situation. It becomes the benchmark for all future relational, academic, occupational, and social transactions. How accurate do you think such views are?

There is no doubt that our personal experiences matter in that they tell us something about ourselves. But how much do they really tell us? Do they tell us all about what we can be or how far we can go?

While our personal experiences do give us information about ourselves, they do not tell us the whole story. They show us only a fragment of what has been, never the whole story and never what can be.

The lens of our experiences is good in that it shows us what strengths and weakness were brought out under given situations in the past. I have seen students who earned straight As in high school but did very poorly in college and university. On the other hand, I have seen students who did not earn high enough grades to enter university but graduated with honours from community college. Some of these same students continued on to university and graduated with honours. This tells us that the condition under which an experience of failure or success occurs plays a critical role in the performance itself.

A woman might have had two failed relationships but flourished in the third, leading to a good marriage, simply because the relational environment created by each potential husband brought out strengths as well as weaknesses in her. In this case, the third man in her life, whom she eventually married, may have created a better environment more conducive to the emerging of her better qualities.

How we see ourselves through our experiences should be tempered with the knowledge that different conditions affect us differently and that no single and discrete situation can completely define who we are in the present and who we can be in the future.

The Lens of the Future

One of the most fascinating things about humans is that self-definition is not confined to our comparison with others or the expectations of others or even set within the limits of our own past and current experiences. The image we see of ourselves can actually transcend what comes from the past and what exists in the present to what we can located in the future. We can be in a failing situation but see ourselves as having the capacity to succeed in the future. Although we've experienced several failures we can refuse to believe we are failures and instead see ourselves succeeding in the future.

People who persevere under duress and trying situations are those who see themselves through the lens of the future. They are able to look beyond what is toward what they can be. The moment you begin to see yourself through the lens of the future you lift yourself beyond your present situation. When you do this the present situation loses its total effect and control over you. You can see yourself as possessing the capacity to be a capable and competent person even though you are failing in the present.

Remember, failure is not self-defining. All it tells is that you have failed at something under a certain set of conditions. It does not tell you if you will acquire the ability to succeed in the future. It is you who must see yourself in such light. It is you who must create the positive image of what you can be and what you can achieve.

Conclusion

Our embedded relationships with others have defining characteristics, and therefore care must be taken when we view and define who we are and what we can do. While the social part of us desires to be with others, and necessarily so, we must balance the influences others exert on us with our sense of self. In the next chapter we explore how to see with our minds and not with our eyes.

chapter five

Vision:
SEEING BEYOND
What Is

Vision helps us look beyond what we are, where we are,
and what is toward what we can become,
beyond what is to what can be.

Sight is one of the most complex and fascinating senses we possess. It combines both sensation and perception. It is easy for us to mistakenly believe that seeing something is entirely a function of the eye only. Our eye along with its complex mechanisms are only half of what's involved in the event of seeing. The human eye only functions as the sensor and converter of visible light into nerve impulses, which are then sent by way of the optical nerve deep into the brain to a region called the occipital lobe, located at the back of the brain. In other words, the eye transforms the raw sense material of light into a form (nerve impulses) that can be recognized by the brain. Once these impulses reach appropriate regions in the brain, they are transformed into images representing the object from which the light was sensed by the eye. This is known as perception.

The event of seeing requires the function of complex mechanisms in the eye as well as sophisticated operations of specialized cells and regions of the brain. The initial stages of visual processing take place in the eye through the work of sensitive sensory receptors in the retina. Once these receptors convert light waves into neural impulses they are then sent to specific regions in the brain for further processing. Not until the brain receives the impulses from the optic nerve do we know what the eye has sensed or can we say that we see something. Seeing, then, is the combined effort of both eye and brain.

This chapter takes you beyond the physical and neurological mechanisms and processes of sight toward the mind's ability to see not merely what is but what can be. It is about seeing without the flow of optic nerve impulses and the limitations of optical mechanisms. It's about employing the mental powers of the mind to see beyond people, objects, and experiences that are bounded by time and circumstances to a present sensory reality. It's about employing the service of the mind at a higher level of intention and consciousness.

Seeing Without Your Eyes

Earlier we discussed the sharp and powerful vision of the eagle and its ability to see small prey at a great distance. Vision is one of the most developed senses in birds, and eagles are distinguished for their sharp and powerful eyesight. They have large eyes (as large as those of humans), which allows for a larger retinal area where the visual image is projected. The retina of the eagle's eye contain a larger number of concentrated cones (receptor cells that convert and send sensory sight information to the brain) than those in humans. This allows them to see with excellent visual accuracy as well as with detailed colour perception.

The back of the eagle's eye is larger than that of humans, which means the image formed there is larger. This gives them not only a longer range of sight but also greater visual sharpness and accuracy than humans. Imagine that you and an eagle are on a high mountain peak, and a rabbit is situated about one mile away on a plane in the distance. Try as you will, you will not be able to see the rabbit. The eagle, on the other hand, will see the rabbit with great visual accuracy and sharpness.

Eagles also have two foveae or centres of focus while humans only have one. The fovea is a special area of the retina where there is a large concentration of vision cells. In the human eye, the fovea is located at the centre of the retina, an area as small as the period at the end of this sentence. When you view an object directly, the image of the object is focused on the centre of your fovea, which is the clearest point of your vision. Our one fovea allows us binocular or forward vision. This means when viewing an object we focus both eyes toward it. In the eagle's eye, one fovea is used like the binocular (forward) vision in human; the other fovea gives them the ability to look sideways. Consequently, having two foveae allows them the ability to see frontward as well as sideways at the same time.

Sight is a natural ability for humans and most other creatures. From the day we were born our eyes were opened naturally to the world of visual sensation.

No one taught us how to see. All we had to do was open our eyes, and even that came with the package of sight. As we began our visual journey no one informed us that we actually possess another visual ability, one that allows us to see without the use of our sensory and visual mechanisms, one that gives us the capacity to look beyond a present condition into a possible future and to conceptualize what the future can be and even to work out its detail through imagination.

This awesome non-sensory visual ability, like that of the eagle, has more than one fovea on which there is a concentration of countless vision cells, allowing us to see far and wide. In fact, without the ability to access this awesome ability people will even struggle with their exercise of faith. Faith is about seeing with another eye; it is about seeing beyond the material furnished by sensory perception. Visioning then is akin to faith.

One of the major obstacles to seeing into the future is that some people are unable to close their eyes to their sensory experiences. The extent of their sight is set within the borders of their single-fovea sensory world. When they look at their present experience they focus on it and are unable to see anything but what their single sensory experience allows them to see. It is this limitation set by the world of sensory experience and perception that prevents many from viewing the horizon of a new and different experience.

By *sensory experience* is meant the experience of the world around us. We experience the world through our senses. Everything around us makes up our sensory world. This includes our experience of realities such as hearing the singing of birds, seeing the sunset, and feeling the warmth of sunshine. Sensory experience includes but is not limited to these physical realities. It includes our interactive experiences with people and situations; the hurt and the failures we experienced or is experiencing. It also includes negative information and messages we continue to get from the people around us. All these work to influence as well as set limits on our feelings, thoughts and perceptions of the events in our everyday experience. They can work to inhibit our mental visual ability or can help us discover it.

There is absolutely no doubt that our present sensory world is important. For one, it furnishes us with the experiential material necessary for human development, relationships, and growth. The sensory world of sight gives us information about our world that no other sense can. It allows us to see things as they are in the present. Without sight, the world would be dark and colourless. Sight, then, is one of the most precious abilities humans have. This is why most people fear blindness more than any other disability.

However, connecting to and experiencing a present reality is but one function of our mind. We have the capacity to imaginatively experience and see more than what is in the here and now. The capacity of our mind to see surpasses its keen ability to perceive tangible objects and experiential situations. It possesses the awesome capability of visualizing possibilities, of seeing beyond what is into the conception of what can be. It can gaze into the future and create a possible situation far brighter, more complex and bigger than what experientially exists in the present. When directed and channeled, the mind can bring into focus an image or representation of any situation of any magnitude of a future state of affairs.

The ability of our mind to formulate a mental picture of a possible future situation and what we can become is known as visioning. Once conceived, this vision of the future is larger and brighter than our present perception and image of the way things are. Vision always deals with the future. It is really where the future begins. Not only does vision look toward the future, but it has the capacity to paint the picture in a much bigger frame with brighter and clearer colours than in the reality of a past or present experience. Although always conceived within the context of a present situation, a vision is never defined or confined to the limits set by such circumstances. Vision bridges the present condition with a possible future situation. This is illustrated in figure 5.1 following. Notice that the size of the conceived vision is many times larger than the situation in which it was conceived. Its magnitude is limited only by our imagination.

Figure 5.1. *The Illustration of Vision*

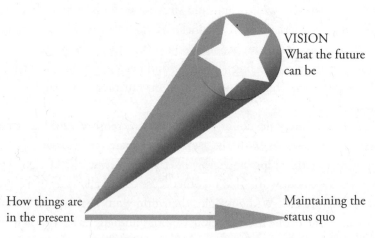

VISION
What the future
can be

How things are
in the present

Maintaining the
status quo

Although the mind's ability to perceptively construct images from sensory data is associated with its ability to visualize or constructively conceptualize, its ability to visualize is not set within the boundaries of sensory information. In the field of psychology, for example, perception is considered to be the process by which the brain acquires, interprets, selects, and organizes sensory information. From a psychological perspective, then, perception in one sense deals with material brought in from the sensory world through our senses.

This sensory material deals with the here and now. Many people find it difficult to move beyond this here-and-now reality. Their perception of the present situation becomes the ongoing reality to which they are imprisoned and shackled. To visualize is to go beyond this reality created by sensory perceptions bounded in the here and now. It is seeing yourself in the future doing something you would like to do that is impossible in the present.

No one can write about vision and dream without mentioning Dr. Martin Luther King Jr. In a time when it was difficult for African Americans to hold good jobs and share equal rights on all levels with whites, one man dared to dream, dared to look beyond what was and into the future and conceptualize what could be, regardless of what was. Dr. King conceived of a future where black people and white people would live together in equality, where people would be judged not by the colour of their skin but by the content of their hearts. Although the conditions in which he lived were discouraging and disappointing, Dr. King was not blinded by these but was able to look beyond them into the distant future and dream of how things could be different and better. His inspiring, passionate and memorable "I have a dream" speech at the Lincoln Memorial at Washington, D.C., on August 28, 1963, imprinted a legacy not only on the hearts of those who heard it but also on history itself.

Dr. King forever changed the way people of colour would view their future. He taught us that present conditions, regardless of how discouraging and demoralizing, should never be the measure of what the future can be. He taught us that the future is a product of visualizing and hard work. He taught us that satisfaction and complacency with present unsatisfying situations will never create a better future. Finally, he taught us that the vision of the future is always conceived from right where you are in the present but extends beyond it.

As we have already noted the election of Barack Obama as president of the United States of America not only confirmed aspects of the dream of Dr. Martin Luther King Jr.; it also demonstrated the truth that the future does not have to look like the past or the present. It took a special type of sight and imagination to conceptualize and paint the future as different from the present. We now turn to the topic of imagination.

Imagination: *The Paint Brush of Your Future*

A casual observation of the design of God's creation from the simplest to the most complex demonstrates an imaginative capacity beyond our finite comprehension. It is from this awesome mould of imaginative genius that God patterned our human imaginative and creative capacity. In designing our human mind, God did more than give us the capacity to visualize what the future can be; he gave us the mental tool kit to paint our future in ways that will make our lives colourful, meaningful and productive.

Vision gives you a macro view of how things can be in the future; it allows you to see the big picture. Imagination, on the other hand, allows you to see and work out the details of it. Here imagination is the creative capacity of the human mind. It is considered one of the faculties of the mind that allows you to see as well as form mental images and generate sensations and impressions with or without the aid of information drawn from the physical senses. Not only does imagination allows you to form images; it allows you to modify and change it as you wish.

We use our imagination almost every time we think about the past, present and future, as well as when we think about people, situations and objects. Although ultimately your imaginative materials have roots in sense experience, they are by no means limited by the range of these sense experiences. Imagination not only permits us to extend across the three dimensions of time—past, present and future; it also allows us the ability to

1) conceptually reframe past experience so that they affect us differently,
2) conceptually move beyond a present unfavourable situation so that we are not limited or negatively affected by such, and
3) project ourselves into the future and create a possible situation different from the past or present.

Here we can think in terms of what has been, what is, and more importantly, what can be. In fact, with our imagination, not only are we not bound by any of the dimensions of time; we are not limited by the boundaries of space or location. Imagination is only limited by the extent and exercise of our thoughts. With our imagination we can place ourselves in just about any place we wish and at any time we desire. Furthermore, it allows us to not only conceptualize and visualize possibilities but also to transform these possibilities into reality.

With our imaginative genius we can create, modify and recreate possible events. We can draft plans for each and evaluate their possible outcomes, as well as visualize how to overcome possible obstacles. Not only does imagination provides us access into the unknown world of the future; it furnishes us with the navigational tools necessary to chart our way deep into the territory of this unknown future state of affairs. In fact, by bridging the present with the future, imagination makes the unknown future becomes familiar to us. Two of the major factors of imagination are the mental workspace and the paintbrush of imagination.

Your Mental Workspace

As a mental workspace, imagination is both reconstructive or interpolative and constructive or extrapolative. It is reconstructive in the sense that it operates on our past experiences by reaching back and synthesizing aspects of our past memories into new and different mental paradigms, allowing us to see and experience the past in new and different ways. It can do this by using our experiential material from the past in conjunction with those in the present. This interpolative or reconstructive ability of imagination allows us to renovate and reframe our past experiences, therefore altering their effects and influence on us in the present, as well as nullifying the extent of their negative potential influence on our future.

A person's inability to use imagination in such reconstructive or interpolative ways may mean being trapped in a domesticated and limited frame of reference by incapacitating experiences. Your reconstructive imaginative ability can serve to unshackle you from any experience in the past that prevents you from moving your life forward.

Many psychologists and psychotherapists employ the techniques of reframing and reconstructing when working with clients who have past experiences from which they are unable to recover by themselves. Such techniques allow them to help clients see and experience a different view of their past. Seeing the past in a new light leads to changes in the client's present perception of it, thus breaking the stronghold the past has on his or her life. Although the reality of memories of events and experiences in the past is not erased, their negative effects become manageable or nullified.

The mental workspace of imagination is also constructive or extrapolative. This characteristic of imagination deals more with the present. This means it helps us create meaning from our present experiences. It allows us to view a present experience from many angles by imaginatively constructing different scenarios of the same event.

Take the example of a person who has just lost his job at which he has worked for twenty years. His entire financial life is built around the salary he gets from this job. How he views this loss and the level of his distress will depend on the nature of what is going on in his imaginative mental workspace. It is here that he presents the distressing situation, and it is here that imagination goes to work in constructing different scenarios from which the best alternative can be selected. If he is not very imaginative, he might come to the conclusion that he can do nothing to change his situation. If he is imaginative, he can think of the possibility of using his acquired skills to start his own business or conceive of job situations in which he could use his transferable skills.

The constructive process of imagination also allows us to extrapolate and build bridges from where we are to far into the unknown future. While it is often said that one cannot cross a bridge before one gets to it, it is the act of crossing bridges in the imagination that puts some individuals far ahead of others in this world. Individuals who dare to build bridges and cross them in their imagination are those that have and continue to effect great and positive changes in human history. Those who build bridges in their imagination are those who seem to arrive in the future long before others even dream of it.

This means imagination makes it possible for us to think new and fresh ideas outside the confines of our present perceptual reality. In this imaginative mental workspace, although we consider past and current experiences, the ideas we can form are not set within their limits. We are not bounded by what has or is being experienced. Tapping into new ideas is a constructive process that allows us to see the future in new ways. In this way, imagination functions as the architect of our future state of affair. It creates and fashion without the constraints set by present circumstances. In fact, imagination is at its best when it uses the material furnished by our present experiences to form new and fresh ones. It can build something new and fresh from present material while at the same time not being limited by it.

In our mental workspace where the genius of your imagination is at work, anything is possible. The imaginative material and possibilities are virtually limitless. In this workspace of the mind you can construct and modify your future as you see it.

Stop for a while and imagine yourself in the job of your dream, at your dream vacation spot, driving the kind of car you like, making the kind of salary you would like or living in the house of your dreams. Did you feel limited in your imagination? You can sit in contemplation all day and never run out of imaginative material. While some of these material borders on fantasy, we can imagine what can actually be.

Bear in mind that vision only gives you the picture of what the future can be, but it is the task of your imaginative workspace to make the picture your own, personalize it and shape it to fit your potential. It is important to note that although imagination is unlimited and powerful, it can never make the picture a reality. Although you can visualize exactly how you want it to be, it will remain a mere dream if it is not brought forth. This, however, is the first step in the process.

The Paintbrush of Creativity

Imagination not only constructs scenarios and create new ideas; it paints you a picture of exactly what the future can be. This means it can paint in outlines, definitions and colours. Imagination is driven by creativity, and there is no limit to its creative genius. It is not boring and mundane. It is full of colours, shapes, contours and life. The right picture of the future will always be appealing, captivating, inspiring and motivating.

This tells you that people who live boring lives are not very imaginative. Your imagination can paint you a picture so beautiful that you just can't wait to get to it. Although painting may come as a natural talent to some, unless it is cultivated and developed you may never become an expert painter.

Similarly, while all people have the capacity to think and imagine, few will develop the ability to control and appropriately direct what enters their mind. Some people allow their imagination to do as it pleases, go astray, run havoc and even dwell on unprofitable mental images, leading to addictive behaviours. Your imagination without conscious control or direction will do things without your permission and can lead your mind into captivity. People who lack the ability to direct and channel their imagination often have difficulty moving their lives forward in productive ways.

If you allow your imagination to run riot, your life will be an uncontrollable mess. But if you consciously begin to channel your imagination, allowing it to focus, you will not only attain self-control; you will also define your future and begin to change your life in accordance with your vision.

If your imagination of the future is not motivating you, you may not have painted the right picture, or the picture may lack completion or arousing definition and colours. The degree of your motivation to move toward your vision depends on how appealing the picture of the future painted by your imagination is.

Bear in mind that you can imagine using all of your five senses. You can imagine the sensations of sight, touch, sound, smell and hearing. This means you can actually visualize or imagine feeling, seeing, tasting and hearing in a future situation. Bringing all these into the picture painted by imagination will have a profound effect on motivation and desire. It is not difficult to see that with imagination you can paint yourself into any possible future situation across the bridge of time, space and circumstances. You can even paint as you plan and plan as you paint.

The creative power of imagination is visible all around us. For example, imagination is necessary if one is to design or invent an instrument, write a book, paint a picture, or even plan how to arrange the furniture in a house. Without the use of imagination, success in the fields of arts, science, technology and even ministry would be significantly impeded if not impossible. Had it not been for imagination, we would not have books, buildings, houses, schools, motor vehicles, airplanes, space rockets, telephones, cellphones, computers, the Internet, Facebook…and the list goes on. Imagination has changed our lives and continues to do so.

Some people will say, "I have no imagination." This is obviously not true. There is no such thing as a human being without imagination. It may be that their imaginative ability is weak and underdeveloped, but everyone has it. In the same way that people can develop their ability to concentrate, they can develop their inner ability to see what can be.

An underdeveloped imagination leads only to idle daydreaming and unprofitable fantasizing. On the other hand, a well-develop and strong imagination provides you the tools necessary to create and recreate, remodel and change your entire life.

Going back to the eagle, remember that its eye has a great number of concentrated receptor cells called cones located in the retina. These cones are used to see colours in detail. Because the eagle has many more of these than humans they are able to see the fine detail of colour even at a great distance. This is why an eagle can spot a small animal at great distance that may be invisible to the human eye.

Imagine creating a vision in the distant future and painting it with the brush of your imagination; to you it is clear, distinct, possible and quite achievable. This may span a distance of five or ten years or more. Now consider trying to communicate it to a person who does not have the eagle's eye, meaning they possess neither the imaginative sharpness nor the visual accuracy for locating a goal across many years. They might laugh at you and think you are out of your mind. Why would they react to your vision in such a way? Don't they possess imagination as you do?

The answer is, they are domesticated and have not learn to access and appropriately use their imaginative powers. They have lived too long as chickens and have never lifted their heads and peeked into the distant sky. They have never employed the full use of their imaginative and creative abilities. They cannot see far into the future as you can. They cannot bridge their present circumstances to the future and paint themselves on the other side of the bridge of time as you can. So they naturally think your vision is too far-fetched, difficult, indistinct and unrealistic.

If directed, the paintbrush of imagination can also paint sad and unhappy situations in the future. If you consistently visualize negative situations in your future, you might end up fulfilling them. But why use such awesome creative genius of the imagination for such unproductive and self-defeating tasks when you can create and paint any meaningful situation in the future? Others have done it, and so can you.

Visioning and Imagination are Human Responsibilities

Much like how we are responsible for finding a job, a life partner, the house we would like to live in, the kind of car we would like to drive and for the proper maintenance of our health, we are responsible for the creation of a vision for our life. Why would God have given us the awesome tool of imagination if he did not expect us to be responsible for its use? What do you suppose would happen to an animal or bird that never uses its instinct? The animal's instinct is built into its nature so that it can survive and take care of itself. If its instinct fails it would not be able to navigate its way in its world and thus would become easy prey for predators.

Using our ability to visualize is a human responsibility. We cannot blame God or anyone else if we fail to use what we have been invested with. We will not be able to find our way around any of the three dimensions of time productively without the appropriate use of our imagination. With imagination, we can conceptually go backward and forward while at the same time make changes in our mental models of the past, the present and the future. This means having a bad experience in the past does not have to hold us back, because with our imagination we can reframe and reinterpret the past in such a way that its effects on us in the present and the future become manageable. Furthermore, not only can we imagine what the future can be, we have the ability to paint ourselves in it in ways that differ significantly from how things were in the past or how things are in the present.

Let's explain this with the use of another example. We have been given the apparatus necessary for sight. What will happen if we decide to walk with our eyes closed? Whose responsibility is it to walk with open eyes? As a driver, I have been frustrated many times when I saw pedestrians walking across the street while talking on their cellphones with no care as to what is happening around them. They yield the responsibility for their lives to drivers, who themselves might be distracted.

In a similar way, we have been given the ability to visualize the future and therefore do not have to walk into it with blinders on or with our imagination blocked by fantasies of unrealistic proportions. People can guide us around objects and even describe what the world is like to us, but they can never truly see and appreciate what is visible for us. When we see, we feel and are aroused by the sensations provided by sight. We are stimulated in mind and body by the fragrance from the variety and nuances of life around us. No one, no matter how masterful they are in describing the world to us, can transfer these visual sensations and impressions to our mind. It is in this sense that no one can see our future or imagine how things could be different in ways that we can. No one can paint the nuances, colours and definitions into our future; these are unique only to us. This responsibility is on our shoulder and ours alone.

It is not possible to not have some imagination of our future. This is because our minds cannot totally block out the future. However, it is possible to not give it any specific meaning or definition.

Think of going to a city you have never been in. You can have a vague and sketchy picture of what you think this city is like, or you can put pieces of information together and paint yourself a more detailed picture of what to expect on arrival. People who have not invested time in visualizing and painting themselves a workable picture of their future will only see bits and pieces of images that the mind naturally provides. These people who have not invested their imagination in their future will have no plans in place for it. This means individuals with no vision and no plan for their future are walking into it with blinders on. Consequently, the future for these individuals will be determined primarily by the random arrangement of the variables in their life.

While we cannot control all the variables in our lives, we are not created to be so helpless that we cannot plan to control those that are controllable. Is it not true that we can determine to a great degree our professions, our spouses and where we live? Are these not all variables that fall within our control? So then, let us stop thinking like chickens and begin taking responsibility for our lives and future.

It is important to note that sometimes life throws us a curve ball. When everything seems to be working according to careful planning, something unexpected suddenly happens. What happen next will determine our ability to take responsibility for and control over our lives and adjust ourselves to changing circumstances or control the controllable variables of life.

Remember, if you throw up your arms and give up, the variables or conditions of your life will take control and lead you in directions you would not have taken if you were at the helm. No one is responsible to chart your future but you. No one is responsible to bridge the present to your future but you. No one is responsible to make your life a success but you. People can help you, but ultimately it is you who must make the final decision that points you in the direction of your preferred future.

There are those who appeal to faith by saying they live by faith and not by sight. By this they mean that they do not need to visualize and plan for their future because God will take care of them in their day-by-day experience. So they close the eyes of their minds and walk by what is known as blind faith. Blind faith is really toxic faith that produces absolutely no work but a lazy and unproductive life. These people forget that the Bible teaches that God gives wisdom only to the wise and helps those who are willing and ready to co-operate with his divine will (Daniel 2:21).

In the book of John chapter 5 we read the case of the man who was crippled for thirty-eight years, who sat by the pool of Bethesda waiting for someone to help him in when the water was divinely touched. One might expect that when Jesus saw the man in this condition he would have immediately healed him. Instead, Jesus came along and asked him if he wanted to be made well. Was this not obvious? The truth is Jesus was willing to help him if he could recognize that although he did not have functional legs he had a functional mind.

The lesson here is we must stop focusing on the resources we do not have and begin using the ones we do have. So you don't have the necessary amount of money to start the business of your dreams, but you have a functional mind with the ability to imagine how you can get the necessary resources you need.

If God wanted to carry you around he would not have provided you with legs. If he wanted to be your eyes he would not have provided you with eyes. If he wanted to think for you he would not have given you free will and a mind with the ability to generate thoughts.

Who is a wise man but one who plans the cost of building and the place for building his house (Luke 14:28–30, Luke 6:48)? The Bible also says that people who refuse to work should not be fed from the produce of those who are working (2 Thessalonians 3:10). Faith is not a blind leap over a cliff into the darkness. Rather, it is a leap over the cliff in the darkness with the confidence that God promises to be there to catch you (even though you cannot see him). But remember, it is you who must do the jumping. The choice to jump is yours, not God; God is not in the business of pushing people off so he can catch them and prove to them that they have faith.

The Transforming Nature of Vision

Vision is transforming in the sense that it has direct effects on thinking, feelings and behaviour. The moment you launch a goal in the future you begin to change. This change takes place in several ways. The first change has to do with your thinking. The moment you decided and resolved that in the next four years you want to finish university or own your own business, you will begin noticing a shift in your thinking. The way you think about life and self begins to take on new meaning. This shift in thinking relates to the demands your goal sets as necessary requisites for its acquisition.

You cannot achieve such an impressive goal as a university degree or owning your own business without making some adjustments in thinking in the present. Your thinking will shift to accommodate the requirements for achieving this goal. Your thinking will become more focus and ordered, and your choices in the present will be made with consideration of the goal at hand. You will become more cognizant of the choices you make and how they might detract from your goal. The very exercise of planning to own your own business requires you to begin thinking and seeing things in different light. How you think about money, saving, investment, planning and so forth now takes on new meaning.

The second change has to do with your motivation. If the thought of achieving your goal does not arouse your motivation from its current level, your vision or goal cannot be considered transformational. Your goal only takes on life when you burn with desire for it. You feel its attainment before you get to it. You imagine already having it before you reach it.

Furthermore, staying the course through the challenges of the visionary journey will take more than a good desire. Between the point where you launch the vision and the point where you actually acquire it will be multiple challenges that will not be easily navigated with just good desires. Your motivation to achieve the goal will depend on the degree to which it has transformed your thinking.

The third change you will notice after launching your goal is your behaviour. Vision defines not only your thinking but also your actions. Only when your goal has changed your thinking and aroused your motivation will your behaviour follow in step. The nature of your actions is critical to the attainment of your goal. If what you do in the present is not in step with what you hope to achieve in the future, it will be difficult if not impossible to attain your goal.

How to Create a Vision

There are some basic steps in how you can begin to create your vision.

Step One: *Begin with a question about your need that focuses on your future.*
Creating a vision for your life requires you to take a first step and ask yourself any one or a combination of the following questions:
- What do I want to become?
- What would I like to be doing?
- Where would I like to be?
- What would be more meaningful for me?

While you are asking yourself the question, project yourself and look into the distant future, anywhere between two and ten years. The answer to this question will become your vision for the future.

Step 2: *Transform the answer to your question into a vision or a mental image of what you would like to accomplish in the future.*
Your vision is your answer to the question you asked regarding your future. Remember, your vision must be bigger and brighter than your present. If your vision can be accomplished where you are and with the resources you presently have, it is not a vision of the future but a mere project. Your vision must extend beyond where you are presently and into the distant future and be impossible to achieve in the present. To transform the answer to your question into a picture requires you to use your imagination. That is, the vision you want to achieve in the future must be created and painted with its details in your mind in the present.

Step 3: *Draft a one-paragraph personal vision statement.*

Your personal vision statement will guide the choices you make each day, influence how you order your activities, and provide you with specific life directions. It will provide you with light for your journey during the dark and discouraging moments of life as you journey toward your vision. Before you write your vision statement, resolve in your own mind that you can and will achieve your vision. Your vision statement tells others what you believe you can and will achieve in the future.

Remember, when you speak of *can* and *will* you are saying two different things. By indicating that you *can* you are actually saying that you are able to, have the necessary resources, or that you have the ability or capacity to do something. By indicating that you *will* you are saying that you have resolved in your mind to do it.

Besides, your personal vision statement allows you to visualize yourself living in your future before you get there. It also contains information about your future aspirations and expectations. For example, if someone is reading your personal vision statement they will immediately know what your plans for the future are.

There is no specific formula you have to follow in order to write your statement. Here are two basic examples of vision statements:

Example 1

Within three years from now I want to own my own business. In five years I would like my business to be making an annual profit of no less than $1 million. I see myself helping others and my company making a difference in the lives of unfortunate and poor individuals in my city and abroad.

Example 2

Seven years from now I will attain my medical degree. I see myself standing on the podium at my graduation as I am awarded a doctorate in medicine. I look across at the audience and hear my family and friends cheering, and I feel a profound sense of pride and accomplishment. With this degree I know I will make a difference in the lives of people suffering from various medical conditions and even work to find ways to cure some long-standing illnesses.

Your personal vision statement allows you the opportunity to transform the mental image of your imagination into words. The act of transforming your vision into words is your first step in making it objective and real. You not only see it in your mind and feel it in your heart; you can use words to clearly and accurately describe it in detail. Only when you can create it in your mind through imagination and describe it with words in your personal vision statement are you ready to move to the next stage.

Step Four: *Create an action plan.*

Your action plan is the stage that brings sharpness and definition to your vision. This is where your vision or mental image of the future begins its transformation into reality. Your action plan specifies what needs to be done along the journey toward your vision.

The completion of one action step should pave the way into another. Sometimes your first action step is the hardest because it is your starting point and requires willpower and determination to break old ways and patterns of thinking and behaving. It is your road map into the unknown and uncharted territory of the future toward the mental image you created. You cannot move your life toward your vision without having an action plan; you will only get lost in the uncharted territories of the uncertainty of what lies ahead. As you follow your action plan you move closer to what you imagine your future to be.

It may be necessary for you to modify your plan or make adjustments to your visual image of the future as you move forward. No plan must be set in stone. Be flexible in your thinking and planning, for life holds many surprises and uncertainties for which we may need to make necessary adjustments and change.

Do not be discouraged and become a victim of circumstances along your journey toward your goal. Remember, you are an eagle within; you have the ability to view many sides of a problem and look beyond what is toward what can be. You are not limited to the present but have an image of what the future can be. With the tool of imagination you can paint and repaint, change lines, modify contours, take out and replace images as well as add and remove colour as you wish. Remember, in your mind you have no limitation but your own thoughts.

Your action plan serves two main purposes. First, it is one of your navigational instruments that will guide you safely to your destination. Once you begin your journey toward your vision you are in unknown territory and can get lost easily. Getting toward your vision requires that you follow a well-worked out plan or path. As each step is achieved successfully, you will know that you have arrived at a signpost or milestone that tells you what distance you have covered and how far you have left to go.

Your action plan also serves as bridging material. There is a great chasm between where you are and where you have located your dream in the future. Between this gap are challenges that are not easily traversed. Getting through to your vision on the other side requires that you build a bridge that connects where you are with your vision. It is your plan that makes it possible to get to the vision on the other side. With an action plan you have left nothing to chance or luck. Clearly, then, without an action plan your vision can never be achieved.

Having a carefully worked out action plan does not mean that things cannot go wrong. Things can go wrong, and they often do. There are variables in life we cannot control. This is where trust in the divine guidance of God comes in. We trust God to give us wisdom at those times when we face unplanned variables and are not prepared to deal with them. His wisdom will become the resource we need to navigate these variables of uncertainties as we push toward our goals. In this, God is not left out of our plans or goal; he is the partner who takes care of the unknown variables and supplies the wisdom necessary to travel through uncharted land.

Step 5: *Review and evaluate.*

Because no plan is perfect, it is important that you review your plan and evaluate or measure your progress periodically as you move toward your goal, even if you think your plan is working fine. You may find that you may need to make some adjustments and modifications to the plan or the vision as you move forward. As mentioned earlier, life is not always a smooth and level playing field; neither is it without sharp turns, high hills and low valleys. Evaluation helps to measure your progress in terms of how well you are doing and how far you are from your intended goal.

Remember that within your action plan is short-term measurable goals that must be accomplished as you move along your visioning journey. Ensure that each of these short-term goals is being achieved successfully and according to the timeline of your action plan and your vision. Without periodic evaluation of your plan you will not know how you are doing, what needs improving or changing or how well current strategies are working given changes in your life situations. Take your vision seriously; this is how your life will move to the next level and where your control over your future begins.

Step 6: *Cultivate productive and strategic habits.*

The final step in creating and achieving your vision requires you to *cultivate productive and strategic habits.* Your habits are your acquired patterns of behaviour. They are the behavioural patterns you follow on a regular basis. They have been followed so regularly that they are carried out almost automatically. Some people developed the habit of always seeing the negative side of things when faced with challenges. Others have the habit of always looking at the bright side. No matter how great your vision, how clear and precise your personal vision statement and how detailed your plans, you will not reach your goal unless you cultivate the habits or patterns of life that facilitate the attainment of such a vision.

Not any or every habit of life will get you to your vision. Great vision requires specific and strategic patterns of thinking, feeling and lifestyle. Your habits have direct effects on whether or not you actually get close to and achieve your vision. The wrong habits will lead you in directions away from your goal. To achieve your goal you must cultivate habits that are in keeping with your short-term and long-term goals and ultimately your vision.

If you are not sure about the utility of your habits for your vision, ask yourself "Does this habit help me get closer to my vision? Does it negatively affect my ability to achieve my goals?" How important your vision is to you will be determined by how prepared you are to change habits that negatively affect its fulfillment and to develop new habits that support it.

Some habits do not need to be changed; they merely add spice to your life. Depending on the nature and demands of your vision, some habits will definitely have to be eliminated. If you have a habit of watching too much TV with not enough time left over to do your schoolwork when you are working on your college diploma or graduate degree, then surely that habit would need to be changed. If your spiritual and ultimate life goal is to enter God's Kingdom and to reign with Christ, then your lifestyle, habits and patterns must be compatible with this life goal.

Earlier we talked about chicken routines. Well, habits that negatively affect the attainment of your dream are called chicken routines. Be conscious of routines and thinking that divert you from working consistently and seriously toward your goals. Seriously measure everything you do against the vision of your life. Evaluate your thought life and be conscious of your routine way of thinking, feeling and behaving. Bring these to the conscious surface of your mind for evaluation.

Later we will delve more into the thought life. For now let it suffice to say that you need to identify and eliminate those thinking routines and behavioural patterns that work against your goal. Great visions require great routines. In the following chapters you will learn that once these negative, unsupportive routines are gone, new and more productive ones will take your life to new heights.

Conclusion

You possess the visualizing ability to see beyond what is toward what can be, to utilize the tools of imagination to shape a desired future. The following chapter will discuss another ability of the mind you must access in order to take your life forward.

chapter six

BELIEVING IS
Becoming

We change to the extent that we believe. With vision we see what can be;
with imagination we paint in the details of what we hope it can be; but
only with belief can we make the vision real and our own.

Why do we believe? Is belief necessary for living a productive life? Is belief a necessary requirement to reach our goals?

Before we delve into answering these important questions let us look at what the term means. If you believe something, you simply accept it as fact or true. I believe my mother is who she said she is, that is, the woman who gave birth to me. I have accepted that to be true and have been given no reason to doubt it. The moment I begin to doubt that my mother is who she said she is, I stop believing she is my mother.

One cannot believe that something is true and doubt that it is so at the same time. If you doubt, you do not believe. Your belief gives you the ability to embrace what you perceive as real. It is the mind's power to grasp and hold something with strength and authority.

Beliefs are not just opinions; they are statements of conviction we make about ourselves, events and things in our lives and our world. These statements of conviction can be negative or positive, true or false. Either way, they have the power to hold us at given points in our lives or undo the shackles of the present and move us forward toward a visualized future.

The Necessity of Believing

The fact that the act of believing is universal suggests that it has a strong biological as well as a psychological basis. This means we are created with the capacity to believe. Our ability to believe is one of the defining features of being human. You cannot live as a human being and not exercise the capacity to believe.

Everyone has the desire for truth, to be right, to belong, to be loved, and for meaning. All these require the ability to believe. If you could not believe you would not know when something is meaningful, true, false, or even when you are right about something.

Believing is a necessary component of a healthy and productive life. When we have strong belief in something we produce conviction and actions for it and feel justified in the actions chosen. This is true for the Christian experience as well as every other aspect of our lives. While not all beliefs are healthy and productive, we cannot live productive lives without the vital component of healthy beliefs.

Believing is necessary for several reasons. First, believing is necessary for you to conceptualize or see something that is not within your natural visual reach. You cannot come to know God if you cannot believe he exists without seeing him with your natural eyes. It will be difficult for you to visualize having a multimillion-dollar business if you don't believe you have the capacity to attain it. It is belief that triggers the spark that ignites into the flame of a great vision. The moment you believe that something in your future falls within your capacity to attain, you have already begun creating the possible future. The fact that some people don't believe in themselves might be one of the reasons why they fail to create visions.

Second, believing is not only necessary for conceptualizing a vision; it also plays a critical role in making it your own. It is not difficult for a person to imagine himself or herself in a certain position of greatness in the future. Just about anyone can generate such imagination. The problem arises when such a person must put ownership on the vision. The furthest some people can reach is imagination; that is, they stop short of claiming the vision as their own.

Vision allows you to see what you desire in the distant future; imagination paints in the nuances and characteristics of what you hope to achieve; but it is by believing that you make the picture your own and create an action plan to get to it. It is quite possible to imagine yourself in the future as a great researcher or scientist, an accomplished writer or singer, a millionaire or effective missionary, but unless you believe you can be such you will never produce the attitude and actions necessary to transform the vision into reality. This is because you become and are transformed to the degree that you believe.

Believing is your conviction in motion. It is accepting those things that are still in the imagination as though they are real and can actually be achieved by you. In other words, imagination paints you into the future, but believing brings the future into your grasp. You can see it and experience the pleasure of its acquisition right in your present circumstances.

Third, believing is also necessary to maintain hold on your vision. Many people, after establishing visions of grandeur, somewhere along the visionary process give up on their dream because they no longer believe they can achieve it. Yes, it is possible to have strong belief in your ability to achieve a vision and then give up on that belief and let go of the vision somewhere on your journey toward its fulfillment. This happens when the conditions of life bear down relentlessly on you and lead you to feel that you don't have the necessary strength and ability to get to your vision. It is the strength of your belief in what you can achieve that allows you the willpower to endure the challenges of the present. The strength of your belief determines how strong and how long you can maintain hold on your vision.

Finally, belief is necessary because it is belief that makes things happen. It arouses and activates motivation and determination. The following discussion explores this topic in great detail with use of the model of the eagle.

The Talons of Belief

The eagle is known for its strong muscular legs and the gripping power of its mighty knife-like talons. The eagle's talons are known to have an impressively strong vise-like locking system. Once a prey is caught and these extremely strong talons lock into its flesh, escape is almost impossible. Many experts believe that the eagle's talons are so powerful that they can even crush some bones in its prey. It is estimated that some eagles can carry prey as heavy as themselves great distances in their talons.

Like the eagle and its remarkable vise-like talons, your ability to hold your vision in view and carry it to completion depends on the gripping strength of your belief. Your vision can easily slip away and fall from view due to the many and varying challenges that lie between where you are and the future where your vision is located. You may have to carry it through criticisms, disappointments, failures, life changes, unexpected circumstances and various other setbacks. Many people start out with large and impressive visions only to lose them somewhere in the storms and circumstances of life. Great visions are like large prey that must be carried at a great height and to far distances against the current of strong winds of circumstances. Like weak talons that cannot grip and carry great weights through the strong current of changing winds for long distances, fragile and undeveloped beliefs will give up on great visions because they lack the tenacity to endure the strong and shifting tide of life's circumstances.

The Mind-Body Connection

The impressive vise-like locking system of the eagle's talons depends on the muscular force of its legs. For the talons to lock into place the strong muscles in the eagle's legs must first contract. When this happens a leg-talons connection is triggered.

In a similar way, when you truly believe that something is possible a mind-body connection is activated. Suddenly there is a mobilization of physical energy. Your nervous system becomes activated in response to the conviction and knowledge that you can actually do something. All the needed energy becomes available for use. The conviction of believing helps you find the energy to fuel your determination and resolve to keep going even under tremendous pressure and duress. Here you find the strength, tenacity and locking power of the will not to give up. The strength of your resolve is contingent on the strength of your belief.

You will find that your mind will surprise your body if you keep telling yourself that you can and will achieve your goal. People usually give up on their dreams when they no longer feel the determination to keep pushing or when they no longer believe they have what it takes to reach the end and attain their vision. Often the only thing that stands between a person and his or her vision is the energy and determination to continue moving forward and the belief that he or she can achieve it.

Your chances of success in reaching and achieving your vision can be gauged by the degree of your belief in your ability to achieve it. Your mind will begin working for you only when you turn on the ignition of your belief. It is only when you start believing that your mind mobilizes your internal resources and ignites the spark of your will to do.

The Authority of the Mind

When it comes to capturing and carrying off its prey, the gripping power of the eagle's talons is its authority over its prey. No prey can dispute with such authority when held with such a powerful grip.

When we believe we give the mind the authority to act on our behalf. Believing is the mind's cue for action. The mind only knows that it can achieve when we begin believing we can. Determination and tenacity flow from a mind that is fully convinced and convicted about the reality of something. The mind has no authority to act and act decisively if a person is undecided, unresolved, unclear or in doubt about something. If we are unclear, unresolved, or in doubt about whether we can achieve the goal, we have already limit our ability to achieve it. If not supported by belief, our mind has no gripping power, no authority to act and no conviction to hold on to our vision.

The capacity to believe is a gift from God. In fact, the Bible tells us that unless we believe we cannot be saved; unless we believe we cannot receive that for which we hope. It is a necessary condition to be saved, to hold the Bible as God's divine word, to receive the promises of God, and to even accept the very existence of God.

It does not stop there. Belief is also necessary for almost all human endeavours, including solving problems, buying a house, going to and completing school, finding a life partner and inventing a new product. How can you buy a house without the belief that you are able to make the payments? Why would you pursue an education without the belief that you can complete it, achieve a career and secure employment?

Belief triggers the mind's power to produce determination, motivation and action, all of which are in line with your vision. Action will be produced in line with your belief only when certain levels of motivation and determination are attained.

When these three components are in place, the locking system of the mind is completed. I call this locking system the *talons of belief.* I have distinguished between motivation and determination. Motivation is your inner driving force, your inner incentive or your reason for moving forward. Determination, on the other hand, is your resolve and your willpower in action. In short, your determination is the tenacity and regulation the mind imposes on itself to pursue and complete a task.

So then, when you begin to believe that you can achieve your vision you trigger the full locking system of your mind. As the Bible says, faith that produces no action is dead (James 2:14–17). In the same sense, beliefs that produce no motivation, determination or actions are weak. Such beliefs can be classified as mere tentative opinions and therefore lack the tenacity to hold up under pressure. Strong beliefs activate the powerful resources of your mind and provide you with the last word on the matter. They are your signature on the document of life. When you believe you affirm your ability and will to do.

The mind's authority to move forward regardless of the challenges and pressures of life reaches its greatest strength when the talons of belief lock around the vision. Though the storms of life may rage, the winds of indifference may blow, and the disturbances of hardship may come your way, the mighty vise-like talons of your belief allows you the holding power to carry your vision to its realization. The strength of your belief is your mind's authority for change. When you believe you sanction and consent to change in your life. You give yourself the approval to attain your goal and achieve your dream.

Believing Is Transforming

Intentional change requires belief. We change in line with our vision to the extent that we believe we can reach and attain it. We gradually develop into any condition we desire if our belief about our ability to achieve it is strong enough. Believing releases the mind from its present restrictive and limiting conditions and allows it to see opportunities where before there were only difficulties and obstacles.

Unbelief inhibits the mind's ability to see possibilities and to conceive the prospect of change. Unbelief has restrictive powers that hold you in a position of helplessness. The moment you believe, your perspective of the world and the conditions in your life begin to change. You no longer see conditions as mere obstacles, barriers and impossibilities. You begin to see these as challenges that can be overcome and as problems that can be solved.

Unless you believe that you can move your life forward to the attainment of your goals, your perceptions will be forever limited to your present conditions. It is your capacity to believe that pulls you out of your present limiting conditions and positions you in a more favourable future state of affairs.

The very act of believing starts an internal process of self-repositioning, self-reconstruction and change. This means the moment you begin believing, you no longer see yourself as a feeble, weak, limited and incompetent person incapacitated by his or her past or present circumstances. Most of the healing that Jesus did during his ministry required people to activate their belief. I think this is because believing does something on the inside of a person. It enables and ignites the spark within. To believe is to unlock the mind's ability to do what it does best, that is to break barriers, solve problems and achieve goals.

How we see ourselves and the opinions we have of ourselves are strongly influenced by our beliefs about who we are in the context of the present as well as in the future. In other words, we are defined by the present and the circumstances therein to the extent that we can conceive of a vision and position ourselves in a future situation. Although Dr. Martin Luther King Jr. was situated in a discouraging situation, he was by no means defined by it. By believing in a dream that transcended both his time and circumstances he redefined and repositioned himself as an agent of change.

Believing Is Igniting

The purpose of an automobile's ignition system is to create a spark that is capable of igniting the fuel-air mixture in the cylinder of the engine, leading to the vehicle's ability to be driven. When you turn the key in your vehicle's ignition system to the "on" position you bridge a connection between the vehicle's battery and ignition coil. The 12 volts from the battery are converted by the ignition coil into an extremely high voltage, somewhere between 20,000 and 40,000 volts. The ignition system then sends this extremely high voltage to spark plugs in each cylinder in the engine. The spark occurs when this voltage gets to the gap at the top of the spark plug. The spark created must be strong enough to ignite the air-fuel mixture for combustion. You can guess that if the spark is not strong enough the engine will not start and consequently your vehicle will not have the power to move.

In the same way, when you believe you ignite the mind's spark and unleash the spirit's passion. When the spark of the human spirit is ignited it mobilizes your internal resources toward the attainment of your goal. Suppose that whenever the idea came to you that you could one day own your own business or dream home or become a brilliant lawyer, an effective speaker or preacher, a successful CEO or a great scientist or achieve the career that you believe would satisfy you, you always dismissed it. Now consider how you would feel if you began to believe that in fact it is really possible, that you could actually achieve the dream of your life. Passion is a product of believing strongly in something. Because some people have so long lived in conditions that are far from what they would like their lives to be, they eventually give up on their dreams and come to define themselves by these same conditions. They continue to live out their lives in expected routines that work to maintain the status quo.

Consider how you would answer the following questions.

1) If you were given the power to perceive certain things in your life differently, what two things would you begin to view in different ways?

2) If you were given the power to see yourself five years into the future, what would you see yourself doing and what would you see yourself as?

3) If you were given the opportunity to believe that you can accomplish something great, what great thing would that be?

4) If believing in yourself would transform your perception of the present and situate you in a future situation, what would you believe about yourself?

5) If you were told that you actually had the power to do all of these things, how would that make you feel?

Well, believe it or not, you do actually have the ability. Purposeful change begins with believing that change is needed and is indeed possible. We achieve only to the degree that we are willing to activate the conviction that we can. What we really and strongly believe in is what we generate the greatest passion for.

The problem is not that people lack the capacity to believe or do not believe they can achieve something. Rather, it is simply because their belief in their ability to achieve has not been raised to the degree that it ignites their spark and starts their fire. There is simply nothing else within humans that ignites our fire and sets motivation in gear other than believing.

Try completing the following exercise:

- Consider where you are now in your life and ask yourself if this is where you want to be in the next three or five years.
- Make a list of the things or situations in your life you would like to eliminate from your life or change going forward.
- Make a list of the things you would love to accomplish within the next five years.
- Reduce the list to one or at the most two primary goals through which all the others could become possible.
- Identify several possible strategies you believe you could employ to bring this goal to pass.
- Select the most workable strategies or plan.
- List several beliefs about yourself that you need to develop in order for this goal to be achieved.
- Write the beliefs as statements about yourself. Make sure they are statements about you that are linked to the achievement of your goal.

Beliefs Can Sabotage Your Dream and Disable Your Life

There's an old saying I heard as a child: "Belief kills and belief cures." Your belief can give you the determination and motivation to produce actions that will bring you to your vision, or your belief can shackle you to your present discouraging conditions. Your beliefs can work to sabotage your vision and cripple your life. The following discussion explains this further.

Beliefs Function as Expectations

What are your expectations of yourself and of your future for the next three or five years? Whatever your expectations of the future are, they are based on the beliefs you hold about your ability to achieve something great in the future. If you expect something, you are looking forward and anticipating it to occur. Furthermore, if you expect something to happen, you believe it will happen. If you expect to own a home one day, you believe that you will be able to own a home one day. This is because your beliefs function as expectations. Your expectations are the function of your beliefs. If you belief then you expect; you expect because you believe.

If you expect to fail or do poorly on an exam, it means you believe you lack the necessary skills and ability to do very well on it. Consider this statement: *If A, then B.* In this statement, *A* is the necessary condition for *B* to exist. Unless *A* is present *B* cannot be. How can you expect something to happen if you do not believe it can or will? Or, if you do not believe you have the ability to accomplish something great, how can you expect to do something great?

Imagine that two novice mountain climbers stand at the foot of a steep and high mountain. None of these two men has ever attempted such a climb. One of the men (let's call him Jake) remarks, "I don't believe I have the expertise to make this climb; it is too difficult."

The other man (let's call him Mark) says, "Yes, it does look challenging, but I believe if I take it slowly and carefully I will reach the top."

What separates these two men? If your answer is their belief, you are absolutely correct. While it is by no means impossible that Jake could make the climb, his belief could work to cripple any attempt to begin the climb. Mark, on the other hand, believes it is possible and in fact expects to make a successful climb given that he takes it slowly and carefully.

Do your beliefs work to inspire or incapacitate you? Beliefs that work to limit or fracture your expectations of the future are sabotaging beliefs. These beliefs are dream and vision killers. They poison the root of your capacity to dream and visualize. They are like blinders that block your vision of what can be while at the same time holding you captive to your present situations. These beliefs invade your conscious and subconscious mind and create one-sided realities, set limits and create inhibiting automatic responses to experiences and situations in your life.

Origins of Sabotaging Beliefs

Where do sabotaging beliefs originate? Why is it that some people find it so hard to shake free of them? To begin with, most of the beliefs we have of ourselves originated from our developing years as children and adolescents. They could very well have started with the types of attachment we had with our caregiver and the treatment we received as children, which could have worked to predispose some individuals to believe certain things about ourselves. Also, as children we received messages about ourselves from significant people in our lives, including family members, relatives, peers and teachers. Some of these messages were positive and empowering, but others were negative and self-limiting. In some cases, children suffer forms of abuse that influence the development of negative beliefs about themselves, people, and the future. These work through both the conscious and the unconscious to affect how they think and interpret situations and how they create meaning from experiences in their lives.

Sabotaging beliefs can also develop as a result of flawed perceptions of failure in our lives. It is quite easy for a person, after trying over and over to do something right and failing each time, to give up with the belief that he or she is just not good enough or not capable enough to succeed. Is it not natural, though, that some of us will not be able to do certain things right, even after several attempts? So then what is wrong with a person saying he or she is just not capable of succeeding at a particular task? The problem is when it becomes a statement of belief that creates the expectations we have of ourselves. Therefore care must be taken in the wording of the statements we make after failing at tasks. For example, notice the words "just not good enough." Embedded in this statement is a belief about the self that is sabotaging and limiting. Let us phrase it in the form of an "I statement" in the way it would be received: "I am just not good enough." It is a statement of belief about the ability of the self. Here the self is believed to not possess the type of qualities or capabilities needed to succeed at a particular task.

Let's expand our understanding of this with an example. Barry is fifty-five years old and has been learning to drive for the past four years. He has attempted the driving test five times and each time has failed. Here is Barry's statement of belief: "I am just not cut out for driving. I have tried so many times and have failed. I just don't have what it takes to pass this driving test." These statements are fundamentally the same. They are underlined by the same belief about the ability of the self.

Does failing at something several times means that you should believe you do not possess the capability to succeed at it? What about finding out what you are doing wrong and improving on it? What about finding out the particular skill or knowledge you are short on and acquiring it? Remember, your beliefs create your expectations.

Let's revisit and reword these statements of belief. "I am just not cut out for driving" becomes "It is obvious that I have not yet acquired the necessary knowledge (or skills) to succeed at driving in order to pass my driving test." "I have tried so many times and have failed" becomes "I am consistently failing my driving test because of lack of skills in reversing, turning, and changing lanes." Notice how different these statements are from the originals. None of these statements are sabotaging or limiting. In fact, they open up possibilities for self-improvement and change. Later in chapter 10 we will deepen your understanding on this topic when we discuss how to extend the limits of your thinking.

Review the following list of sabotaging beliefs and the expectations they create.

Summary of Sabotaging Beliefs
- My ability is fixed and cannot change.
- I don't have what it takes to do something.
- I am not good at this sort of thing.
- This is how my mind works, and I can do nothing about it.
- Once I have this in place, I will.

Beliefs That Sabotage Your Ability to Perform
- Statement of belief: I will never be able to do this right; I am just not good at this sort of things.
- Expectation: You expect to fail if you try again.

Beliefs That Sabotage Your Desire for Change
- Statement of belief: I don't believe things will ever get better; it has been this way for ever.
- Expectation: You expect to fail in your attempt.

Beliefs That Sabotage Your Growth Opportunities
- Statement of belief: This is too difficult. I will never learn how to do this right.
- Expectation: You expect to remain the way you are because of the belief that your abilities are fixed.

Beliefs That Sabotage Your Personal Agency
- Statement of belief: There is nothing I can ever do to change the way things are.
- Expectation: You expect your situations to remain the way they are.

Beliefs That Sabotage Your Self-Esteem
- Statement of belief: I am not important; no one cares if I live or die
- Expectation: You expect no help or assistance from others.

Beliefs That Sabotage Your Ability to Act in the Present
- Statement of belief: I will have more time to do it later.
- Expectation: You expect to have more control over the variables and the activities of your life at a later time.

How to Challenge and Change Your Sabotaging Beliefs

The power to challenge and transform a sabotaging belief resides only in the present moment. It matters not how long these beliefs have dominated your life; you can do something about them now. Although beliefs can be strong and enduring, no belief is carved in stone.

Remember, beliefs are statements of assumption we make. Beliefs can be changed, modified or even eliminated depending on how they hold up under careful examination and challenge. No matter how strong you think your belief is, it can change given the right exposure and challenge.

The following five tips will give you a starting point in challenging and changing those beliefs that are limiting and sabotaging your life.

Tip One: *Identify the beliefs.*

Your first task is to identify your sabotaging beliefs. To do this, keep a journal of all your statement of beliefs. You can begin identifying them in your conversations as you interact with others, encounter challenging situations or think of your future in terms of change in your present condition. If you have trouble identifying sabotaging beliefs, try identifying your expectations. You can also identify them using the if-then statement (If A, then B) discussed earlier.

You can also identify these sabotaging beliefs by asking probing questions. Here are some examples:
- What do I believe about my ability to achieve great things?
- What do I believe about my ability to change the way my life is?

• What do I believe is stopping me from advancing my life?
• What do I believe people think about me?

Phrase the answer to each of these questions as statements of belief. Once you have done this you have identified your sabotaging beliefs and are ready to move to tip 2.

Tip Two: *Recognize their function.*
Your second step is to recognize the particular function played by the belief you have identified. Remember that every belief has a function. It does something to you as well as giving you particular information about yourself, your future and the world around you. Ask yourself in what particular way this belief is affecting or will affect you. Here are some examples of how to recognize their particular function:
• What is this belief telling me about my ability?
• How am I seeing myself through the lens of this belief?
• How is this belief hindering me from making the necessary changes in my life?
• How is this belief influencing my decisions, motivation and actions?
• What is this belief telling me about possibilities in my life?
• How has this belief affected my feeling about myself?

Tip Three: *Challenge their usefulness.*
Your third step is to challenge the usefulness of the sabotaging belief. Beliefs are not easily discarded. You can't just throw a belief out the window or put it in a bag and dump it in a garbage bin. Beliefs develop over time and have roots that connect to various aspects of your conscious and subconscious states. This means they are part of your thought life, motivation, expectations and emotions. Beliefs are not just transient thoughts but are part of the very structure of our mental world.

In this case, there are specific things you need to do before you change or discard them. Care must be taken when challenging your sabotaging beliefs. You wouldn't want to damage or remove productive beliefs along with the sabotaging ones. When a surgeon is about to operate and take out a tumour he or she has to ensure that only the tumour is removed and not part of an organ to which it may have attached itself. Therefore, before discarding the belief, challenge the underlying reason why it exists in the first place. Challenge its usefulness in your life by asking how it has served or is serving you.

Think of this in the way you would challenge a deductive argument. You never challenge the conclusion of a deductive argument. This is because the conclusion is logically deduced from two or more premises or statements. In order to cast doubt on a conclusion you first must show that one or more of the premises are incorrect. Once a premise is shown to be incorrect the entire argument becomes unreliable and the conclusion is no longer valid. In order to render a belief invalid you have to ask specific questions relating to its usefulness in your life. Once its usefulness cannot be validated, the belief begins to disintegrate.

The following are examples of how you can challenge the usefulness and validity of your sabotaging beliefs:

• In what particular way has this belief served my life in the past?
• What benefit has it brought to my life in the present or can it bring in the future?
• Am I empowered, inspired or motivated toward accomplishing any useful goal when this belief is activated?

The answers to these challenge questions will become your cue that these beliefs are not working for you but are in fact working against you. These questions will aid you in getting to the roots of these beliefs and removing them without affecting other necessary beliefs.

Once you have completed this step you are now ready to use the next tip.

Tip Four: Revoke their tenancy and silent their voices.

Sabotaging beliefs impose authority onto your life. They act as your advisors and counsellors. They tell you how far you should go, how high you must reach and what you can and cannot do. It is you who have allowed them tenancy for the time they have endured. Now it is time to revoke their right to live in your mind.

Once you have challenged them and find them to be unproductive, censure them from your mental repertoire of beliefs. Consciously decide not to listen to their voices when they raise their heads. Render them mute with the belief that they will do more damage than good to your life. The more you consciously put them in their place, censure and denounce them, the more silent they will become. By taking these actions you are cutting these tumours of unproductive beliefs from your conscious and unconscious mental life.

When they become silent it means you have cut out their roots from the delicate organs of your mental world. Once you have managed to do this you will be ready to use the final tip.

Here are some examples of how you can silence their voices:
- With this type of belief I will never change my life.
- If I continue to hold this belief I will always be what I am and where I am; I will never be able to move my life forward.
- I will no longer believe this is all I can be and all I can do. The evidence is overwhelming that I can do better.
- I refuse to believe that my ability is fixed and cannot improve.
- I refuse to believe that others can and I cannot.
- I refuse to allow my past failures to imprison me.
- I refuse to believe that I am helpless and cannot do something to change my situation.
- I refuse to believe that I am not capable of greatness.
- I believe that while I cannot change what has been, I can change what can be.

Tip Five: Restructure or replace.

The final tip in the process of challenging and changing your sabotaging beliefs is the restructuring and rephrasing of the sabotaging beliefs so they reflect your new ideals. The moment you begin to challenge a belief, if the challenge is strong enough, the belief will begin to crack and eventually lose its strength and fall apart. If a sabotaging belief cannot be restructured, then it must be replaced entirely with a new one.

Here are some examples of how you can restructure or replace sabotaging beliefs:
- **Beliefs that sabotage your self-esteem**: *I am not important; no one cares if I live or die.*
Restructured: *I am important, and even if no one cares if I live or die, I care.*
- **Beliefs that sabotage your growth opportunity:** *This is too difficult; I will never learn how to do it right.*
Restructured: *This is sure challenging, but I believe with more practice and knowledge I will surely get it right.*

After you have restructured or replaced a sabotaging belief, the new belief will increase your motivation and empower you. This comes with patient and practice. Some of these beliefs are well rooted and may be difficult to uproot. Some have been planted for so long that they, like cancer, may have spread to other areas of your conscious and subconscious life. The only way to uproot them is to continue to follow the five given tips. You must develop the belief that anything is possible if you keep trying and do not give up.

Conclusion

We have been equipped with capacities that are undiscovered and therefore unused in productive ways. At this point in your journey of discovering the eagle within, you might be asking what else is left to be said. We are not fully there yet. The following chapters take you deeper into the working of the mind to the discovery of the power of your thought world and the ability you have been divinely given.

chapter seven

Thoughts THAT DO NOT Soar

Wings are to flight what thoughts are to success.
It is your thoughts that determine your ability to ascend to elevation
of greatness or keep you grounded in the rut of life.

In the previous chapter we discussed the importance of believing in one's ability to achieve. Our primary model of comparison was the locking system of the eagle's talons. We saw that the human mind is equipped with capacities and mechanisms that when activated can allow us to hold on to our vision amidst the challenges and storms of life. We are not meant to stagnate and die in the rut of life. We saw what the power of believing can do.

This chapter is the first chapter in a series of chapters that will discuss the awesome mechanisms of thinking. Here again we will use the model of the eagle, particularly the eagle's wings, to explain how our thought world functions.

Usually when people think of wings they immediately think of flying. By the same token, it is difficult to think of birds and not think of wings and flying. In this case the association is not always true, because some birds have wings but do not fly. Wings on penguins, for example, are not used for flying but for rowing or paddling underwater. For other birds that do not fly, wings are used for balancing as they run. The ostrich is an example of a running bird. They can run up to forty-five miles per hour and are one of the fastest running birds.

Another incorrect association is between wing flapping and soaring. It is incorrect to believe that the rate at which a bird flaps its wings determines soaring ability and height. Although some birds have the ability to flap their wings at a tremendous speed, it is not meant to take them to soaring heights. Such flapping ability is used primarily for hovering and stationary flight.

Hummingbirds are one example. While they can flap their wings extremely fast, such exercise does not take them to any significant height but only provides them the ability for hovering and stationary flight. To observe a hummingbird in stationary flight is amazing. Some experts estimate that they can flap their wings up to 4,800 times per minute. It is important to note, then, that the frequency of wing flapping does not determine height and soaring ability.

Not all birds are equipped with the type of wings that allow them to soar to great heights and maintain such flight for a great distance. The shape and wingspan of a bird's wings determines its flight ability. Not all wings can support flight, height and distance. Some birds are equipped with long and narrow wings that allow them to cover great distances in flight. Some have short and rounded wings that allow them to cover very short distances. Still others have wings that allow them to fly from branch to branch and from tree to tree within a very short distance. The eagle can ascend to soaring heights because it has the wing design and wing power that makes it able to lift its body and support it in flight. This is clearly not so with all birds.

To show how some styles of thinking work to limit the potential of the thinker, we will look at four types of birds, the penguin, hummingbird, ostrich, and chicken. It is the writer's hope that as the reader engages this chapter he or she will become more conscious of the fact that our thinking plays one of the most important roles in the course and quality of our lives. What's more, our thinking determines whether we end up on the mountaintop of productivity and success or stuck in a pothole somewhere in a dark alley of life.

Paddling Thoughts

Penguins are birds with wings that are not designed to support flight. Their wings appear disproportionate to their body size and are designed for paddling in water instead of flying in the sky. They fit perfectly with their watery environment. Their wings provide them with the necessary skills not only to navigate but also to master their watery world.

A close look at the penguin's wings will show that they look more like paddlelike flippers than wings of birds. We will use the *term paddling thoughts* or *penguin thinking* to describe the type of thinking that people use to keep themselves fitted to particular paddling situations of life. While it is important that thinking be flexible and adaptive, it can be unproductive if thinking adapts to situations that hinder the acquisition of a successful and productive life. This is exactly what paddling type thinking produces. Thinking that allows us to merely paddle our way through life and around the same situations does not get us anywhere but in the same mess of a life. Living beneath our God-given potential when clearly we can engage life with passion and motivation gives glory to no one but the enemy of our life. We have been created to succeed, but we continue to make excuses as to why we cannot get ahead while at the same time continuing to be depressed over life's conditions.

Paddling thoughts are your everyday no-effort form of thinking that provides you with no soaring power. This type of thinking allows you to merely cope with your circumstances, not challenge and transcend them. People with paddling thoughts or penguin thinking can be classified into two groups. These are *deferred thinkers* or "*I should*" *thinkers*.

Deferred Thinking

People who defer a task that needs to be done in the present for a later time are said to procrastinate. They know that something in their lives needs changing in the here and now but tell themselves that tomorrow or later will be a better time to get it done. When "later" arrives, the task is again deferred to yet a later time and eventually never gets done. The following are examples of deferred thinking:

- I will do it later because I'll have more time.
- I don't have everything I need now, so I'll wait until later.
- I don't have enough time right now, so I'll do it later.
- I can't do it the way I want to, so I'll wait until…
- I would love to start school now, but I'll wait until…
- I am tired; I will get to it later.

These statements are patterns of excuses on which the deferred thinker consistently draws. He or she usually has a large range of these excuses available. These excuses aid the thinker in avoiding immediate action. Over time these patterns develop into a deep-rooted mental laziness that is difficult to break, which most people label as procrastination.

Procrastination is really a symptom of a thinking problem that goes deeper than merely putting things off to a later time. It is a deep-rooted and flawed pattern of thinking that is similar to addiction. Although people who are chronic deferred thinkers are generally aware that their procrastinating is working against them, they are often unable to consciously change their thinking. They use excuses as justification to avoid doing something in the present.

Because people addicted to deferred thinking generally have seemingly good reasons for putting things off, they usually do not think of themselves as procrastinators. The primary difference between people who are chronic deferred thinkers and those who sometimes put things off to a later time is planning. People who put something off with the genuine intent of getting to it will put a timeline and plan in place to actually do it. Chronic deferred thinkers put things off with no definite timeline or plan in place for accomplishing what they put off today for tomorrow.

"I Should" Thinking

The second type of penguin thinking is referred to here as *"I should" thinking*. This thinking style has a dual effect on the thinker. First, it has a motivating or arousing effect that gives the thinker the feeling that he or she is actually going to get to a task. Put another way, it is an internal instruction about what should be done in the immediate present. While these thinkers often recognize that they need to get things done in their lives and are even able to generate thoughts that on the surface offer them some arousal, the thoughts they generate only serve as paddles. This type of thinking offers people a type of comfort zone to which they return each time they are faced with the need for change in their lives. Telling themselves that they *should* really get something done gives them the feeling that they know what needs to be done, which generate a sense of being responsible.

The following are some examples of this type of thinking:

- I should really get this done now; I shouldn't be so lazy.
- I really should pursue that university degree. I shouldn't continue to procrastinate.
- I will never get anywhere with this type of performance. I really should pull myself together and practice more.
- I really should try to make my life better. I shouldn't just sit back and let the world pass me by.
- I shouldn't really let my negative thinking get in the way of getting this done. I really should change my thinking habits.

The second effect "I should" statements have on the thinker is self-rebuke. It is important to note here that the habit of using these statements is not really to create change or a shift in position but as a means of generating guilt through a self-rebuke statement.

The "I should" statement usually consists of two parts. The first part of the statement identifies the need for the task to be done and a sense of urgency for getting the task done. The second part is a rebuke of the behaviour that is presently hindering the completion of the task. Merely sitting back and not speaking to oneself about what needs to be done would seem very irresponsible on the part of the thinker. Therefore, in order not to feel irresponsible, the thinker engages in self-talk in which the task to be done is identified followed by a self-rebuke about the behavioural condition that is serving to prevent the task from being done.

Consider the following example: *I really should try to do something to make my life more productive. I shouldn't just sit back and let opportunities pass me by.* Here the first part suggests a sense of urgency about a task to be done, and the second part is a rebuke of a current non-action regarding the task.

The result of this self-rebuke is guilt. Consequently, people with "I should" thinking usually feel guilty for not achieving a goal or developing their lives in more productive ways. Because these thoughts do not give them the wing power of flight, they are limited to what is and never able to visualize and achieve what can be.

Paddling thoughts do get you somewhere in life but not to the sky and beyond the circumstances of the past and present. People with this thinking style find that they cannot think outside the ocean of their circumstances. Their thoughts carry them in a circle within the circumference of their situations. Paddling thoughts do not have the capacity to move beyond the here and now and visualize possibilities.

People with this thinking style continuously complain about their circumstances but never seem able to rise above them. There is an ever present sense of frustration and boredom with the way things are but little or no thought power to create change and move forward.

Hovering Thoughts

In addition to paddling thoughts, some people produce what is referred to in this text as *hovering thoughts*. This is a type of thinking that keeps them suspended over the same condition and issue in life year after year. Like the hummingbird, which has to generate a great number of wing flaps to stay in stationary flight, people who produce hovering thoughts usually generate a great deal of ideas and thoughts, are always planning but never seem to be accomplishing anything. Their lives remain in the same stationary status every year.

The hummingbird is one of a class of birds that do not use their wings for soaring but for hovering and stationary flight. Their wings allow them the ability to stay in a stationary flight position while extracting the sweet nectar from certain plants and flowers. As noted earlier, it is estimated that these birds can produce up to 4,800 wing flaps per minute while in stationary or hovering flight. The hummingbird metaphor for a thinking style helps us understand why some people who have great thoughts and plans for their lives are unable to move their lives forward and seem fixed in the same situation year after year. Like hummingbirds extracting nectar from plants while in stationary flight, these thinkers derive satisfaction from the ideas of grandeur they conjure up. They are always full of ideas of what they are going to accomplish. The problem is, they never seem to be doing anything about moving toward accomplishing any of these ideas. This is because their satisfaction resides only in the ideas, not in the actual achievement of them. They fail to understand that ideas of greatness are merely the first steps in the visionary process, not the accomplishment of the task. Somewhere in their lives they misunderstood what it means to move their lives forward. They are unable to move toward the accomplishment of these ideas because their thinking style does not provide them with the type of soaring power to move beyond current circumstances.

Hovering thoughts can be divided into three categories: when/then thinking, wishful thinking and redundant thinking.

When/Then Thinking

The *when/then* thinking style is a form of convenient thinking or procrastination in which the thinker declares that he or she will perform an action in the future but only if certain conditions in the present change. This thinking is considered convenient in the sense that the thinker uses it to avoid feelings of guilt and self-punishment. It is similar to the deferred thinking style, but it is used not merely to avoid an action but to avoid feelings of guilt for not pursuing a task. Here the thinker claims an existing condition is the reason why he or she has not attended to the task.

The when/then thinking style has two components, a *when* component and a *then* component. The first part of the statement consists of a condition that the thinker presents as an obstacle in the pursuing or completion of a task. By establishing the *when* condition as a criteria for action the thinker is free to procrastinate in the present and therefore free of the guilt of appearing irresponsible.

The second part consists of the expected action to be performed only when the condition is resolved. The statement goes like this: When A, then B. Here "A" is a present condition that needs resolving, and "B" is the intended action to follow the resolution of "A." In other words, resolving "A" becomes the necessary condition for the action "B." Therefore, unless "A" is resolved, "B" cannot be initiated. The following statements are examples of this thinking style:

- When things change in my life, *then* I am going to…
- When I find the time, *then* I will…
- When I have things sorted out in my life, *then* I will…
- When I am free of this, *then* I will…
- When all this is over, *then* I will…

While each of these statements can be a genuine reason for not attending to a task, when the use of them becomes a pattern of excuses not to act the thinker will remain in the same life position for a long period of time. Because the thought of getting to the task in the future often takes away feelings of guilt, the thinker uses it as a comfort zone, or a type of sweet nectar if you will, and thus becomes suspended over the same condition of life. Consequently, people who are chronic when/then thinkers are always setting up conditions that need resolving before they can move their lives forward. Because the reasons given for not acting seem perfectly acceptable to them, when/then thinkers are not generally worried about their lives. They feel no guilt and are in fact pleased with themselves to know that they have the mind to act when a condition is resolved.

Wishful Thinking

Wishful thinking is a form of thinking in which the thinker wants something to be true and believes it to be true. In this case, the thinking is based on a wish that the thinker believes is true without any evidence in reality.

Wishful thinkers can be classified into two groups: the *predictive* wishful thinkers and the *daydreaming or make-believe* wishful thinkers. In predictive wishful thinking, the thinker makes a prediction (or a declaration) about a future state of affair that he or she would like to see happen and believes that it will be so. On the surface this might seem like an exercise of faith, but a closer examination reveals that such thinking only serves to keep a person suspended over the same condition for indefinite periods of time. Let us explore this type of thinking a bit closer by examining the following statement. When asked what he is doing with his life, Colin, who is twenty-nine years old, replies, "One day I am going to complete college and open my own business." Notice here that Colin makes a prediction about how his life will turn out in the future. However, Colin is not in college and has no plans in place to attend college. Because predictive wishful statements are usually strongly believed by the thinker, the contentment derived from them is usually enough to hold the thinker in the same position time after time.

In predictive wishful thinking there is a disconnection between the thinker's wishful thoughts and his or her resolve or will to do. This missing resolve is why the thinker never gets beyond wishful thinking. While there is nothing inherently wrong with wishful thinking, the thinker's inability to transform the wish into reality is the problem. To transform a wish into reality requires a decision, a plan and actions. The idea that something will happen without careful planning is wishful thinking.

The following are examples of predictive wishful thinking:
• Within a few years I am going to be a successful businesswoman [with no plans in place].
• Before I am thirty-five years old I am going to own my own business [with no plans in place].
• My financial situation will change significantly over the next few years [with no plans in place].

The second type of wishful thinking is the daydreaming or make-believe type. To daydream is to evoke certain desires and fantasies into consciousness while awake. It is a process of allowing oneself to imagine how things could be. Daydreaming can have positive effect in that it can arouse and improve one's creative ability as well as increase one's motivation toward an identified goal. It is negative if it serves only to provide a person a way of escape from responsible thinking and reality.

When daydreaming is positive it usually has at its focus a goal the thinker is pursuing or intends to pursue. When it is only a way of escape from responsible thinking and reality, the power of the imagination is used merely to conjure up and paint images in the mind that induce a sense of pleasure in the thinker. Because the wishful thinker usually believes that the probability of achieving the wish is extremely low, he or she does not exert any effort or set any plan in place to achieve it.

Let's say that John wishes to be a pilot. In daydreaming he imagines himself as a pilot flying the latest and most sophisticated aircraft. In reality though, he believes that achieving this goal is near impossible. The experience of daydreaming allows him to fulfill his wish in a wish world that requires no responsible action.

Homeostatic Thinking

Ostriches are birds with wings that do not support flight. Their wings are primarily use for balance when they run. Like the ostrich, some people generate thoughts not to take them toward success but to create and maintain thinking equilibrium. Thoughts are generated to suppress or cancel thoughts that would upset an undisturbed state of being. People who are homeostatic thinkers are usually afraid of change and uncertainty. They are content with the familiar, mundane and routine state of things. They regulate their thinking in such a way that it maintains a stable and constant mental environment and life condition. If change means significant cost or a large shift in the balance of things, then it must be challenged or ignored. They usually have a repertoire of thoughts available that work to keep intruding thoughts of change at a safe distance.

Two types of thinking characterize the homeostatic thinker. These are economic thinking and default thinking.

Economical Thinking (Cheap Thinking)

People who are economic thinkers are *sensitive to the cost of change.* The cost of commitment, time, effort and money are foremost on their minds when presented with the idea of change. If the cost of change is too great, then they consider the change too risky or too difficult to pursue. They usually do not put much effort into thinking that challenges the need for change. They admire the effort and achievements others make and often wonder where they find the time and commitment for such a life investment.

These thinkers do not despise or have no desire for change. It is the cost of change they fear. They are inherently cheap thinkers. They will continue to live in a status quo situation if they perceive that change will cost them too much. When confronted with a challenge for change they compare themselves with the magnitude of the task. For example, when asked, Why don't you pursue a university or college degree? their response may be something like "I don't have the money to spend on school right now," I don't have the time to spend in school" or "I don't have the brain power to study so hard." Notice carefully that in each of these statements there is concern over the cost of the pursuit. It could be money, time or effort. This is because the cost involved requires them to change a current state.

In each of these statements there is an underlying philosophy that prevents individuals from extending themselves beyond where they are to what they can be. If the step forward means extending themselves beyond their comfort zone, the cost is considered too great and the risk too high. This cheap thinking limits their reach and keeps them in a state of mental poverty and an imprisonment of potential.

The following are some examples of economical thinking:

- It's too difficult.
- It will take too long.
- It's too risky.
- I don't have the time.
- I've never done this before.
- I don't have the skill.
- It will take too much energy.

Default Thinking (Preset Thinking)

The term *default* means "failure to act." In the world of computer programs and computerized devises, the term *default* refers to a particular action that a program, software or operating system will execute when the user does not specify overriding instructions. Most electronics systems come from the factory with preset or default codes and programs, which the user is instructed to change for security reasons. Unless the user overrides these codes with new ones, the system when activated will continue to operate according to the defaults. A factory default code may be an on/off code, a timing code or a programming code that determines certain operating parameters. Unless these codes are changed by the user they continue to direct the operation and function of the system according to the factory's default settings.

People who are default thinkers have preset patterns of thinking. These default patterns work to keep them in a homeostatic state of thinking and being. They can rightly be called comfort-zone thinkers. Like economical thinkers, default thinkers are afraid to upset their lives' balance. However, while economical thinkers are afraid of the cost of change, default thinkers are more concern about *their ability to maintain change*. They are afraid of failure, particularly failure to maintain change or complete what they have started. In view of this, whenever they attempt to initiate something new and the idea of failure comes to mind, they revert back to a default pattern of thinking that works to keep them from upsetting their lives' balance and mental equilibrium.

Their fear of failure is more overriding and powerful than their desire for change.

Default thinkers are not void of ideas or desire for change. It is the fear that they may fail to complete the task that continues to pull them back into default or comfort-zone thinking.

Many people never bother to change the default codes or programs that come with their newly purchased electronic devices. One reason for this is the idea that doing so is too complicated. Some people fear that because they are not knowledgeable about computers and computerized devices they may do something that will damage or compromise the operation of their new device. For them it is easier to use the default settings that come from the factory than to try to change them. Although a programming manual always comes with a new device, going through it seems a tedious task to some people. I must admit, some manuals for simple devices are just too complicated for people untrained in electronics and computers. In the same way some people continue to use the default codes and programs that come with their devices because of the perception that it is too complex to change. When faced with new challenges, default thinkers continue to use familiar ways of thinking drawn from past experiences.

Although sometimes old and familiar ways of thinking fit well with new experiences and challenges, there are other times when what worked in the past is incompatible and ineffective with new challenges. In such cases thinkers need to be prepared to adjust their thinking or generate new forms to meet with new experiences. While for some thinkers this is not difficult, for default thinkers this is an almost impossible challenge. Past experiences and early conditioning have a way of unconsciously programming default thinking in people, compromising their ability to approach new challenges with new and fresh thinking. This is why, unfortunately, some people unknowingly continue to use these default patterns when faced with new situations for which such thinking is ineffective.

Default thinking is a form of mental shortcut. This means when a person is confronted with a challenge that appears to be similar to one experienced in the past or under similar circumstances, he or she, instead of engaging the mind in a conscious and deliberate process of thought generation, accesses a default or familiar pattern of thinking. Default or familiar thinking patterns are triggered easily or come to mind without much effort. They are like pop-up screens that are immediately activated once your cursor comes in contact with them, leaving almost no room for the activation of other thoughts. If the dynamics of some new experience or challenge bears similarity with past experiences, the default thinker without much mental deliberation immediately accesses his or her familiar pattern of thinking, thus compromising his or her ability to be creative and to move forward successfully.

Default thinking can exert an anchoring effect on the thinker's mental world. When we think of an anchor we picture a heavy object that is dropped by a cable into the water to keep a floating vessel in a stationary position. When thinking acts like an anchor it holds the mind at a particular point or creates a reference point for thoughts from which the mind cannot easily deviate. When faced with new problems and challenges, we tend to draw upon solutions from the past to try to resolve them. People do this because it seems to be a quick, easy, safe and comfortable way to deal with problems. It is, however, a sort of mindless thinking that requires little effort in problem-solving. People inadvertently switch on, as it were, an autopilot by reaching back to the past for a quick solution. In this the past become the standard and reference for problem-solving and thinking.

Default thinking from past experiences can limit the type of thoughts people can generate in new and different situations, thus holding them in an anchored state of being. For example, a person who has experienced a number of failures may come to believe that he or she is incompetent or lacks particular ability to succeed at certain other things in life. Given a new challenge the thinker becomes unable to generate anything different from the patterns that have been used in the past. Thus the past pattern becomes the anchor or standard for present thinking.

Another example of default thinking is the tendency to think of a single negative event as a general pattern for all other similar events. Generalization in thinking occurs when a person develops a negative interpretation of a single unpleasant situation and extends it generically to a multitude of other situations. Generalizing a particular event to a wider range of situations is a fundamental error in thinking. Here it is not merely the event that is generalized but also the thinking that goes into the interpretation of the event. This irrational in-the-box thinking style of making generalizations works to prevent the thinker from trying different alternatives to a problem. Because the default thinker expects the same negative outcome in a different situation, he or she is inhibited from thinking about different options. In this case the prediction that the same negative result will occur creates the fear of obtaining the same result.

The following are some examples of the default thinking style:
• I'm afraid I will fail again.
• I've never done it that way; I'd rather continue the way I am used to.

- I'm afraid I may start and not able to complete it.
- I'm afraid it will not turn out right, just like the last time.
- I'm afraid of what others will say.
- I'm afraid I will do all this work for nothing.
- I'm afraid that when I finish it might not turn out as expected.
- I know if I attempt this the same thing is going to happen as the last time.
- I'm just not good at these things; look what happened when I tried doing that last project.
- My high school grades are proof that I am not cut out for college or higher learning.
- Relationships are just not for me; look what happened to the last two relationships I was in.
- How can I ever be successful at anything when I did so terrible in school?
- This is what my experience has taught me.

Recycle Thinking (Non-Creative)

When a thing is recycled it goes through a procedure that makes it usable again. The essential form of a recycled product is never changed. For example, you cannot recycle metal by changing its essential element to plastic or paper. You cannot recycle paper and change its essential element into iron. The key to recycling is to collect something that is considered waste and remanufacture it so that it can be reused in a similar or close application. In this case, no new element is created, only a manufacturing of the waste itself into a different product or form having the same basic substance. The practice of recycling is believed to be a useful and beneficial endeavour for the environment.

In the same way people recycle waste products, some people tend to recycle their thinking. While recycling material is useful in the world of waste, in the world of thinking it can work to incapacitate one's ability to think in new and creative ways. While all humans are equipped with the capacity for creativity in thinking, only a few will discover how to use it productively. This is because it is always easier to use forms of thinking we have become familiar with.

Although not all forms of thinking we have used in the past are wasteful, many people continue to approach new situations and challenges with forms of thinking that have not helped them in the past. These unproductive patterns of thinking continue to be recycled and applied to new and different situation and endeavours.

Not all recycle thinking was unproductive in the past. It may have been very useful at one time during a particular experience or stage of one's experience. Consider the words of the apostle Paul, who said that when he was a child he spoke as a child, he understood as a child, he thought as a child, but when he became a man he put away childish ways (1 Corinthians 13:11). What were appropriate and useful forms of thinking in the past may be unproductive in the present or even wasteful under a different set of conditions. To carry over such forms and believe them to be effective when clearly they are not is recycle thinking.

Recycle thinking shares some similarities with default thinking. For example, both thinkers fail to produce forms of new and creative thinking when faced with new and different situations. Both continue to depend on forms of thinking used in the past. The main difference lies in the way the form of thinking from the past is brought into the present. While default thinkers are passive and reactive thinkers, recycle thinkers do not use preset ideas and thinking. Rather, they actively rework their old approach or way of thinking to try to make it fit with a new situation. By doing this they introduce nothing new in their approach, and in cases where new and creative thinking is critical, they fail to achieve productive outcomes.

For example, if in the past a person's approach to facing a challenge was to find someone to blame, find a way to avoid it or fail to take responsibility for developing a strategy toward a resolution, then merely recycling such thinking patterns will produce similar results as in the past.

Let's try to explain this with an example. For five years Barry ran a small business but couldn't make it succeed. Taking the advice of his wife he hired a business consultant, which did not help. He got a sizable loan from the bank, but that too did not help to move his business forward. At times he felt he was making some headway, but that did not last very long. He eventually had to close his business, which was almost sinking into the ground anyway and drawing all the family's financial resources with it. Finally, Barry concluded that he did not get the kind of support from those around him that would help his business. Three years later, Barry again tried to start a business. His family and friends wanted to help and invested heavily in his dream. Slowly the business began to decline after only eighteen months.

Now what would Barry's excuse be? He had adequate help from friends and family, which did not help. Why did Barry's business fail again?

Although there could be many reasons, a couple of things can be highlighted here. First, Barry had come to the wrong conclusion about why his business failed in the first place. Second, he thought that having enough financial support would make his business grow. It is clear that he had not introduced anything new in his thinking. He failed to critically evaluate why he really failed the first time. He brought his old ways of thinking, doing things, planning and organizing into his new business and again had to face failure. Maybe now he would blame his customers for not being consistent and dedicated customers. It can be predicted that if Barry starts a thousand businesses he will fail a thousand times if he fails to change his thinking about how he does things.

Could Barry's problem lie in his inability to plan and organize, lack of professionalism with customers, or lack of knowledge and appropriate business skills? Failure to recognize why one was not successful in the past will result in recycling and reusing the same pattern, leading to similar results.

Domesticated Thinking

As we discussed earlier, chickens are easily given to domestication. They have wings and can fly but cannot lift themselves to a great height or maintain a long duration of flight. In an earlier chapter we explored the world of the chicken and found that they are birds that can live out a comfortable existence in domestication. They generally do not try to escape or seem perturbed with their ongoing controlled and extremely dependent condition.

The fact that chicken can fly at limited altitude and cannot maintain a long duration of flight fits well with the type of thinking that some people generate. Three types of thinking styles characterize chicken thinking. These are contextually controlled thinking, in-the-box thinking and scapegoat thinking.

Contextually Controlled Thinking

Thinking that is contextually controlled is a type of contingent thinking in which the thoughts generated depend heavily on the immediate situation. Contextually controlled thinking lacks the ability to raise the thinker beyond a present condition. The dynamics of the situation totally determine the type of thoughts generated.

For example, imagine after working at a job for twenty years you are suddenly informed that your employment is terminated. You have no other source of income. What type of thoughts would be going through your mind? Regardless of how strong you are, the power of the situation would immediately impose sad and discouraging thoughts on your mind. The concern here, however, is not the initial thoughts that are impressed on us by the power of the situation; rather, it is our ability to impose control on our own thinking after the initial shock of the situation.

When a person fails to exert control over his or her own thinking, by default he or she allows the force of the situation to assume command. This is what is referred to as domesticated or chicken thinking or, more precisely, contextually controlled thinking.

There is no greater example of our inability to use our minds effectively than in situations where we are challenged with discouraging and disabling dynamics operating within a situation. When our perception of the challenging nature of our situation inhibits our ability to generate thoughts that can raise us to new levels, see opportunities and uncover possibilities where there appear to be none, we become domesticated and helpless victims of the circumstances themselves. Knowing that we are capable of raising our thinking beyond the thoughts and feelings generated from the immediate influences of a potentially disabling circumstance is a necessary step toward breaking chicken thinking.

More times than not, however, we simply yield our right to control our thoughts to the negative circumstances that bear upon us. As a result, like the domesticated chicken whose life is lived out in a controlled environment, contextually controlled thinkers never attain the level of flying power that can lift them out of the coop of their disabling life situation.

Contextually controlled thinkers need to understand that we have the capacity to see the same situation in a different light and therefore interpret it in ways that allow us to transcend its potentially disabling effects. This means we are able to impose a new perspective on the situation, thus experiencing it in a way that moves us beyond its potentially negative control. What we create with our perception is what we experience, and what we experience becomes our reality. If we perceive something in a negative way, that is the effect it will have on us. On the other hand, if we perceive something in a positive way, that is the effect it will have on us. It is therefore not hard to see how our thinking can become contextually controlled by our own perceptions of situations in our lives. Contextually controlled thinkers need to become aware that although they live in the here and now, they do not have to be limited by circumstances therein.

One noticeable characteristic of contextually controlled thinking is the tendency to see things and to speak in absolute terms. Absolute terms are words that allow no exception. Most people do not realize that the words they use when speaking have significant effects on their feelings and actions as well as on other thoughts they generate. Absolute words include *only, no, must, always, no one, everyone, never, all* and *none.* Unknown to these thinkers the words they speak reflect the interpretation they give to a situation and the meaning they impose on it, which in turn has a direct effect on their feelings and behaviour. When a person says "I am *always* failing," "I will *always* be a failure," or "I will *never* be able to do this right," he or she in turn generates emotions in steps with these statements. In fact, over time a negative thinking style becomes easily triggered by situations that bear similarities to past experiences.

The following are examples of contextually controlled thinking:

- This job was all I had; I will *never* get a better job. My life is going to be so messed up from here on.
- This job was my life; I don't know what else to do. I will *never* be able to lift myself from this dump of a life.
- The house was my dream; I will *never* be able to own another one.
- I tried so hard to pass this exam and ended up failing. I am just *no* good at academics.
- Why couldn't I do that as well as Susan did? I am *just* a loser.
- He was my life and all I had. Now that he has up and left me, my life is over. I am *nothing* without him.

Each statement reveals two thought components. The first is the thought relating to the situation itself. There is emphasis on the significance of the situation, in this case a significant loss or a task considered important to the thinker.

The second thought component relates to an inability in the thinker to positively respond to the situation. There is a negative thought reaction to the situation. Notice also how the thinker sees a single unpleasant event as an absolute and never-ending pattern of defeat. Failing an exam, the thinker believes he is *no* good at academics. Losing her house, the thinker believes she will *never* be able to own another one. Because the thinker failed to do a task as well as Susan, she believes she is *just* a loser. Here the second component reflects a negative and absolute thinking pattern that unless broken will control the generation of subsequent thoughts, imposing control over the entire thought life of the thinker.

In-the-Box Thinking

The term *thinking inside the box* or simply *box thinking* is a phrase used when referring to situations where thinking fails to move beyond the familiar ways we are accustomed to seeing things. In-the-box thinking is the opposite of thinking outside the box. In-the-box thinkers are unable to see the familiar in new ways and are fundamentally afraid of the magnitude of the challenge.

There are three types of in-the-box thinkers. The first type is those who are unable to see the familiar in new and different ways or to see a problem from different viewpoints. While default thinkers are primarily afraid of change, in-the-box thinkers are unable to extend the reach of their perceptual and imaginative powers beyond the present situation. Such inability to see things in new and different ways or from different perspectives keeps them in the same domesticated or controlled conditions of life.

The ability to see the familiar in new and different ways not only frees us from the constraint of a disabling situation but also allows us to recognize opportunities and create possibilities. While it is true that we possess such ability, the in-the-box thinking style inhibits the use of it in some people, thus limiting their thinking to the ways they have always seen and understood things. There is a prevailing sense of helplessness in these thinkers. They tend to approach every new challenge with the same mentality. They never seem to be able to move forward, and as a result they are often left frustrated with feelings of helplessness. Furthermore, this inability to transform their perception of a current situation into new insights significantly limits their perceptual reach and imaginative ability. While they desire change and often long for it, their failure to think outside their routine patterns prevents them from initiating the changes they desire.

The second type of in-the box thinkers are those who believe that ambitious visions and projects that require them to extend their thoughts beyond their familiar circumscribed style may put them in potentially dangerous or compromising situations. Their main problem is not with making changes, as long as those changes do not extend them outside their familiar environment. Rather, their primary problem lies particularly with the size of the change as well as the potential danger and possible compromising position they think they might find themselves in trying to extend toward an ambitious venture. You may have heard the statement "Don't put your hat where your hands can't reach it." Well, this is the attitude of these thinkers. The statement simply means do not extend yourself into a situation you are not easily able to afford or maintain. When used with wisdom, this statement can provide a good guideline for decision-making. On the other hand, it can also provide an excuse to not think beyond a present situation. It makes perfect sense to the in-the-box thinker to hang his hat within comfortable reach.

If you think about it in terms of the purchase of a $70,000 car where the buyer has no reasonable plan or means to make the monthly payments, you will see the wisdom of the statement. On the other hand, if you think of it in terms of a thinker visualizing an impressive five-year goal larger than his present condition can afford, you will see that this statement does not apply. The problem with in-the-box thinkers is that they are unable to distinguish between these two scenarios. They have the tendency to see all ambitious thinking as putting your hat where you will have difficulty reaching it.

At the core of their thinking is the fear of stretching themselves beyond what they perceive to be a familiar or comfortable region. They fail to understand that every ambitious dream and vision requires the thinker to stretch beyond comfort levels and move beyond the familiar. This makes sense because you are reaching for heights you have never reached before and to distances you have never gone.

Let us go back to the phrase again. Until you put your hat at a height you cannot reach with familiar strategies, you will never know what you can do, how far you can stretch or how creative you are. This is one sure way you can distinguish between thinkers who are domesticated by their conditions and thinkers who are not.

Another type of in-the-box thinkers are those who, while not afraid to entertain big dreams, due to their years of small or box thinking are unable to generate the type of strategic plans necessary for big-goal acquisition. While they can think big they lack the ability to formulate the type of plans necessary to get them to their vision. They fail to understand that visions of grandeur require extensive thinking and careful strategic planning. Merely having a picture of a beautiful house in your mind does nothing to transform it into reality.

People who all their lives have been accustomed to thinking small will find it difficult to extend their thinking to a range required for big-goal acquisition. Big dreams require big thinking. Like the chicken that is unable to achieve great heights or long duration in flight, even if these thinkers manage to acquire a significant life ambition it dies or fade away because of the lack of the ambitious and strategic thinking needed to keep the dream alive. We see this in business, industry, education and many other areas of life endeavours.

A person may acquire a great deal of cash and become motivated to open a dream business only to watch it dies not long after it is opened. Others may begin college or university as a dream they wish to accomplish only to drop out after a few months or years. Although the ability to lift off the ground is important, the ability to maintain flight for reaching a goal is just as important.

The ten spies in the book of Numbers chapter 13 illustrate in-the-box thinking well. One man from each of the twelve tribes of Israel was sent to spy out the land of Canaan. Ten of the spies came back with the report that the challenge of taking the land was too great for the people. Several things can be identified in their report that suggest that these ten men were domesticated or in-the-box thinkers. First was their view of the goal itself. They saw occupying the land and defeating its inhabitants as a goal too large and too overwhelming for them. In verse 32 they reported that the land they saw *devoured its inhabitants* and that its people were of great size.

Like these spies, in-the-box thinkers usually compare their present size, ability, resources, situation and so on with the magnitude of the vision. If the goal requires them to think beyond what they are familiar with, they will perceive it as too overwhelming and dangerous. The idea that they have not done this or have gone this way before is common in their thinking. They fail to understand that what people can accomplish in the future is not totally dependent on their circumstances of the present or experiences of the past. They will never dream and dream big and believe they can reach it if they constantly compare where they are coming from, what they possess and where they are in life with where they can reach or what they can accomplish.

The second thing that is noted is the spies' perception of themselves with respect to the intended goal and their assumption of how others perceived them. In the latter part of verse 33 we read *"and we were like grasshoppers in our own sight, and so we were in their sight."* One of the most identifiable characteristics of chicken thinking is the thinker's perception of himself or herself when compared with others or the challenge of an ambitious goal. These spies not only lacked faith in their God; they also lacked the type of thinking required to see themselves succeeding at something bigger or greater than past accomplishments. In their minds, the likelihood of failure greatly outweighed the possibility of success. Consequently, they preferred to remain where they were or to return from whence they came rather than challenge a big dream. They'd rather return to Egyptian bondage or remain in the barren land where they were than to engage the challenge and acquire the goal God had told them they could achieve.

It is interesting to note that these spies were selected for the task because they were considered leaders of their respective clans. It is clear, however, that the true test of leadership and courage resides not in the position one holds, where one comes from or where one is in life, but rather in one's ability to face a challenging task that one has never faced before and for which one is required to extend thinking beyond that which is familiar.

At the core of chicken thinking is an underlying fear of the unknown and of the uncertainties that lie beyond their domesticated and familiar fence. When faced with situations that challenge them to think outside the box, they usually ask their favourite question: "What if?" By asking "What if?" in-the-box thinkers propose a worst-case scenario, which in turn prevents them from generating thoughts which would extend their thinking and paint the possibility of success. While "what if" statements can be a healthy way of thinking about possible negative situations and aids in preparing the thinker for possible challenges, it can also become a routine way of thinking that limits thoughts and blocks visions and ultimately success. Here it is clear that big goals or dreams require you to think beyond who you are in the present to who you can be in the future. Remember, your dream for the future is dependent not so much on what you are in the present or where you have been but more so on what you can become and where you can go. In this simple exercise of thinking, these men failed and as a result caused the death of many.

The implications of this type of thinking are far-reaching. For example, business leaders who are chicken thinkers may fail to move their business or department to new levels of success. Pastors who are chicken thinkers may fail to move their ministry and church to higher levels of growth. Many churches remains stagnant not because they are short of sincere Christians but because they lack the type of leadership that is not afraid to think outside the box. Chicken thinkers are afraid to lift their feet too far off the ground, and if they manage to lift themselves in flight, they lack what it takes to maintain height and flight, and consequently like chickens they return quickly back to the ground and into their coop.

The following are statements of in-the-box thinking:
- I don't know how I can do this differently.
- I am afraid if I do this I may end up in a greater mess.
- What if it doesn't work out as planned?
- What if I end up losing everything?
- This project is just too big. I don't think I'm ready to start it.
- I've never done this before. I think I will only end up failing if I try.
- This church building is too large for our small congregation; we will never be able to fill it.
- I would rather stay with what I know than try something new that I'm not familiar with.
- What if I start and it doesn't work out? What will people say?

•I am willing to give it a try, but the moment I see things going bad I will return to what I am familiar with.

Scapegoat Thinking

The third and final type of chicken-style thinking is the scapegoat type. The concept of scapegoating comes from its use in ancient biblical times when a live goat was released into the wilderness on the Day of Atonement, also known as Yom Kippur, after the high priest symbolically confessed the sins of the people over its head (Leviticus 16). The goat was then said to bear the sins and guilt of the people. The term *scapegoat* has come to mean one who is made to bear the blame of others. By placing the blame for something on an innocent party you have made that person a scapegoat.

When applied to thinking, scapegoating is when a thinker, when faced with failure or a challenging situation in which he or she feels helpless, finds a way to blame others for the perceived predicament. Scapegoating is an insensitive practice by which thinkers shift blame and responsibility away from themselves toward others. When someone blames others, he accuses them or finds fault with something they did or did not do that he believes led to his failure or a disabling situation. By blaming others, the thinker does not have to take responsibility for the situation or deal with it head on. Scapegoating is a clear indication of chicken or domesticated thinking in which people are motivated to avoid facing and solving their own problems

A review of the story of the fall of the first humans in Genesis helps us understand where this scapegoating style of thinking came from. When Adam was found at fault for sinning against God's instruction, he immediately shifted the blame for his action from himself. By saying "*The woman whom You gave to be with me, she gave me of the tree, and I ate*" (3:12), he was blaming not only the woman but God for his predicament.

It is important here to be reminded that God hates excuses and scapegoating. While God is merciful and forgiving, it is difficult even for him to forgive someone if they fail to take responsibility for their own thinking and actions. Does this mean that others are not in some ways responsible for many negative effects in our lives? Many of the issues and challenges we face in our lives are consequences of the actions of others. Remember that Adam's eating of the fruit was a consequence of Eve's action. Note also that physical or sexual abuse of a child can influence later behaviours. With all this in mind, how can we say that blaming others is necessarily wrong?

In answering this question we must first put things in their proper perspective. First, people whose actions directly or indirectly affect others are not guilt-free. They are responsible for all of their actions. What would their victims say if these abusers said that it was not their fault but the fault of their parents or caregivers, who abused them? The fundamental truth here is that while our thinking and behaviours are heavily influenced by factors operating in our lives, the actions that result from our own thinking are our responsibility and ours alone. So, if our parents were poor and did not provide us with any financial legacy, once we become responsible for our lives we cannot make them scapegoats for our inability to own a house or buy a car, etc. Rather, we must generate the type of thinking and initiate the kind of plans that move us beyond where our parents may have left us. By continuing to blame others we fail to see opportunities and reach beyond where we are to where we can be.

Why people, when faced with failures and challenging situations they perceive they cannot change, blame others is an interesting question. The answer may vary depending on who you ask. Several reasons stand out. First, by blaming others people *make themselves victims* of circumstances. Some people make themselves victims when they want others to act on their behalf or come to their rescue. While many people are true victims of circumstances and deserve help, scapegoaters make themselves victims simply because they have no desire to engage in responsible and ambitious thinking that would upset their comfort zone and move them beyond their domesticated life conditions. They love handouts, and as long as scapegoating others keeps them on the receiving end of things, they make it their dominant lifestyle.

Second, by blaming others scapegoaters *free themselves from being responsible* for making hard and critical decisions for change. Decision-making that moves one out of a circumscribed situation and into unfamiliar territories requires serious and strategic thinking. Such thinking would involve reflections and projections as well as consciously visualizing and creating possible future scenarios unlike anything encounter in the past or present.

You may be surprised to know that some people do not have a clear view of their possible future. Others live one day at a time with no definite plans for their future beyond a few weeks or months at a time. Where we end up in the future rests heavily on how we think about the future in the present and the responsibility we take in making decisions in the here and now to move us toward it. If you think about it, where you are now in life and the things you have or have accomplished are the future of your past. The choices you made or did not make in the past are being experienced in the here and now. If five years ago you had visualized how things could be in this season of your life and made plans accordingly, would things have turned out differently? Consider, then, the many people today who are unsatisfied with where they are in life, only to look back with regrets and blame others for how things turned out. Here scapegoating frees the person from some self-dissatisfaction and provides a way to ease the discomfort that results from no decisions to move one's life forward. Five years from now, if you are a scapegoater, you will look back on where you are now and find someone or something to blame for not having arrived at some successful point in your life.

The third reason why people scapegoat others is the perception of *loss of control.* No one wants to feel that in some way they have lost control. That can cause a person to become afraid and put him in a vulnerable and anxious state of being. Some people panic and become scared when they sense that they are losing or have lost control of a situation. When this happens they try to restore their sense of being in control by scapegoating others.

Many things can influence a person's perception that he or she has lost or is losing control. First is the inability to maintain the course towards a vision. This may be due to lack of careful planning, lack of big thinking to match the size of the vision, unrealistic thinking about one's ability to achieve the particular goal, lack of the type of determination and resolve needed to bring the vision into reality, lack of imaginative skills or simply lack of proper evaluation of the vision along the journey toward its attainment.

The second reason is the unforeseen variables that pop up along life's journey. Because scapegoat thinkers usually do not factor unknown variables into their planning equation, they are more often unprepared to deal with them. While it is true that no thinker, no matter how skilled, can be truly prepared for unknown variables, effective thinkers factor in contingencies and are usually prepared to either modify their thinking about the goal or to change or make reasonable adjustments to the goal so that it can accommodate new conditions.

Conversely, because maintaining control in the face of such challenges requires reflective and strategic thinking, scapegoat thinkers find it easier to cast the blame on others. By casting the blame on others for their own inability to meet the challenge of unknown conditions, they hope to feel some measure of justification for their failure.

The fourth reason why people scapegoat others is because they *are unable to accept negative outcomes.* People tend to blame others when something negative happens in their life that they find hard to accept. As noted earlier, many of our problems are a result of the actions of others. However, should we blame the car manufacturer because our car caught fire on the road due to our own carelessness in ensuring that we had enough oil or coolant in our car? Because our parents did not finish college, should we blame them for our own academic failing? Because a good friend introduced you to the person you got married to, should you now blame your friend for the failed marriage? When people learn how to appropriately accept challenging events and failures in their lives, they never blame others for such. When people scapegoat others for their failures, such blame only works as a defense mechanism against the anxiety they feel for not being able to deal with their issues head on.

The fifth and final reason why people scapegoat others is to *save face*. Saving face is a type of defense mechanism against appearing ineffective or incompetent in the presence of others. In the face of a challenge or failure in which the scapegoater perceives that he or she will look bad before others, the burden of and liability for a personal failure is immediately placed on some innocent party or parties. At the core of the saving-face mechanism is insecurity in one's ability to act and be successful. When people are incompetent and ineffective in managing their lives and taking it to new levels of achievement, when they are unsuccessful in facing and dealing with critical issues and challenges in their lives, to save face they turn on others with the subtle assault of scapegoating. It is a subtle form of aggression in which an innocent party has to carry the blame for something he or she is not guilty of.

The scapegoat suffers helplessly under the critical gaze and ridicule of onlookers. This is a true depiction of what happened to Christ. The scapegoat on which the high priest confessed the sins of the people represented Christ's ministry in which, though innocent, he carried the sins and guilt of the world on him to the cross, where he paid for them with his own life. His journey from the garden of prayer through his trial to his final moment on the cross was one of utter humiliation and scorn. Many laughed at him, mocked him, spat on him and even called him inappropriate and blasphemous names. This is exactly what people do to others when they scapegoat them for issues and failures they should take responsibility for and face up to themselves.

Note here that the person on whom the blame for the situation is placed has to bear it openly. Here the ultimate goal of the scapegoater is to let others see and know that what is happening or what has occurred is no fault of his own but that of another or others. Consequently, the person on which the blame is cast is looked down upon by others, while the one who cast the blame goes free and becomes justified in his or her failure.

The following examples summarize the thinking styles of the scapegoat thinker:

- If only my parents were better off, things would have turned out differently for me.
- If only I had married the right person, my life would be better.
- If I had not been so deprived as a child, I would be in a better position now.
- If my parents had paid more attention to and punished my inappropriate behaviours when I was young, I would not be in this predicament.
- Working for that company has made me an angry person.
- Having Mr. Jones for a teacher has caused me to fail the course.
- Had it not been for the lack of support from my friends and family I would certainly have succeed at the project.

As seen in some of these statements, scapegoating is directed toward not only people but also experience. There are times when, because no one can be found to blame, the scapegoater places the blame on circumstances or experiences. In either case, the blame for failure or the inability to face up to and solve a current problem is shifted away from the scapegoater.

The Dark Side: *A Summary of the Power of Negative Thinking*

The negative aspects of thinking can be rightly called the dark side of thinking. Like most things in life, thinking has a negative or dark side as well as a positive or light side. In the *Star Wars* movies, the force has two sides, both powerful enough to exert influence on reality. In a similar way, our own thinking can work to make our lives a failure or a success.

When we use the term *negative thinking* we have in view a pattern of thinking that, when activated, has little or no positive effects on life's challenges and circumstances. Negative thinking can kill the mind's potential while productive thinking can unleash its power. With our thoughts we can transcend our circumstances, and with them we can bury ourselves in the rut of life. Negative thinking has no power to move your life forward; its power lies in holding it back. When negative thinking occurs it disables and blocks every mechanism that can produce positive change in a person's life.

Let's examine some effects of negative thinking.

136

Origins and Effects of Negative Thoughts

Negative thinking has its roots in flawed beliefs we have acquired over time about ourselves, others and the world. In an earlier chapter we noted that sabotaging beliefs can originate from early development or perceptions formed from consistent negative experiences in our lives. Because understanding, closure or resolution to these negative experiences were never attained, over time negative and consistent thought patterns emerged. The fact that beliefs give rise to thoughts of like manner helps us understand the origin of negative thoughts. In view of this, you cannot eliminate a negative thought without first changing the negative belief source from which it is produced. The duration and degree of strength of the belief can give you a clue as to the extent of its negativity and ultimately the power such thinking can exert on the person's life. Note the following effects of negative thinking:

It kills motivation and cripples determination: When people think negatively they find it hard to move forward. Their own thoughts prevent them from creating necessary change in their lives. They approach problems with a defeated attitude. They tend to see the world from behind the bars of their own negative thinking. Their thinking incarcerates their ability to create resolve about positive change for their future. The only motivation and determination they feel is that which tells them to stay locked up within the walls of their own failures.

It closes out possibilities: Negative thinking closes out possibilities and blocks opportunities by allowing the person to interpret new experiences and challenges in light of past failures and unsolved issues. The tendency of most if not all of us when faced with new challenges is to draw some reference from past experiences. While this is quite normal, some people do more than this. They interpret the present situation in light of what happened in the past. By doing this the past becomes the anchor that keeps them from moving forward. When we interpret new experiences only from the perspective of the past, we turn off the key of creativity and close the doors of possibilities and opportunities. In other words, when the past is used as a mirror for new experiences, you will only see who you were and not who you can be.

It pays attention to what is least likely to work: Negative thinking focuses a person's attention on aspects of a situation that are the least likely to work rather than on those features that easily give themselves to possibilities and change. While most if not all situations have positive and negative aspects, some people find it hard to focus their attention on the positive. By focusing their attention on the negative aspects of a situation they develop the tendency of mind to look for the negatives in every situation they encounter. However, if they paid more attention to aspects of a situation that are workable and positive, things would appear quite different.

It assumes that bad events last forever: In negative thinking, the thinker generalizes that the negative and unresolved experiences of the past continue to define reality in the present and ultimately the future. The thinker collapses the three dimensions of time—the past, present and future—into one time dimension, the past. For this person, there is really no future. The future is nothing more than the past relived.

It imprisons potential: By blocking the person's view of possibilities and inhibiting his or her capacity to move forward, negative thinking imprisons the potential for change. Potential is what can be. Nothing can be if its potential is imprisoned.

It promotes psychological and physiological distress: By holding the person in a stagnant position in life, negative thinking leads to feelings of frustration with life and self, thus promoting levels of physiological, psychological and even spiritual distress, compromising health and well-being in all domains of life.

Conclusion

It is clear from our discussion that thinking occupies a defining and central part of our lives. We do not become to the extent that we think but rather to the degree that our thinking takes our lives beyond the limiting circumstances of the past and the present. Merely having thoughts in our heads is not what gets us to the sky and toward change and success.

As was illustrated in the metaphors of the wing types of various birds, although all birds have wings, not all wings are designed for soaring flight. This was also shown to be true of thoughts; although we all think, we do not all produce the types of thinking that lift our lives beyond failures and debilitating circumstances.

In the next chapter we will explore thoughts that are not only able to lift us into the sky but are capable of taking us to heights of grandeur and success in life, education, business and ministry.

chapter eight

Thinking LIKE AN EAGLE: THOUGHTS THAT *Soar*

When we think, we set in motion the most powerful force in the universe.
When we think correctly and effectively, we unleash a creative
and imaginative power unmatched by anything else
God has in his genius created in the material world.

I n the previous chapter we saw that thoughts are to success what wings are to flight. We also saw that like language, effective thinking has to be acquired and mastered. Unless people become more aware that most of their failures in life are due to their own inability to think in correct ways, they will forever remain unsuccessful in their endeavours of life.

In this chapter we explore the type of thinking that aids the thinker not only to see difficult issues as solvable but also to reach beyond what is to what can be. To achieve this end, we use as a metaphor the wings of the eagle to demonstrate the type of thinking necessary for taking the thinker toward successful endeavours.

Eagles are known to have wings that allow them the ability to both soar to great height and fly to a great distance. As noted in chapter 3, eagles have a wingspan of up to eight feet. The shape and size of the eagle's wings are designed to allow it to fly at a great speed and soar and maintain flight at a great altitude, even in changing wind currents. Its wings are not weak or fragile; they contain strategically located strong muscles through which they work to support the eagle's entire weight when lifting, flying and soaring.

Humans do not have wings, but here we conceptualize thoughts as wings necessary for taking our lives to great heights. By employing the metaphor of the eagle's wing for thinking, we are able to understand how thoughts function to take thinkers to an elevation of success with incredible soaring ability. We can say that effective, strategic and purposeful thinking are to humans what wings are to eagles.

Of all the creatures on this planet, humans alone possess the capacity to take their lives and their existence beyond what is seen in the present to what can be conceptualized in the future. They can achieve this only through the power of their thoughts. If it is true that thoughts are to humans what wings are to eagles, it stands to reason then that thoughts and thinking are the only means available to humans whereby we can move our lives upward to the unfolding of our God-given potential.

If you had never thought seriously of buying a house, would you have been moved to buy one? If you had never thought seriously of a career, would you have pursued and achieved one? The truth is, we are either derailed or directed by our thoughts.

The following are types of thinking that direct us toward positive outcomes and are true representations of the wings of the eagle. These include what I consider three of the most powerful and effective thinking styles, which are ambitious, incubative and strategic.

Ambitious Thinking:
Thoughts That Take You Beyond the Ordinary and Familiar

The term *ambition* means a strong desire for personal growth and achievement. People who are ambitious are usually those motivated to bring out the best in themselves in what they do. *Ambition* is associated with such terms as *desire, aspiration, goal, dream* and *purpose*. Most scholars believe that ambitious thinking is more a personality trait through which people are motivated to excel and advance themselves beyond the ordinary. In fact, it can be said that most people who are high in ambition are also self-motivated initiative-takers and have a strong internal locus of control.

A person with a strong internal locus of control is not easily swayed by external failures or what people think or how bad things appear. He or she is not easily deterred by disabling and discouraging situations. At the core of ambitious thinking is the persistent motivation to become, to move forward, to achieve, and to excel at what one does. An ambitious thinker sees the outcome before the first action step is planned or taken toward the goal.

Put another way, the end result is painted in the thinker's mind before the journey toward its achievement starts. Here, the thinker knows how to begin planning and what direction to take. The goals and vision of the ambitious thinker are usually great and impressive and at the same time realistic and achievable.

While it is true that there are times when ambition can go wrong, ambitious thinking is nonetheless a desired trait in people. For example, when ambition goes wrong people tend to become arrogant, impulsive, foolhardy and overconfident, leading to errors in judgment. On a positive level, however, several characteristics distinguish the ambitious thinker. These are visionary, out-of-the-box, purpose-driven, investment, and progressive thinking. Let us examine each of these.

Visionary Thinking

Vision is the ability not merely to see what is but to conceptualize what can be. The ambitious thinker is a *visionary* thinker. (Although we have discussed vision in an earlier chapter, we again discuss it here as a type of ambitious thinking.) Visionary thinkers are those who possess the ability to see beyond a present situation far into the future. They can conceptually and easily locate themselves and their church, ministry, organization or business in a new and better situation in a future scenario. They are not get-by thinkers who merely paddle or balance themselves as they go through life. They are breakthrough thinkers who are able to see and lay legitimate claim on the future.

This is unlike the type of thinkers discussed in the previous chapter who find it hard to transcend the present or past. For visionary thinkers, the future depends on the past or present only in the sense that they provide a reason or starting point to move forward. What's more, visionary thinkers do not believe how a person starts a journey determines how he or she ends it. They can conceptually and practically dissociate any relationship between situations of the past or present and how things can be in the future. This may be one of the most desired characteristics of the visionary thinker. Not many people can divorce crippling circumstances of the past or present from how things can turn out in the future. Non-visionary thinkers are unable to paint and locate themselves in a situation different from the one they have experienced or are experiencing.

Another desired characteristic of visionary thinkers is their perceptions of small beginnings and growing pains. The launching and fulfillment of great and impressive visions can sometimes have extremely weak and unimpressive beginnings. It is during these challenging times that some thinkers throw their hands in the air and give up. They do so because they are unable to see beyond what is to what can be. Successful people and leaders who have worked toward the achievement of big dreams and the growth of ministries, successful companies and organizations are acquainted with the growing pains that must be endured from the very start. While this can be discouraging and a turnoff for non-visionary thinkers, visionary thinkers are not dispirited by such a start. Rather, they embrace it as a challenge that must be tolerated as they move forward toward the big goal. They are aware that although circumstances may allow for only a small and weak start, such a start does not have to negatively affect how the journey ends. It is the conceptualized future, not the challenges associated with the journey, from which visionary thinkers derive their motivation and determination.

The visionary thinker is capable of taking *great mental leaps.* This means they can conceptually move beyond the domain of the known and expected into the realm of the uncharted and unfamiliar within their mental world. Regardless of what the present situation looks like, the visionary thinker is able to conceptually resolve this situation in the future. This is why they are not held back by circumstances of the here and now but are drawn forward toward the big picture of the future. It is not where we are but where we can go, not what we are but what we are capable of becoming that characterizes and fuels their thinking.

Visionary thinkers have a *pioneering spirit,* which makes it easy for them to break out of restraints that imprison non-visionary thinkers. When there seems to be no way out of a restraining situation, they introduce something new or make changes to whatever exists in order to break out and move forward. They are able to see the familiar in new ways and find alternatives for the conventional when faced with challenging situations. They are prepared to do what others have not done and go where others fear to go. When the journey becomes unclear, uncertain or even blocked by obstacles and seems impassable, they are prepared to chart new paths and lay new tracks. Their pioneering spirit allows them to see what others cannot or can only vaguely see. Like the eagle they can spot opportunity and possibility far into the distant future.

Visionary thinkers are *independent thinkers.* They do not sit back and wait on the ideas of others to make a breakthrough or to conceptualize how things can be in the future. While they welcome and can work with the ideas of others, they are not inhibited in thinking if others do not have ideas. Their pioneering spirit allows them the ability to look deep into the future while at the same time understanding their present situation.

Out-of-the-Box Thinking (Creative Thinking)

Out-of-the-box thinkers share many of the characteristics of the visionary thinkers, including big thinking, forward thinking and independent thinking. Three of the outstanding characteristics of out-of-the-box thinkers are (1) their ability to conceptualize and transform current problems into solvable conditions, (2) their ability to be innovative and (3) their ability to easily identify opportunities where others see only problems.

They are never perturbed about the magnitude or complexity of a problem. They know that a complex problem is usually made up of small issues, which when identified can be easily resolved. This means they not only see the big issue; they are also cognizant of those component parts that give rise to its size.

Because they are not afraid of new ideas they easily innovate when faced with outmoded and stagnant situations for which no solution is readily available. While others search in vain for solutions in what exists, they innovate and create changes to what is. In other words, where thinkers who are afraid to think beyond the familiar get stuck, out-of the box thinkers introduce something new or make changes to what is in order to move forward. Their ability to recognize opportunities where others see only problems rest in the fact that they can step out of the box and look at the situation with a different set of eyes. This allows them not only to be open to new experiences but also to entertain multiple perspectives on an issue.

Unlike in-the-box-thinkers who are afraid to extend themselves beyond the familiar, out-of-the-box thinkers are not afraid to think independently and break with traditional or conventional ways of seeing and doing things. For them the type of thinking that gave rise to a problem situation must be changed if a solution must be arrived at. This means if a problem was caused by or was maintained by a particular style of thinking, the problem or maintenance of it will be changed only if thinking changes. For out-of-box thinkers, goals are achieved and dreams realized only when people are willing to think outside the expected and the norm and create necessary change to what is to give way to what can be.

Out-of-the box thinkers are realistic and at the same time unconventional and creative in their thinking and approach to problem-solving and planning. For them, if something is no longer working, then new ways must be sought to replace the norm or the outmoded. They are not afraid to upset the status quo or the conventional in order to achieve a worthwhile goal. While they are capable of seeing things as others see them, their vision is not blurred or blocked by the circumstances surrounding a present situation.

Purpose-Driven Thinking

The third category of ambitious thinkers is the *purpose-driven* type. These thinkers are self-motivated and internally driven. Purpose fuel motivation and gives definition and direction to plans. Purpose always drives a person forward.

The material from which purpose is derived can be drawn from any of the three dimensions of time, the past, present, future or a combination of any two or all three. Whatever triggers purpose, once aroused it always points forward and away from the point of defeat, hurt or failure. When purpose is ignited in a person, it mobilizes the will to move and to do.

Purpose-driven thinkers, like all ambitious thinkers, begin with the end in view. In this, the gap of time between the thinker and the goal is bridged. This means the entire scope of thinking, from the first thought to the final reflection, is influenced by what the thinker hopes to achieve at the end. James Allen, in his book *As a Man Thinketh,* says it well when he notes that "They who have no central purpose in their life fall an easy prey to petty worries, fears, troubles, and self-pity, all of which are indications of weakness, which lead just as surely as deliberately planned sins…to failure, unhappiness, and loss" (Allen 2008). People with no innermost purpose for their lives are those whose thinking lacks the power to break free of redundancy and traditional moulds and limitations. People who contribute to positive changes in the world are those who are driven by purpose.

When we connect purpose to thinking we set in motion internal dynamics of motivation and energy. It is this internal fire that moves people toward what appears to others as a difficult and often impossible dream. Purpose-driven thinkers are not confused about what they need or where they need to go. While they are fully aware that there will be challenging conditions on the way toward their goals, the vision to be attained is never one that is unclear or vague. There is no doubt in the purpose-driven thinker's mind that the goal can be achieved. This is so because the end is always in clear view. They are not easily defeated by what is in the present but are drawn forward by their unfolding purpose in time.

Investment Thinking

The fourth type of ambitious thinkers is the *investment* type. These are thinkers who plant today to secure a harvest in the future. They are long-range thinkers who seriously and meticulously plant their seeds of thought in the here and now with hope to achieve some gain in the future. They are not inhibited by how meagre or desperate things appear in the present or how limited present opportunities are. Their thinking is characterized by the idea that small things if invested well can turn into great gains in the future.

What do we really mean by investment? Depending on whether you ask a finance professional or an economist you will get a slightly different answer. At the core, however, investment is really the careful utilization of resources in order to produce some increase in the future. This means that every investor must be able to see the future as a fertile and profitable marketplace of opportunity that can yield some gain. Investors must also be able to conceptualize it as the coming present. This is because the gain they invested for can only be acquired when the future becomes the present.

In addition to seeing the future as an opportunity for gain, the investor must be able to recognize investment resources and opportunities in the present. The gain expected in the future determines the nature and quality of the investment made in the present.

Like a true investor, the investment thinker sees the current state of affairs as giving way to a future that will one day becomes the present. Furthermore, the investment thinker understands that tomorrow's gain begins with an investment in the present. It is with this in mind that he or she creates and invests in a dream bigger and better than anything in the present. Instead of worrying over what is, the investment thinker looks forward toward what can be in the future.

Does the investment thinker not care about what's happening in the present? It is because the investment thinker is concerned about situations in the present that he or she desires to ensure that the future is better than the present. Because investments must begin with the resources one has in hand or can access, the investment thinker is wise in utilizing current situations as investment opportunities. This is done by reframing a current situation, regardless of how desperate it appears, into a reason or motivation to move forward and look toward the future. It is by transforming the perceptions of a current situation into an opportunity for change that the investment thinker deposits the first investment for a future gain. Remember, investment is really using the resources one has to secure a gain in the future before you get there.

There are four important things to consider when we think of investment.

1. The Investment Goal

It's the nature of the future goal that determines the quality of present decisions and actions. The investment thinker is *gain-driven* and can be rightly called a *gain-driven thinker*. This means the future must yield more than the past or present, not less. The central goal of investment thinking is to have a more productive and purposeful life in the future. This may pertain to ministry, family, business, career or personal growth and development. For the investment thinker, overcoming the challenges of the present and charting a more productive future is not an option but an imperative that can and must be achieved.

Having a central goal for your future is critical for several reasons. First, it determines the type and nature of the decisions you make in the present. Major decisions made in the present must be linked to a goal in the future. For example, would a goal to buy a house in three years affect your everyday financial decisions in the present? Would a goal to enter ministry in the future affect your life decisions in the present? I am sure you would agree with me that the answer to both these questions is an emphatic Yes!

Second, the goal of the future must shape your behaviour in the present. How we behave in the present has a lot to do with the goal we set for ourselves in the future. People who have no central goals for their future live lives that go around in circles in no particular direction. At the beginning of every year, they find themselves no farther than the year before. The investment thinker knows that not any behaviour will get him or her to the goal. If your behaviour in the present is incompatible with your goal, you will not achieve it. Goals and behaviours must be in harmony.

Third, having a goal stimulates hope in a person. Hope stimulates energy and inspires motivation and passion in people. Hope is always linked with a future goal, not with a past situation.

2. Assets

How assets are identified, allocated and used is critical for any investment. Assets come in many forms. They can be tangible as well as intangible. For example, money, houses and land are tangible assets. On the other hand, such things as skills, talents, knowledge and even time, motivation and tenacity are intangible assets. The investment thinker uses both types to achieve his or her goal. The investment thinker takes care not to waste intangible resources on things or in areas of life that cannot be turned into a future profit. For the investment thinker, to waste time, energy and motivation on things that do not profit is to waste valuable assets and resources.

How many people do you know who sit around doing nothing or waste time on things that yield no productive outcomes and have the guts to say they do not have time when it comes to tasks that can yield profitable life gains? For example, they tell you they don't have the time to advance themselves in a career or education. Yet these same individuals spend hours watching television or talking on the phone. These same individuals complain about the boring jobs they have been working at or the low levels of competence they possess or their lack of knowledge of important subjects. People who are not investment thinkers usually enter a future that is no different from their past. The wasted past is what they bring into the future, thus creating their future in the exact image of their past.

3. Opportunity

The investment thinker is aware that many great opportunities are created within unfavourable circumstances. In view of this, where some people see challenges and disappointments they see opportunities for change.

It is interesting that when difficult situations arise in our lives it is usually then that we feel we are the weakest. The investment thinker is aware of these moments but also believes that's when gates of opportunities swing wide open. Instead of searching for the opportunities provided by a bad situation, the first thing most people do is react negatively. It is similar to people who constantly focus on their one weakness and never give thought to the several strengths they possess.

Successful investors know where and when to invest. Where others are afraid to invest they see opportunity that can turn over into significant gains in the future. Like a careful investor, the investment thinker embraces the challenges of the present and carefully evaluates the timing and moment for strategic investment.

4. Risk

Every investor knows that the higher the risk, the more potential for higher returns and also for loss. For people in business this is not rocket science but a simple way to understand the nature of investment. In the real world nothing is ever as it appears; there are always deeper levels of uncertainties and unknown variables to things that we see and experience on the surface. Consequently, no matter how carefully we plan, how many variables we account for, there are always margins of errors in our thinking and planning that can lead to undesired outcomes.

Where there is a great chance of success there are also great challenges to be encountered and great risk of failure. This is like saying the higher a person climbs, the more he can see and the greater will be his fall. Although investment thinkers are aware of the risk, they are not afraid to think and plan for big returns.

Weren't there great challenges for the children of Israel going into the land of Canaan to possess it? Wouldn't they encounter great and powerful people in the land? Was the possibility of loss significant? Absolutely! But see what happened when some focused only on the challenges and failed to think of the profits.

No one would invest if they only focused on the possibility of loss. The same can be said for serving God. To serve God is to invest our lives for a future gain. However, this eternal investment requires great sacrifices and comes with great challenges and many trials. If we focus only on the challenges and trials we will no doubt be tempted to pull out of the investment. It is, however, not the trials and challenges but the reality of being with our Lord eternally that draws us forward.

The investment thinker knows full well that many of the circumstances of the present are results of no investment or bad investments in the past and can only be changed or altered by reinvesting in the future. For example, a person may have made a bad choice in dropping out of school in the past but is considering going back to school in the present. Going back to school is considered an investment for the future. For the investment thinker, a past failure is an opportunity to improve in the future. With this in mind, they are able to turn current disappointments into opportunities that, instead of holding them in a disabling state, can create new prospects as well as new ways of preparing for the future.

People who go through life without much consideration as to how their future will be and who waste their mental resources on worrying over *what is* will come into a tomorrow that is empty and even more depressed than their past. In fact, for these people, their tomorrow is essentially no different from their today or their yesterday. They have not invested and therefore have nothing to gain. Life for them is nothing but a constant recycling of the same old material of the past.

Progressive Thinking

The fifth type of ambitious thinking is the *progressive* type. Like all ambitious thinkers, progressive thinkers look toward the future and have big dreams. However, because they primarily focus on the next stage in the process of reaching their goal rather than the final goal itself, they can be rightly called stage thinkers. They think mostly in stages.

While they do have long-term plans, like all ambitious thinkers, unlike the visionary thinker who takes mental leaps they are more concerned with taking *what is* to the next stage of *what it can be* without fully upsetting the traditional mould in the initial phase. They prefer to proceed in a step-by-step manner, having the next stage as their primary target. They seek to constantly improve a current situation until it is totally transformed into what it can be. These thinkers are not hurried. Rather, they make timely plans and achieved them easily. Their goal is to arrive at their vision through a process of gradual change.

Incubative Thinking:
Thoughts That Produce New and Extended Ideas
Ambitious thinking helps you bridge the gap between where you are in the present to where your vision is located in the future. Without such thinking people would never be able to move beyond where they are in life. However, because life is a complex mix of various dynamics and challenges, sometimes people with great ambition will be overwhelmed in trying to find workable solutions as well as in deciding which path in life to take. It is with this in mind that you are introduced in this section to what I call *incubative thinking*.

The term *incubate,* according to *Webster's Dictionary*, means "to cause to develop : give form and substance to." Incubation is usually a slow and deliberate process of allowing something new to take form from an existing incubating material. When applies to thinking, incubation describes a type of thinking in which the thinker is not hurried and does not act immediately on an idea but chooses rather to push it into the unconscious so it can germinate and produce more ideas and possibilities.

You have heard the phrase "Let me sleep on it," or simply "Sleep on it." This refers to giving the idea or decision a period of incubation when the unconscious aids us by providing new insights into the decisions we are about to make or ideas we are planning to implement. Because we live in a fast-moving world filled with multiple arrays of stimulations, it is easy for people to get confused and feel pressured when challenged to make quick decisions as to how to proceed in a life path.

Incubative thinkers intentionally draw upon the unconscious powers of their minds. They are long-range thinkers who can delay gratification and set forth ambitious goals or dreams and intentionally not work out any immediate plans for their acquisition. Instead, they push their ideas into the deepest domain of their minds (or the unconscious domain) for incubation. They are not rushed in their thinking but believe that, given a period of time, their minds have the capacity to sift through confusing thoughts, expand on their original idea, giving them deeper insight, generating new perspectives and producing solutions and even giving clarity to ambiguous and complex ideas.

This does not mean that these thinkers go around putting off decision-making while they push ideas into their unconscious and sit waiting for something to just pop up into their consciousness. On the contrary, they are not procrastinators but careful reflective thinkers who have developed the tendency to work with how their minds function.

When we say that one pushes an idea into the unconscious it does not mean just intentionally forgetting everything about the original idea. They do not allow their ideas to slip away but write them down for further reference. If you are an incubative thinker you know that the more you reflect on an idea, the deeper it is processed by your mind, and the more incubation takes place, the more ideas are generated. In view of this, incubative thinkers usually journal or commit their ideas to paper as they are generated. They keep records of the insights generated by their minds on the subject of their plan.

Although we are far from understanding the full capacity of the human mind in the area of the unconscious, we do know that it is capable of incubating ideas. When our mind gives us what appear to be spontaneous insights and bright ideas, these are not impulsive or random stuff falling out of our unconsciousness. Although random stuff does occurs in our minds, not everything that appears random is accidental but is generated from unconscious processes resulting from some previous deliberate conscious operation.

I am almost certain that most individuals have experienced what I call unconscious pop-up insights in which, days after an idea is given birth to, the original idea is transformed or extended by new insights that seem to spring up in the mind from nowhere and without any conscious effort or deliberate reflection. A careful examination of some of these pop-up insights will reveal that they are really not accidental thoughts but extensions, deeper insights, new forms or reworkings of the original idea.

While this happens to all of us, not many people intentionally tap into this ability. Consequently, because they do not understand this ability of the mind they usually don't recognize incubated outcomes as significant for applications. Individuals who are aware of this awesome ability understand that many of these insights are not just random pop-ups but incubated results of a much deeper unconscious process of actual conscious material.

The next time you have a challenge you cannot solve immediately or a goal you wish to accomplish, write it down and muse upon it for a while. Pay careful attention to and be prepared to write down the extended thoughts and ideas that will be generated from your mind days later. This will surprise you!

It is important to note that some of the insights that we receive are not from our own incubation process but directly impressed on our minds by the Spirit of God himself. While God has given us this awesome ability he still reserves the right to impress insights and inspiration on our consciousness. The fact that we have been endowed with both a conscious and an unconscious capacity of mind means we are expected to employ them in our everyday life effectively.

Strategic Thinking:
Thoughts That Position You for Change and Relevance

The next type of thinking that takes us to soaring height is strategic thinking. The term *strategic* has been applied to such processes as planning, leadership, management and even military operations, to name a few. The term is usually used to describe the way in which a process is carried out, decisions made, plans developed and executed, resources configured and challenges met.

In this text we describe strategic thinking as a type of thinking that is a creative, adaptive, resourceful and insightful way of generating and using thoughts as well as planning for the future. It is also a thinking style that situates the individual in a position of relevance and anticipatory change.

Although strategic thinking shares many of the characteristics of ambitious and incubative thinking, it is distinguished by its capacity to position the individual for change and relevance. The key characteristic is its *positioning* and *relevance creating* feature. In the following discussion we will explore the process through which strategic thinking works to achieve its positioning and relevance effects. Let us begin by looking at some key factors in strategic thinking.

Key Elements in Strategic Thinking

In the world of business, strategic thinking is considered by many to be the basis for successful and effective planning, managing, organizing and leading. In fact, staying on the competitive edge of effectiveness and keeping an organization relevant in a changing world depend heavily on strategic thinking.

Let us examine two fundamental bases that give rise to strategic thinking. First is the *awareness* of the nature of situations in the present environment. The strategic thinker has a keen awareness of what is happening in the world around him or her as this relates to self, organization, leadership task, church, family or personal ambition. Having an ambitious goal is good but not good enough. One must go beyond just having a goal to the extent of becoming aware of how current forces can work to influence the acquisition of such a goal. Having an understanding of the dynamics of these forces will help in positioning oneself, one's organization, or one's church or ministry for success in the future.

Forces operating in a present circumstance can have far-reaching influence on future plans and goals. The strategic thinker knows that developing plans for a future situation without careful consideration of influences from forces in the present is setting up one's self, organization or ministry for possibly failure. Business leaders who fail to recognize the effects of forces in the present as well as the influence they can exert on the future will also fail to remain competitive and consequently will not be prepared for changes in the future. It is the strategic thinker with his or her awareness of the dynamics of present forces that can position a business, organization, church or ministry to remain relevant in the present and in the future in spite of changes and challenges in the market or in society, respectively.

People who resist change that is intended to keep an organization competitive and relevant are not capable of taking their organization, church, ministry, or life toward success. For example, people who only think of the Internet as evil fail to see that the good outweighs the negative. Parents who believe the Internet is evil and refuse their children access to it are not thinking strategically. Managers of small businesses who refuse to utilize the Internet to advertise their products and enhance their business will find that the sales of their produce will begin to decline. This is because people in today's society no longer look for products or company in the Yellow Pages but on the Internet. If someone even wants to find a church they go to the Internet. So then, strategic thinking applies to positioning not only a business or your life but even a entity such as a church.

Let's examine this a bit. Would you say that having the Internet at your church is a bad idea? Some traditional thinkers might think so. Because the Internet can connect us with so much bad material, it is easy for people to dismiss it as overall evil. To expect only good from this world is wrong thinking. What we need to do is carefully filter out the good from the bad, not throw out everything.

Having the Internet at your church is beneficial for several reasons. First, a pastor can easily access information that would otherwise take him days to get. A preacher can integrate video clips from the Internet to strengthen and enhance his teaching or sermons. It is also a teaching tool and resource for all ages in the church. Sermons and teaching and even the worship service can be streamed live through the Internet so that shut-in members can gain access. Further, responsible use of the Internet can be taught. Sessions can be developed for older members where they can learn to use the Internet and find sites that could be a source of help for them. The health ministry can use it to provide insight for church members on health and wellness.

As you can see, the list of benefits is long. On the other hand, churches that refuse to utilize this awesome technological tool are failing to remain relevant in a world of change. Of course there is always the issue of people misusing and abusing the Internet. While this is valid, it should never be an argument not to use it. Steps can always be taken to prevent unauthorized or inappropriate use of the church's Internet.

Second, in addition to being keenly aware of the forces at work in a present situation, the strategic thinker has an insightful, innovative and creative approach in the development of effective responses to meet the challenges of the present and those anticipated in the future. In this case, strategic thinking leads to strategic planning. Strategic planning is like a road map that bridges the present to the future.

The strategic thinker asks two simple but profound questions. The first is "What are the present issues that must be responded to?" The strategic thinker then answers this question by becoming aware of the forces at work in the present. This is what we discussed as *awareness*.

The second question is "How can we remain relevant and effective in the midst of change, both now and later?" The answer is to think and plan strategically. To remain relevant is to think about the present as well as the future and position oneself or one's organization in such a way that you remain relevant.

For example, imagine that you have been working for a company for twenty years, doing pretty much the same thing year after year. Do you consider that, given the current changes in technology, outsourcing and downsizing, your particular skills might soon not be needed? Or do you just continue to do what you have always done for the past twenty years, hoping that you will be spared? This is clearly not strategic thinking. People who think like this are the most likely to get depressed and feel hopeless when they realize they are not prepared for the changes in their life or organization.

A strategic thinker would first become aware of the forces at work in the present situation of the company and in the world of business and then ask how his skills could be upgraded to remain relevant and effective in view of coming changes. A strategic thinker would begin making plans to upgrade his skills in order to keep them on the competitive edge. He may need to learn how to use the computer and Internet better or use some new software or to go back to school for additional training or upgrading in particular area of competence or expertise. In other words, strategic thinking has to do with how you configure your resources in a changing and challenging environment for the greatest success in the present and in the future.

When it comes right down to it, strategic thinking has to do with how your personal and professional life, organization, ministry or church can function at its best, given the challenges and changes in the present. Success in a world of change means remaining relevant and staying in step with change. This applies to your personal and professional life, your business or organization and even your church and ministry.

The strategic thinker makes decisions in the present with the understanding of how situations will change in the future and how such changes might affect him or his organization. Consequently, his professional life, organization or church will always be in a position to meet the challenges and changes of the future, simply because he thought about it and made preparation for such in the past.

The strategic thinker is adaptive to change. This means he or she monitors events and trends and make timely changes to self, the process or organization that is being led. The need to adapt to change is born out of the need to survive and remain relevant. Whether this applies to self, organization, a church or ministry, the strategic thinker must confront several challenges.

The first relates to identity. The question then becomes "What type of person am I?" or "What type of organization, church or ministry are we?"

The second relates to mission. The question then becomes "What activities should I be involved in?"

The third relates to vision. The question then becomes "What type of person should I become?" or "What goals should we be pursuing?"

The fourth relates to others. If you are leading an organization or church, the question you are challenged with is "How are people affected by forces operating in society, and how are they changing as a result of these forces?" The next question you have to confront relating to people is "How are societal or environmental changes affecting people's attitudes?"

Only when you can appropriately answer these questions can you strategically position yourself or your organization and church to adapt to change and remain relevant. For example, if you are a leader and do not know how the forces in society are affecting people and their attitudes, you cannot effectively position your organization for the type of change and relevance that will be necessary to withstand the effects of the changing forces operating in society. This means if you are a leader of a manufacturing company, you will not be prepared to meet the changing needs of consumers. If you lead people, you will not understand that changes in their behaviour and attitude are strongly influenced by forces operating in society. If you are a leader of a church, you will not be able to position your ministry to meet the changing needs of people in your community. However, if you are a strategic thinker, these societal dynamics do not go unnoticed. You are alert to them and take necessary action and make appropriate decisions that position your life or organization for continuing relevance and success.

While remaining relevant in a changing society is necessary, change must be undergirded and tempered by values. There is a fine line between conformity and authentic change. Care must be taken that we do not become conformed to trends and societal standards and call it relevant change. Any change that causes you to compromise your core values has taken you too far.

Vigilant Thinking:
Thoughts That Block or Destroy Vision Killers
Everyone who has ever launched a vision knows the challenges that often lie between the inception of the vision and its fulfillment. Great thinkers usually don't have problems with thinking big and launching impressive visions. The challenge mostly faced by these thinkers is what I refer to in this text as *vision viruses* or *vision killers*. These viruses present not only challenges but serious threats to the fulfillment of a vision.

Believe it or not, your vision and plans can and will often come under severe attack from vision viruses. Once a vision virus invades your thinking, it corrupts your vision and renders it useless. Not every type of thinking can prevent vision viruses from destroying a vision. *Vigilant thinking* not only protects against the deadliest of vision killers but ensures that an achievable vision is attained.

A vigilant thinker is mentally alert and attentive to intrusive thoughts. These are beliefs that keep a person's life in a dysfunctional state and work against positive life change and the fulfillment of a vision.

A virus in general is an infectious and corrupting agent that has the ability to infect and destroy a functioning system from within. In a biological system, for example, a virus spreads by inserting its DNA into a host cell. By compromising the normal functioning of the cell, the virus negatively affects parts of the biological system, leading to severe impairment in the system.

In a computer, a virus needs only to attach itself to a document or program to infect parts or the entire operating system. It is usually a self-replicating code that, after gaining illegal access, works itself through the computer system, damaging, corrupting, deleting or shutting down part of or the entire system. The way a computer virus infiltrates your computer often depends on the type of virus it is. Different computer viruses have different characteristics that make them unique and dangerous to the normal functioning of your computer. Some viruses can erase all the information from the memory location on the hard drive, others may display strange messages on your computer screen, and still others can make small changes in your computer programs leading to significant effects in the overall computer operation. Regardless of how a virus infects your computer, once inside it is difficult to remove. It hides in your computer's memory and begins duplicating itself like cancer. When you save your information, you also save the virus, which begins corrupting or deleting critical data, causing major computer and programming issues.

A single virus can bring down a large computer network system, which can leave a company disabled and vulnerable and cost it greatly. To protect their computer operations, companies invest in high-level virus protection software, which is able to detect, block and disable incoming viruses. From the ordinary user to large businesses to government and military operations, billions of dollars are spent every year protecting computer systems.

The human thinking system has some fundamental similarities to a computer system. For example, the computer operates on three basic principles. First is the principle of inputting. The computer must receive input from an external source, which could be keys pressed on the keyboard, words spoken into a microphone connected to the computer, an email coming into the computer through its modem or information coming into the computer from the Internet.

Second is the principle of internal processing. Once information or data is received into the computer it is internally processed by its central processing unit.

Third is the principle of outputting. Once the information is internally processed according to the computer's internal program, a result is outputted on the screen or through a printer, a voice simulator, email or whatever other means the user provides as an output.

Although the human thinking system is much more sophisticated and complex than a computer system, it nonetheless operates on the same three basic principles. Let's examine this a bit closer. Humans are equipped with senses through which we receive information from the outside world. Our senses act as sensory input devices much like the computer's peripheral devices.

The information we receive through our senses is transformed into neural impulses and routed to particular regions of our brain for mental processing and memory storage.

The final stage of this process is the output. Once information from the outside world is processed and stored, the results will be outputted in the form of belief, attitude, words and behaviour. The beliefs, attitudes and actions produced by mental processing become experiential conditions that influence the perception and interpretation of subsequent experiences. This means that a past or current experience can subtly exert control over how a new experience is perceived, interpreted or acted on.

How we process and interpret our own experiences can work to destroy our own dreams and aspirations. We are not destroyed so much by what happens on the outside but more so by what is happening within our own minds. This is because it is through our minds that we are changed and transformed.

This is where your greatest battle is fought. It is a battle for your success, dreams and ultimately eternal destiny. In fact, the greatest weapon again us is not people or external circumstances. Rather, it is the type of thinking that acts like a virus in our minds, turning our own thoughts against us.

Let us examine the virus effect on the visioning process and how vigilant thinking works to prevent such from attacking, corrupting or even disabling the fulfillment of a vision. We will use as examples two of the most dangerous computer viruses, resident viruses and Trojan horse viruses.

Vigilant Thinking vs. Resident Virus:
Overcoming Intrusive and Abusive Thoughts

In the world of computers, a resident virus is a permanent destructive program that resides in the random access memory (RAM), which is the part of your computer where the operating system application programs and data that are in current use are kept so that they can be quickly accessed by the computer's central processing unit (CPU). The information in RAM is only available while the computer is on. When the computer is turned off the information in RAM is lost. When the computer is again turned on the computer operating system and other files are again loaded into RAM.

These resident viruses have the ability to stay in memory after the program closes. When the computer is again turned on and a program is run, the virus is activated and can overcome and interrupt all the operations executed by the system, corrupting files and programs that are opened, closed, copied and renamed.

RAM can be compared to a person's short-term memory and the hard drive to long-term memory. A person's short-term memory, also called working memory, is where tasks being currently worked on take place. You can think of working memory as the workspace of the mind. This is where current processes are worked out, the basis for perception is established, and a host of executive functions, such as planning and decisions for short-term and long-term goals, are carried out. If left unprotected, your mental workspace can become vulnerable to vision viruses or dream killers.

Whenever you generate thoughts in your mind and begin thinking about something, you enter your mental workspace. This is the meeting place for past and current experiences as well as future aspirations. What goes on in this mental workspace has significant effects on goals and ambition.

Because of its importance to vision building and planning, your mental workspace is a primary target for resident viruses. You don't know these viruses even exist until you engage your mind and begin the process of setting impressive goals and executing plans. These resident viruses are nothing more than intrusive or abusive thoughts that take such forms as self-doubt, self-criticism or negative self-talk, to name a few. They are called resident viruses because they reside inside that conscious part of your mind where you generate, modify and create plans for your life and for the attainment of your vision. They are activated when you engage your mind with thoughts to extend the borders of your life, your organization, church or ministry. Once your mental life and plans are infected by these viruses, your visions and dreams will appear to be unattainable.

Here is how these resident vision killers work. First, you do not know they even exist until you engage your mind toward something big. As long as your mind only works on small, mundane routines or everyday expected things, you will never activate these dream killers. The activation of these viruses requires the start-up of particular program in your mental system. They are not designed to destroy your everyday routine, which is not intended to move your life to higher heights. Therefore, as long as you keep your life on the most basic level, you may never experience their deadly and crippling effects. However, the moment you turn on your mental machine and start the program and initiate the command that says you are about to take your life to another level, you immediately activate and release a bunch of resident viruses in your mental workspace. You will begin hearing negative thoughts in your head, telling you things that are meant to destroy any attempt to move your life forward. Here are some of the statements that will be released in your mental command centre by these viruses:

- You are not good enough.
- God will never forgive you for all that stuff you did.
- Why bother taking the risk? You will only fail anyway.
- There is no way you can achieve such an impressive goal.
- You have always failed, and you are bound to fail again.
- There is no way that God can love a person like you.
- No one in your family has attained such a level of success, so why do you believe you will?
- It's too hard, and you don't have what it takes to reach that level.
- You may have to go back to school, and you are too old, it will take too long, and you are not smart enough.
- You cannot accomplish this without some help, and you don't have any.
- No one even care if you succeed or fail anyway.
- You don't have the time and energy to undertake this goal.
- You don't have the kind of resources that would help you succeed, so why bother?
- You don't have the capability that others have to succeed at such a goal.
- Do not interrupt your current life; you will only end up worse off than you are now.
- People are just waiting to laugh at you if you mess up, so why make yourself an embarrassment and a joke in the eyes of people?
- Individuals like you never really attain such a level of lifestyle and achievement anyway.

They are called resident viruses simply because they reside inside your mental world, waiting until you engage your mental program called "potential." The main purpose of this type of virus is to replicate and take action when it is executed. When a specific condition is met, the virus will go into action and infect files in the directory or folder that it is in and in directories that are specified by a particular command. Their intent is to wipe out all traces of your success program and corrupt or rewrite all your vision sub-routines.

Think of the many goals and visions that have been destroyed by these vision viruses, leaving people with feelings of incompetence and uselessness. While most people have good goals and would like to achieve some degree of success in their lives, many will never get close to them simply because of these vision blockers.

Think also of the many people who desperately want to move their lives to new spiritual levels, but every time they think of making a change, their dream is shattered by their own killer thoughts. The goal of these thoughts is to abuse and put you down, telling you things that make you feel worthless, stupid and incompetent. They corrupt or rewrite files where you keep information about your past successes and accomplishments as well as future aspirations. Once these files are overwritten or corrupted, it is difficult to gain access to them, and therefore you have no true reference of success from which to work.

When people can look back in their lives on the small successes they have had, these can serve as motivation toward more success. But if these memory files get corrupted and written over with new and incorrect information, people may believe that these successes were mere luck or not real accomplishments, and they are left with no real basis for knowing what they are capable of accomplishing.

Another type of resident virus is called a time bomb. As its name implies, once it gets into your computer it is timed to release itself and affect your computer at a specific time or when a specific event occurs. Once released this virus can delete or reformat your hard drive and delete or corrupt information throughout your system.

Life can appear fine and easygoing until you decide to make decisions that will launch your life beyond the mundane and the familiar. The moment you spread your wings to fly, you activate the time bomb virus in your thinking world, which works to destroy your ability to fly upward to success. The trigger for these time bombs again is your own thinking. However, they are triggered only by life-changing thoughts. The moment you entertain thoughts to change or move your life forward you set off these mental bombs.

Like a computer system, our mental world has levels of vulnerability for what we have referred to as intrusive or abusive thoughts. Many computer systems continue to operate successfully, not because attempts have not been made by viruses to invade them but because their operators have taken particular precaution to block their entry or destroy them upon their attempt to enter the system. In the same way that a computer system and its programs can be protected from viruses, the mental world of thoughts can be secured against the deadly effects of intrusive and abusive thoughts by vigilant thinking.

Vigilant thinking is to the fulfillment of your vision what virus protection is to the safe operation of a computer system. Vigilant thinking helps you generate thoughts that block abusive thoughts as they attempt to invade your mental world to destroy your ability to change and to conceptualize and accomplish greatness. Vigilant thinking operates much like the white blood cells in your immune system, which search, mark and destroy deadly invading microorganisms intended to disable, infect or destroy whole or parts of your body system. Your immune system acts like a virus tracker, virus blocker and virus killer, which keep your internal system protected and functioning well.

Vigilant Thinking vs. Trojan Horse Virus

According to Greek legend, the Greeks won the Trojan War by hiding their soldiers in a huge hollow wooden horse (called a Trojan horse) and sneaking them into the fortified city of Troy. In computer terms, a Trojan horse is a deadly security-breaking program that is disguised as something harmless. A Trojan horse virus has the appearance of a useful and desired function but in reality is an imposter with deadly intent. Its malicious intent is not apparent to the user at first.

For a Trojan horse virus to spread into your computer you must invite it in by opening a file or attachment. For example, when you click and download what appears to be a harmless file from the Internet or from an attachment in your email, you may unleash a deadly virus that can erase your hard drive or send personal or critical information from your computer to some unauthorized person. Such attacks can cripple entire networks or steal critical information from a computer system or database.

Like the Trojan horse virus, ideas and thoughts that appear useful but are really imposters can get into our mental world, break down our mental security and capture significant part of or our entire life and vision. This type of virus can be compared to advice that we receive that appears useful but has deadly intent. This originates from people who we trust and look up to. These Trojan viruses are really imposter thoughts that enter your mind when you listen to and believe the negatives that people have to say about your goals and vision or about your ability to achieve them. Believing these opinions that have the appearance of useful advice may in fact work to cripple your perception of your own ability to achieve. For example, when talking to a friend about your desire to go back to school and improve on your education or skills, he might say to you, "Are you sure you want to do that now, considering the responsibilities and commitment you have, not to mention how long you've been out of school?" On the surface this might sound like useful advice, but the moment you open this attachment you release a deadly Trojan virus that works through your mental system, infecting your vision and thus disabling your ability to move your life forward.

Vigilant thinking blocks imposter thoughts that can compromise your ability to achieve and change. Vigilant thinking means that before it is believed and acted upon, what people have to say about what you can or cannot do it must first pass through the grid of your own sense of self derived from who you know you are and can be.

How do we acquire the type of vigilant thinking that protects us against negative, intrusive and abusive thoughts? The most effective way is to see and think of ourselves as God's unique creation, full of capability and potential and created for greatness. Believe that in you there is awesome potential waiting to be brought forth; believe that there is an eagle within waiting to be discovered and released.

Conclusion

It is clear that appropriate thinking is not only necessary to move our lives forward but also critical to overcoming and positioning our organizations, churches, ministries and families for success. In the following chapter we will move our discussion from types of thinking to how the mind operates and how thoughts are employed in the process of thinking and change.

chapter nine

The
POWER AND PURPOSE OF
Thinking

Our ability to soar and reach to great heights is not determined by our past experiences or the expectations of others but by our own thoughts. We can only attain the height of our greatest and uppermost thoughts.

Have you ever asked yourself what the purpose of thinking is? What do people do when they think? How do your thoughts and thinking change your life, move you forward or hold you back? How does your thinking influence your health and well-being? How does it help you succeed or cause you to fail in life? Are there laws or principles by which the mind or thinking operates? Some of these questions are the focus of this chapter.

To begin, your thoughts are the source of power and change; they can enable or disable you. They can generate feelings of happiness or feelings of despair; they can work to set you free or to enslave you. When you think of it, deciding everything from what to wear, what to have for breakfast and who to form a relationship with to what career to pursue and where we would like to be in ten years depends on the power of thought. Thinking also helps us make sense of the events in our lives. It organizes events into categories and even creates pattern that inform us regarding what is happening and how what is happening should be interpreted. With our thoughts we steer our lives, move them forward or backward, lift ourselves to great heights or bury ourselves deep in the dust of despair. One of the greatest tasks of thought is creating change in our lives.

When it comes right down to it, your thoughts will have a lot to do with whether you succeed or fail and whether you move forward or lag behind in life. Learning to think effectively is like mastering a new language. Skillful and effective thinking does not occur automatically; it is an ability that must be cultivated, practiced and mastered.

Before we explore the principles and the purpose of thinking, we need first to understand what thoughts are and what thinking is. So here is a two-part question: What are thoughts and what is thinking?

Thoughts are the basic building blocks of mental activity. The definitions of *thought* in most dictionaries suggest that thoughts are the product of as well as the material used in the process of mental activity. As a product of a mental process, thoughts may be defined as an opinion, an idea, or a belief. As part of the process of mental activity, thoughts may be defined as thinking itself.

Mental activity or the process of thinking involves more than just having a thought or thoughts in the mind. It appears to involve but is not limited to the process of thought organization, thought production, thought association, and overall thought management. If the process of thinking involves such complex processes, it is reasonable to conclude that people can have thoughts in their mind without putting them through the effortful process of thinking. Consequently, while we cannot have thoughtless minds we can have minds that lack the appropriate mental management of thoughts. This means that without applying correct and effective thinking to your thought world, your thoughts can be destructive, confused, disorganized, unproductive and even messy.

In this text, when we refer to *thoughts* we have in mind the range of mental processes and activities, including opinions, beliefs, ideas, and so forth, that are both acted on and produced in the mind. When we refer to *thinking* we are more concerned with the management and production processes of these mental activities. This means when we apply thinking to thoughts we modify, extend, replace or eliminate existing thoughts, create new ideas, opinions or beliefs, and even create new images to represent existing or new thoughts. The process of thinking then becomes transformational in that it can change the environment and world of our minds, leading to changes in every area of our external lives. To fully appreciate the nature, utility and power of thoughts and thinking, in this text they are used alongside each other.

While much about thinking and mental processes remains a mystery, this does not mean we are completely in the dark on the subject. On the contrary, in the past twenty years scientists have uncovered and solved many of what were once considered mysteries of the mind. They have linked many of our mental processes with brain processes and can explain some of what was considered too mysterious and complex to be understood. For example, as noted in chapter 1, we now know that thoughts activate and affect chemical brain processes, and these processes also affect thoughts. We know that emotions, memory, self-regulation, imagination, visualization and volition among other mental phenomena are all associated with thinking and brain processes at some level. Scientists now have understanding, at least in part, about how mental activities can activate and affect changes in certain areas of the brain leading to the release of particular brain chemicals as well as the formation of neural connections.

We know that thoughts can be productive or unproductive for physical and emotional health. We also know that thoughts can be organized and controlled toward productive ends or can be random, unsystematic and unpleasant, leading to unproductive ends. For example, if you continue to generate and entertain thoughts that are sad you will feel depressed and become more vulnerable to the illness itself.

Before moving on let's explore the principles by which our minds operate.

The Operating Principles of Our Minds

When we generate thoughts and execute actions we are moving our lives by some known principles. Nothing in the universe just happens outside the sphere of some principles. A piece of paper is carried from your desk into the air as if lifted by something invisible. A leaf falls from a branch to the ground as if carried by an invisible hand. A careful observation will reveal that the actions of the piece of paper and the leaf are following some known principles of physics. Although we are not fully aware of all the principles that govern our world, we know that everything that happens somehow follow particular principles.

We know that events usually occur due to some antecedent factors. You desire a drink because you feel thirsty; you walk because you desire to get from point A to point B; you cry because you are either sad or happy; you rest because you are tired; you feel nervous because you are fearful, and so on. Is it not reasonable, then, to propose that your mind operates according to principles that can be known, as least in part?

A careful study of the thinking process will reveal that our thought world operates and is governed by principles. These principles set the boundaries in our mental world. Although we are just beginning to understand the complexities of the mind, we are learning that there are some internal rules that work to keep our minds from chaos and disorder. It follows that if we are to manage our thinking so that our lives become productive we must understand these basic rules of mind. We cannot hope to create any positive and consistent change in our minds and lives if we are not aware of how our minds work.

There is much being said today about the laws of thinking and the laws of the mind. Some have proposed that the mind operates according to a particular metaphysical law. This law proposes that you can attract into your life what you consistently concentrate on, think about or are in vibrational harmony with. In other words, you have the divine or cosmic ability to control external realities through the vibrational powers of your thoughts. The idea that the mind is divine and can supernaturally affect changes in the physical world merely by thinking has no basis in either science or theology. If such a law of mind exists, why is the focus more on wealth and prosperity and not on world peace, harmony and health? If such a law exists, why are we still plagued by poverty, terminal illnesses, diseases and even death? If through the powers of our mind we can alter physical realities merely by thinking about them, why are we still growing old and dying?

Why do people continue to follow ideas and philosophies that imprison their true abilities and potential? This author believes we humans have the ability, unlike any other creature, to transform our thoughts into physical reality, but only through deliberate and intentional plans and actions. It is more challenging, creative and becoming than to believe we have the ability to control reality metaphysically. In fact, such an idea encourages laziness and non-creativity.

Proponents of this metaphysical idea have even gone as far as quoting Scriptures to validate their claims. This is not a book on biblical exposition or theology, but it is needful for me to refute the incorrect use of Scripture and set forth some clarifications on passages that are clearly misused. Following are a few of the passages drawn from Scriptures used to validate this metaphysical position. Following these passages is a brief discussion on how these texts should be better understood:

"Ask, and it will be given to you; seek, and you will find; knock, and it will be opened to you. For everyone who asks receives, and he who seeks finds, and to him who knocks it will be opened" (Matthew 7:7–8).

"For the thing I greatly feared has come upon me, And what I dreaded has happened to me" (Job 3:25).

"Therefore I say to you, whatever things you ask when you pray, believe that you receive them, and you will have them" (Mark 11:24).

"Assuredly, I say to you, if you have faith and do not doubt, you will not only do what was done to the fig tree, but also if you say to this mountain, 'Be removed and be cast into the sea,' it will be done. And whatever things you ask in prayer, believing, you will receive" (Matthew 21:21–22).

I can do all things through Christ who strengthens me (Philippians 4:13).

Delight yourself also in the LORD, *And He shall give you the desires of your heart* (Psalm 37:4).

Let's briefly examine some of these passages. Remember, the belief that we can attract anything we desire into our lives is about metaphysically altering physical reality with your mind without actually working for it. However, a careful look at the first passage reveals that it has nothing to do with concentrating on things or altering reality to fit with one's desire. The text is simply saying that you must *ask* God for what you want and *seek* what you want. Does asking and seeking sound like concentrating and altering reality with your mind to get what you desire? Furthermore, God, as indicated here, is not the universe. While he operates within the universe he transcends it. The focus of this teaching is not to ask God but rather to ask the cosmic universe.

The second passage is a reference to the plight of Job. Is it true that Job concentrated on bad things and as a result attracted them into his life? Is it not true that many of us fear many bad things in our lives yet not many of these things befall us? The truth is, Job did not bring these things upon himself by concentrating on them. We have been given an insight of what actually happened behind the scene. The Scriptures tell us that what happened to Job was a result of a deliberate attempt of Satan to destroy him, but God used it as a means to improve on Job.

Mark 11:24 is also used to endorse this teaching. The text, however, is saying nothing about concentrating and altering reality. What it is clearly saying is to *ask* or make your petition to God, who can bring this desire to pass, and in asking you must believe that he has already heard your prayer. Through faith you believe that God has already provided what you asked of him, and you wait diligently for it. Waiting here does not necessarily mean sitting around in laziness doing nothing. Depending on the request, you might have to do some work on your part. For example, if you pray for and believe that God will give you a job, are you going to sit in your house day after day waiting for someone to call you, send you an email or show up at your door with the invitation for a job? Or are you going to be actively sending out resumés and going for job interviews? When you exercise faith, your faith is not in the thing or things you desire but rather in the ability of God to provide it or make a way for its attainment.

In Philippians 4:13 it is again clear that it is not your own thinking and concentration that alter external reality; rather, you achieve your goals and desires through God, who provides strength. Listen to what Galatians 6:7 says: "*Do not be deceived, God is not mocked; for whatever a man sows, that he will also reap.*" In simple terms it is saying that if you do not sow you cannot expect to reap, and you reap only what you have planted. If you do not transform your thinking into careful and diligent actions you will not get what you desire or attain it through appropriate means.

Preachers and teachers who want to promote a gospel of prosperity without work and effort will no doubt be attracted to this metaphysical idea. Setting forth a vision and working toward it takes effort and a great deal of work. Taking the Scriptures out of context to support an idea that encourages laziness does nothing more than blocks people's ability to use their minds correctly. We can alter physical reality only when we deliberately transform our thoughts into actions.

It is important before leaving the subject to ask if there are universal laws or principles by which our minds and thinking operate. And if so, are we able to identify and understand them? To consciously change our lives we must be aware of how the mind works. This means understanding its operating principles. The following discussion examines seven principles the author believes apply to the operation of our mind and thinking.

Principle 1:
The mind creates and operates according to dominant patterns.

When you see something for the first time, your mind tries to recognize what it is. If it appears to be disorganized, your mind tries to impose order on it so it becomes recognizable. This means the mind not only has a pattern-recognizing capacity, it can also create and store patterns. The mind has the ability to create and hold dominant thought patterns. A dominant thought pattern is a habit of the mind or a governing, regular disposition or tendency through which it influences behaviour. In other words, the mind is a habit-forming mechanism.

Habits are dominant thought patterns created by the mind that in turn govern behaviour. Once formed, a habit can be triggered into action almost automatically. Why do you park in the same parking space when you go to work in the mornings? Why do you sit in the same seat in class every week? Why do you sit in the same seat at church during weekly services? Why do you sleep on the same side of the bed, even when you are alone in it? A careful observation of your life will reveal patterns or habits created by your mind, many of which are without your conscious consent.

Let's take a peek inside your brain for a bit. When you do something for the first time, let us say consciously selecting a seat in a church service or parking on a particular side of your driveway, this action creates a physical neural connection inside your brain. This connection is quite weak and cannot by itself create a pattern. Every time the behaviour is repeated the connection becomes tighter and stronger, leading to the creation of a dominant pattern inside your mind, which in turn leads to a pattern in how you think and behave.

How does the knowledge of how the mind works benefit you? To begin with, knowing about this operating principle of your mind helps you better understand why you continue to do the same things over and over. It also helps you understand why some things in your life seem so persistent and why some changes seem so difficult to make or maintain. It also helps you understand that if you must make changes to what appears to be long-standing habits, you need to change the pattern of thinking that has created that dominant habit in the first place. Furthermore, it helps you understand that creating new neurological connections in your brain and new thought patterns in your mind requires work and consistency in transferring thinking into action. Once patterns are created, it takes consistent monitoring and practice to shift our thoughts into new frames of thinking, which of course lead to different actions.

Principle 2: The mind is empowered and directed by intentions.
Imagine for a moment that you are sitting in your room, and your mind is completely blank. You are not thinking of anything. What particular behaviour do you think can be produced from that state of mind? If you say none, you are absolutely correct.

Imagine again that you are sitting in your room, and your mind is roaming freely on just about anything that comes to mind. What particular behaviour do you think will be produce from such a state of mind? If you say no particular behaviour, again you are correct. Here we see that while thinking occurs in the mind, the mind is powerless to act purposefully on anything without focus or intentions.

Intentions power the mind and give it focus and direction. To have an intention is to have a particular object of thought. It is to have a purpose, aim, plan or goal in mind. It is the state of mind that answers questions such as "What are you thinking about now?" It also answers such questions as "What do you plan to do with your life? What career do you plan to pursue?" Without an intention the mind is unpowered, unguided, aimless and even weak. It is impossible for the mind to focus and be guided toward a goal without intentions.

You can think of an intention as the result of an internal conversation with yourself in which your mind is brought to focus on an object, goal or plan. This means an intention is not without a conscious deliberate mental dialogue. When we say a person has an intention we are saying the person has his or her internal eyes fixed on some object or goal.

While we are intentional beings, meaning we have the capacity to create intentions, an intention is not a capacity but a generated or created object of the mind. This means that there are times when people may be lacking in intention. It goes even further; without intentions the mind is deprived of enthusiasm, motivation, commitment, determination and resolve. When you think about it, what would you be enthused about, motivated toward or determined to do? These attitudes of the mind are born out of intentions.

An intention not only gives birth to these mental attributes, it strengthens them. In fact, these are the mental states that set the operating temperature of your mind. The argument can be made that the measure of focus that is given to a goal determines the degree of motivation and enthusiasm generated in the mind toward it.

This principle of the mind alerts us to the fact that unless we set productive and meaningful goals and have plans to reach them, our minds will be aimless and our lives void of interest and passion. Our mind works best and moves us forward when it has good and wholesome intentions.

Principle 3: Thoughts attract like thoughts.

Another principle by which the mind operates is the principle that similarity attracts. This means that if a thought is allowed to persist, soon it will attract similar thoughts. This happens because thoughts influence the generation of new and similar thoughts. If you think of buying a new computer, subsequent to this initial thought several thoughts about the purchasing or use of the computer will be generated. It doesn't matter if the thought is new; the mind finds a way to generate similar thoughts unless this initial thought is dismissed. This means thoughts allowed to persist will influence the generation of similar thoughts. You can call this the mind's law of similarity.

The consequence is that when thoughts attract like thoughts they create and cultivate a strong mental atmosphere that is hard to weaken. This can be positive as well as negative. People can be driven toward some action by either a predominantly negative or predominantly positive mental atmosphere. The seeds of determination and motivation for intentions are planted in a mental atmosphere that is well cultivated and nurtured with similar thoughts. This is the principle by which the mind is designed to work effectively. You cannot be determined and be motivated toward something if your thoughts do not share a similar focus. Only when there is agreement of thoughts can you reach a resolve on anything.

While the principle of similarity does exist in the mind, it is easier for a negative thought to attract other negative thoughts than it is for a positive thought to attract other positive ones. One reason for this phenomenon may be because we humans have a stronger bent toward the negative than we have toward the positive. What types of thoughts tend to pop up into our minds when we face challenging situations? Usually the first thing we think about is the worst-case scenario. Then it becomes hard to see the positive side of the situation.

Do parents have to teach their children to do wrong? Children seem to have a natural bent toward doing that which is wrong. You have to teach a child that lying is wrong with the hope that he or she will learn not to lie. But most parents know that to lie is the first option that may come to a child's mind when caught doing something they were told not to do. In fact, parents spend their entire parenting years trying to inculcate positive and wholesome attitudes and behaviours into their children. So then, while the mind operates by the principle of similarity, it may have a stronger leaning toward attracting negative thoughts than positive ones due to our inherent bent toward the negative.

This means that conscious effort must be exerted to encourage the mind more toward the positive. With deliberate effort the mind's principle of similarity can work effectively for the positive. This will happen when you develop an intention and consciously bring your mind to focus on its accomplishments. Don't let the thought slip away; give your mind a rationale for its acquisition, and the mind will automatically evoke its principle of similarity.

Remember, the mind is encouraged and empowered by intentions. It derives its empowerment and focus from such. Remember also that only when there is congruency among your thoughts can your mind generate those forces (determination and motivation) that take you to your goal.

Principle 4: Thoughts can persist for indefinite periods.

This principle of the mind states that thought patterns will persist for indefinite periods if not impacted by other thoughts. If you are acquainted with the laws of physics you will immediately recognize that this is similar to the law of inertia. According to the laws of physics, inertia is the property of matter that keeps it in its existing state of motion or non-motion unless some outside force is brought to act upon it. This means if it is at rest it will remain in that condition; if it is moving in a particular way it will continue in that particular motion without any change unless acted upon by some force outside itself. For example, have you ever wondered why when you throw a stone away from you it doesn't continue on into the distance uninterrupted but eventually falls to the ground after some time? It fails to continue in its state of motion because of the force of gravity, which acts upon it, changing its direction and motion. If the force of gravity did not act on the stone it would continue in its particular motion indefinitely.

Along with inertia is the idea of *permanence.* Permanence is the property of something that allows it to remain in a particular state over long periods of time unless caused to change by some force acting on it. In order to understand why thought pattern can and do exist for long periods, a discussion of these two properties as applied to thinking is important.

In the same way that the principle of inertia can be applied to objects in motion, it can also be applied to our thought life. This fourth principle means that your thought pattern will continue to exist in its current state unless impacted by other thoughts. Think of it in this light: every pattern of thinking people hold has the tendency to persist simply because once created and set in motion it has no force in itself to change its direction or state. The fact is, thoughts tend to persist indefinitely unless impacted by some other thought force.

Bear in mind that thoughts can impact thoughts. This may explain why some people continue to have the same negative pattern of thinking about themselves, their ability and their future year after year. Consequently, the unchanging and consistent thought pattern continue to have the exact same effects on their lives without any change. When we allow an unproductive pattern of thinking to take root in our lives we invoke the principle of thought inertia, which takes over, keeping it in place as long as the force of new thinking is not brought to bear on it. In this sense, the principle of inertia not only help us understand permanence and constancy in thinking; it also helps us understand the type of mechanism necessary for creating change in our mental world. By using the principle of inertia we can see how the force of our own thinking can actually create change in patterns of thinking that have persisted in our lives without change. This happens when we impose a new type of thinking on our current thought patterns.

The human mind has the power to create change only when new patterns are imposed on long-standing dysfunctional and irrational patterns. This appears to be precisely what happens in the process of conversion, when new ways of thinking break old patterns, setting forth a new paradigm in the mental life of a person. As the new convert's mind acquires new thought patterns it influences new behavioural patterns. It is no wonder that the place where the Holy Spirit and God's words have their most potent effects is right there in the mental world of a person. Their focus of change is your thoughts and thinking.

Remember that the materials of your mental life are thoughts; therefore for any change to occur it must occur with new ways of thinking. Stop reading for a while and think of the statements you have consistently used to describe yourself and the negative thoughts and beliefs you have held about yourself for as long as you can remember. Now think of how many times in the past you have really challenged the credibility of these negative patterns. You may surprise yourself to realize that these have persisted for so long in a state of inertia because no significant force has been exerted on them. While thinking is important for change in your mental state, not just any thinking can affect change in thought inertia. Not all thinking possesses force enough to create change in thought patterns that have existed without change for long time. Thinking that has force enough to change the course of thought inertia is called *effortful thinking*. It is through the process of thinking with effort that you break old and consistent patterns that are working against you. For thinking to be effortful it must be underlined by purpose and intentions.

Thought patterns do not only persist because of the lack of force acting on them. They tend to continue their existence because each thought we generate has the property of permanence. This is the ability of something to persist for a long time. With the right support their level of permanence becomes stronger.

Do you think your thoughts are permanent? What about those thoughts that keep coming back no matter what you do? Thoughts can be said to be permanent because they all have the property of *permanence;* that is, they have the tendency to endure for an indefinite period of time, even across the span of a person's life.

On the other hand, many thoughts are transient. This means they do not exist for long periods of time. While they do have the property of permanence, they do not develop durability or persistence, because their effects on us are insignificant and we do not pay much attention to or support them. While thousands of thoughts pass through our consciousness each day, it is the ones we support and pay attention to that develop high levels of permanence. The more permanence a thought has, the more durability it develops and the more influence it has on the words we speak and the actions we perform.

The fact that your thoughts can be either permanent or temporary is good news! There is no doubt that there are thoughts you want to keep for the rest of your life and thoughts you want to rid yourself of as soon as possible.

No matter how long thoughts have endured, under what condition they were created or how powerfully they have exerted themselves in your life, their permanence and effects can be broken. This does not mean you will forget them all. It simply mean their strength, influence and place of dominance will be broken.

Imagine for a moment how many people are living under the assumption that they cannot change their thinking patterns and therefore they continue to be prisoners of their own beliefs and thinking. The unproductive thoughts and negative patterns of thinking that have persisted and have chained you to the past or the present can be rendered null and void in your life. There is no thought, opinion, belief or idea that you have in your mind that cannot be altered in terms of their effects on you. Some may be more difficult to deal with than others, given their degree of permanence, but given time and the right kind of mental influence and force, their effects can change.

Among the reasons why unproductive patterns of thinking continue to persist is that they have being allowed to exist without being forcefully challenged by effectual thinking. What's more, some people just accept the assumption that these thoughts and patterns of thinking are part of who they are and cannot be changed. Some people will even say, "That's just who I am; I can't change." Almost anything can exist and endure for long periods with good maintenance. For thoughts and thinking patterns to continue to exist, they must be supported, maintained and accepted as truth. While you may not be totally responsible for the origins of some of your negative thought patterns, it is you, the thinker, who determines how long the patterns persist in your life.

Children develop enduring thought patterns due to their experiences and the messages they receive from significant others. Many of these patterns persist even into their adult years. While we can agree that children are not responsible for these unproductive patterns, we cannot say the same for adults. Becoming an adult means taking responsibility for our own thoughts and behaviour regardless of when or under what conditions they might have developed. We cannot continue to blame our past for our unproductive thinking and actions in the present. We must discover how current unproductive patterns are being maintained and supported and terminate such support. Once support for a persistent pattern is removed, its permanence in our life begins to diminish. On the other hand, when we give support to productive and wholesome thoughts we activate and increase their permanence.

The good news is, no matter how long you have lived with these thoughts, how enduring they may seem and how helpless you feel when they are activated, you can alter their influence and direction in your life. You can bring the force of mental gravity to bear on those thought pattern that seem to have no end.

The first step in breaking their hold on your life is to embrace the truth that your thoughts are your responsibility and therefore subject to you. The Scriptures tell us that we have the ability to take all undesirable and unproductive thoughts into captivity and make them obedient to the standard of Christ (2 Corinthians 10:5).

As noted, thoughts that endure for long periods of time have been maintained and accepted as truth. One effective way we maintain our thoughts is by developing justification for their existence. Every time we justify something we not only strengthen it; we affirm its right to exist. People who continue to think they are failures look for every mistake, no matter how minute, as evidence to confirm their belief that they are failures.

Over time these justified thoughts move from the status of provisional evidence to unqualified truth. Once the status of unqualified truth is reached, changing them becomes extremely difficult. Although this is a good thing for productive and healthy thoughts and patterns of thinking, it is unhealthy and disabling if these are unhealthy patterns. Clearly then, the level of permanence that is activated in our thoughts depends heavily on the degree of maintenance the thought pattern receives.

Principle 5: Thoughts are manifested in feelings and behaviour.
The fifth principle of the mind deals with the causal effects of thoughts. This principle of causal effect states that thoughts can and do manifest themselves through feelings and actions. Every thought you generate in your mind has the ability to activate some feeling or action in the present or in the future. In this case, a thought is said to have *potential action* or *potential effect* simply because given the right condition it can germinate and manifest itself through some form of action.

Does it surprise you that your thoughts can cause your feelings and behaviour? Next time when you experience an emotion, stop and ask yourself, "What am I thinking about now?" Do not be surprised if you discover that you can change the way you feel simply by changing the associated thoughts.

So then, not only are we capable of creating intentions, but our minds can transform them into feelings and actions. Can you see the implications of this? Next time you blame someone for your feelings or your behaviour think carefully about whether or not they are truly responsible for it. The cause of your conscious behaviour originates in your own thought world. There is no doubt that your thoughts can be strongly influenced by external realities, but what is produced in action is your responsibility. Although there are unconscious processes always at work in our minds and these processes can influence actions, we are nonetheless still responsible for any actions performed by us.

The link between our thoughts and action speaks volume. For one, it tells us that we can have control over how and what we do. Second, it tells us that while we can modify and change our thoughts when they cause an action, the particular action cannot be taken back or changed. Third, and most importantly, it tells us that through our own thoughts we can cause an effect in our lives and in the world around us.

Let it be understood that the effect that is spoken of here is not through a metaphysical process, as discussed earlier, but an intentional transformation of thoughts into action. Your thoughts are your creative powers. Through them you can do marvelous and unbelievable things and accomplish the almost impossible.

Given this awesome principle of the mind one would rightly ask, don't people know they have this ability? Why are some people still stuck in life's potholes? One of the greatest lessons a person can learn is how to think, how to transform his or her own thoughts into positive and productive actions. This is because while the mind has the ability, not many people know how to manage and use it well. Consequently, actions are produced by thoughts that are unproductive, ineffective and unfocused.

What do you think allows humans to be so advanced in science and technology? It is thoughts transformed into actions. What differentiates the lawyer and doctor from the thief and drug dealer is not their ability to think, but rather what they think about and the type of actions created by those thoughts. We are reminded by Scriptures that we eventually become what we continue to think about (Proverbs 23:7).

While this fifth principle states that thoughts are manifested in actions, it is important to note that intentional actions do not follow naturally and automatically from our thoughts. Many people have great thoughts in their minds but produce no corresponding actions. These thoughts manifest themselves into action only when they make a decision to act on them. A simple decision to act is the mechanism by which thoughts are transformed into powerful actions. Figure 9:1 illustrates the concept of the relationship between thought, feeling, decisions and behaviour.

Figure 9.1: The Controlling Nature of Thinking

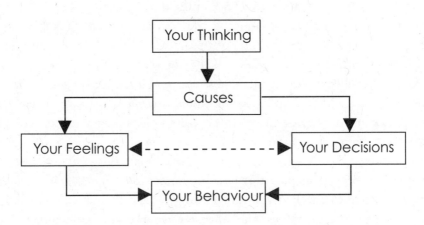

Principle 6: Your thoughts are guided by mental frames.

Have you ever wondered why some thoughts are activated easily under certain situations and not so under others? According to this principle, many of our thoughts are generated in respect to a particular frame of reference already existing in our mind. Let's call these mental frames *frameworks*.

A framework is a structure that serves to hold the components of a system together. A mental framework then is a system in which particular thoughts are organized around a certain aspect of the world. Its purpose is to give your mind automated processes when faced with certain situations in the world. These mental frames help us make quick decisions, take mental shortcuts and filter information easily. While some of these decisions and mental shortcuts may be appropriate and healthy, others can work to limit careful analysis of a situation, as well as creativity.

These frameworks in our mental world are usually formed over time, beginning in our childhood years. As we interacted with and experienced the world we naturally developed mental frameworks through which we see, interpret, understand and respond to the world. Many of these exist in our thought world and act as reference points to our thinking and acting. This means they help us make sense of the world as well as new experiences. They help us form expectations as well as opinions about things, events and people. In this they sensitize our thinking, making it easy for us to generate particular thoughts in certain situation.

While there is no doubt this can serve us in productive and wholesome ways, it can also serve to limit our thought-generating and creative capacity. More times than not, how we react and the thoughts and feelings that come easily to us in particular situations are not consciously and carefully thought through but come about because of the framework we have for the specific situation. For example, imagine if while you were driving to work another driver suddenly cut you off and almost ran you off the road. How would you naturally react? More than likely you would react negatively and maybe even curse him aloud. Notice here that your reaction, including words and feelings, are not something you actually think of in the moment. Rather, they come to you suddenly.

Where do you suppose this reaction comes from? Your reaction emerges from the mental framework you have developed over time regarding expectations of how people should drive. When this expectation is not met it automatically triggers a reaction framework that, in this case, is a negative one. What if your expectation was that while people should drive with care and consideration, they will sometimes make very serious mistakes, which other drivers should anticipate and be prepared for? Would your reaction be different?

What else are these frameworks responsible for in our lives? Perhaps more than you can imagine. We have mental frameworks for many things in our lives. These have persisted even into the maturing and adult years and continue to affect our lives in positive as well as negative and unproductive ways. However, regardless of when and under what conditions these mental frameworks and types of reactions developed, if they are negative, they will work to hinder you from advancing your live forward in productive ways.

The truth lies in the words of the apostle Paul, who said that when we were children we spoke, understood and behave like children, but when we become adults we need to think like adults in mature ways (1 Corinthians 13:11). Adults have the capacity to break with or rework old and persistent mental frameworks. It is unfortunate that a great number of individuals lack the knowledge that they actually have the ability to think differently and use their thoughts to lift themselves.

If someone told you that no one else can think your thoughts, they are your own creation and are therefore unique to you, what would you say? Most people would not have a problem agreeing. The problem is, although we are able to agree that our thoughts are our own, we do not personally manage them so that they can effect necessary and productive changes in our lives. The moment you start thinking that your mental frameworks can change and seriously begin taking responsibility for such change is the moment things begin to change for the better in your life.

Knowing how our minds and thoughts work provides us the first step in taking control over our thought life and eventually our actions. Although mental frameworks can persist for long periods in our lives, they can be modified or changed. You can modify and change your expectations of people and events as well as your reactions and thoughts in given situations. You are not condemned or destined to think or behave in any one way for life but have the capacity to revise your mental frameworks and thought life, leading to more productive life changes.

Principle 7: Your thinking is complex but adaptable.

Regardless of what some scholars think, humans are not moved by raw instinct as animals are. Although like most animals we depend on our senses when we take in information from the environment, we differ from them in the way we process and act on such information. With our ability to process sense information from an internal frame of reference we transcend the capacity of animals. In other words, we have the capability to process and manage the raw information taken in by our senses in ways that allow us to manipulate our environment and move our lives to higher levels.

Our ability to think and to generate thoughts and use them to process sense information in ways that change our lives and our environment is one of the most fascinating features of being human. It goes deeper though. Not only can we generate thoughts, we can use current thinking to generate even greater levels of thinking.

Picture thinking as a staircase in which each step upward brings you to a higher level. The highest thought you can generate is the height of your staircase. You cannot go beyond the level of your highest thought. Your thoughts set the limits of your reach and the distance you can go. Put another way, your thoughts can adjust you to an environment and make you rise above it.

As you have learned in our earlier discussions, while all birds have wings, not all wings are designed for soaring or even flying. Different wings adapt a bird to different aspects of the environment. For example, penguins have wings, but they only swim. Ostriches have wings, but they only run. If you are an eagle you should have wings that are adapted for height and soaring; why then would you adapt yourself to conditions that do not support your ability?

In a similar way that wings adapt birds to particular environmental conditions, your thoughts can adapt themselves to particular life conditions. What you continue to think about will eventually become the environment of your thought life. People who think more about success and growth see more opportunities for success than those who think more about failure. People whose thought life is more adapted to failure thinking tend to see failure even in situations of opportunity. The good news is that because our thought life is not set in stone but is adaptable, we can still change its course for growth and success by adapting our thoughts to positive and wholesome thinking.

What Your Thoughts Can Accomplish

Now that we have a working understanding of the principles by which the mind operates we can turn our attention to the subject of the function or purpose of thoughts, what your thoughts can accomplish. This subject is of the utmost importance because thoughts and thinking are considered the most powerful characteristics of humanity. Without the ability to generate thoughts humans would be no higher than animals. Thoughts are the basic building blocks of reasoning, perception, extrapolations, beliefs, assumptions, and the list goes on. So then, the subject of the purpose and power of thinking is important because it is with the appropriate use of this ability that we move our lives forward and become what we were created to be. It is also with the inappropriate or ineffective use of thinking that our lives become unproductive, stagnant and empty.

To begin, if you were asked to list several purposes or functions of thoughts or thinking, what would your list include? I asked several individuals that question. Here are some of the responses they gave:

- Thought can create your reality.
- Thoughts are the source of power.
- Thoughts can generate more thoughts.
- Thoughts cause actions.
- Thoughts create change.
- Thoughts are used to reflect.

- Thoughts are used to plan.
- Thoughts help you communicate.
- Thoughts regulate you actions.
- Thoughts project you into the future.
- Your thoughts are the forces of your mind.

From these responses you can begin to see that people believe the function of thoughts involves several dimensions, covering almost all areas of mental activities and processes. Note also that taken together the responses suggest that a whole lot about our thought life exists in our consciousness. That is, thoughts fall within our conscious control. It appears that these are dynamic processes that provide us with unmatched power to effect change in our lives. This means in the domain of our mental life we should not be helpless, because we are provided with the type of mental tools and material with which we can transcend the limitations imposed on us by the conditions of the past and present.

Thinking and thoughts provide us with the opportunity for growth and the capacity for change. With this in mind, we will explore some of the dynamics of the power of thoughts and thinking.

Your Thoughts Create Your Reality

Your thoughts create your reality. What you see, imagine and experience in your mind is created by your own thoughts. People have it all wrong when they believe that they feel certain ways because of their circumstances. This is not altogether so. What we feel on the inside results from how we think about external circumstances.

Does this mean that how you feel about your boss who refused to promote you, your ex-husband who left you for another woman, your wife who cheated on you, your neighbour who hurt your pet, or your math teacher who gave you a failing grade when you needed only two points to pass the exam resulted from your own thoughts? Absolutely!

But wait a minute. Didn't each of these persons causes these thoughts to be generated in the mind? Surprisingly, the answer is no. As humans we see things from the inside out. There is an internal world of perception within each of us that is affected not so much by what happens outside us but more so by how we interpret these external situations from the inside. This internal world is our mental reality, which is constructed from our own perceptual thought material. The reality you experience from within you is your own inside job. What happens outside us influences the type of thoughts we generate inside our minds but does not directly cause them.

When we say that a thing causes something to happen it means that the result could not have been otherwise given the same condition. If, given the same external situation, you could have generated a different thought, then the situation did not directly cause your thought; it merely influenced its development. There is a significant implication to the statement "John made me fall in love with him." It means, firstly, you had absolutely no choice in the matter. Secondly, it means neither your choice nor your action are your responsibility, since falling in love with John could not have been avoided. Even with a gun pointed at your head and someone demanding that you break the law or denounce your faith, you still have control over the thoughts in your mind. Throughout the history of the church many Christians when threatened with death if they did not recant their faith chose to die rather than give up their faith. Many people have chosen prison rather than giving up certain religious or political beliefs.

I have often heard people say, "I had no choice; I had to do it" or "I couldn't help myself in the situation." Only when there is clearly no other alternative open to you can you say you had no choice. When you say you are conscious and alive, it is because you are thinking and perceiving. Your reality is what you feel, perceive, understand and experience from the inside.

Put another way, it is the way things, people, places and experiences appear to you and are perceived from within your own mental world from which your reality emerges. If this is true, then no one can make you feel happy or sad but you. No one can make you believe you are a failure or a success but you. No one can tell you what you can or can't achieve in the future but you. No one can truly motivate you but you. While people can tell you what they think about you and your ability or provide stimulation for motivation, only you can create the internal reality that is needed to move your life to higher levels.

To reorganize or modify your thoughts about something is to alter your perception of it, which in turn changes how you are affected by it. What type of reality about the self do you think is being experienced in the mental world of a person who constantly tells himself or herself that "I am just a stupid person" or "I will never succeed at anything important"? Your thoughts have creative power, and the internal reality they create is based entirely on the same thoughts you entertain.

It gets deeper. The feelings you experience at any given time are primarily based on your thoughts. Because these feelings are for the most part created by your thoughts, they have associations with them. Once generated, these feelings now become the environment that facilitates the generation of new thoughts, which follow in the same vein as the original thoughts (refer back to figure 9:1). This means that thoughts produce feelings, and feelings produce feeling-thoughts, which in turn create a cycle of thought-feeling association. Unless this internal unproductive cycle is broken, an individual can become trapped in a mental world of unproductive and unhealthy reality.

Think of the thoughts you have when a driver cuts you off and almost causes an accident. Now think of the type of feelings you would experience in this situation. Which comes first, the thoughts or the feelings of anger? No doubt the thoughts, followed by the feelings. Once the feelings are generated they become the basis for even more negative thoughts. Because your thoughts create your reality, learning to think in ways that serves your best interest will provide the mental foundation for growth and emotional health.

Again it must be remembered that the statement *thoughts have the power to create reality* is not in any way linked with the idea that your thoughts have cosmic power to change reality by your merely thinking about it. Remember that while thoughts can lead to changes in your life circumstances and even in the material world, they do not accomplish these changes in supernatural ways but through the process of transforming thoughts into deliberate actions.

Your Thoughts Can Take Your Life to New Heights

How do you suppose the great people of the past and those of our time got to where they were and where they are, respectively? The Bible tells us that we were created in the image of God (Genesis 1:27). One aspect of that image is our ability to think and reason on levels unmatched by anything else in this known world.

You were created with the capacity to generate thoughts that can take your life to new heights and to great distance. However, while thinking is a natural function of our mind, not all thoughts are created equal and not all types of thinking occur easily. Thinking that produces soaring ability is hard work. Merely putting thoughts together is easy and takes little effort and practically no skill. Such thinking does not give soaring power to our thoughts. Thinking that has power to change our perception, release us from crippling situations and solve problems is produced through effortful and careful mental deliberation.

Why do you think some people don't like science and mathematics? Working through a math problem requires hard, deliberate and intelligent thinking. It requires you to manage your thoughts carefully and effectively. It also requires you to block out distractions as you mentally process complex information and create paths to solutions from within your own mind. For some people any type of thinking that calls for strong concentration and purposeful mental management is too hard and tedious and therefore must be abandoned. For others, if the thinking does not give an instant solution or emotional gratification it is not worth the effort or time. For some people the mere exercise of reading is hard work. It is hard work for them because reading requires the reader to put effort into comprehending what is read. Because understanding or comprehending requires the engagement of complex thinking processes, some people refuse to put their minds through such exercise and consequently remain as they are.

A brief word needs to be said about the modern trend of some churches as relates to the topic of thinking. We live in a time when Christianity has lost its intellectual and true spiritual appeal. In many areas it has become a religion that promotes spiritedness and an emotionalism that borders on emotional addiction. The difference between spiritual and emotionalism has become blurred. People go to church to get a high and call it worship. Churches are filled to capacity on Sunday mornings but are like ghost towns on Bible study or prayer meeting evenings. The people say that they love God but refuse to engage their minds in serious thinking about him. It is so bad that Christians leave good, solid, Bible-teaching churches to follow so-called ministries that provide them with *only* an emotional high. More than anyone, Christians should be at the forefront promoting proper and careful thinking about God and life. It is the church's responsibility to teach people how to think productively and correctly, not to lead them away from using their minds correctly or to refusing to engage in meaningful and critical thinking.

I have heard Christians say they do not need to plan their lives, because they have faith that God will provide. This borders on insanity, not faith or good thinking. More than anything else, God wants us to use our minds guided by his words. In fact he said in Isaiah 1:18, "*Come now, and let us reason together.*" How are we going to reason with God if not with our minds?

Think for a moment of the type of thinking that has been applied to scientific research, which produced the space program that took men to the moon and sent unmanned space craft deep into space, produced medical knowledge and skills that resulted in the ability to perform incredible and complex medical procedures, and gave us satellite and radio communications as well as computers and the Internet. Think also of the type of thinking employed in the development of complex mathematical formulas, some of which have aided scientists in solving some of the most difficult problems, creating breakthroughs in almost every area of science and technology. The people who carefully and intentionally used their minds to make these incredible scientific and technological advancements possible did not do so by refusing to put their minds to hard thinking but by learning how to think in creative and productive ways and to solve challenging problems. Skillful thinking does not come easily; it must be acquired.

Learning to think effectively, for example, is like the formal learning of a language. The educational systems in most developed countries have mandatory requirements for the formal learning of their native language, even for students who were born in that particular country and speak the language. In fact, many high schools, colleges and universities in North America require that their students demonstrate high proficiency in English. Yet most people who have English as their native language have no problem speaking and understanding English in their everyday lives. So why study it again in school? The reason is that the everyday speaking of the language does not allow the speaker to acquire all the forms and rules of the language itself. A great deal of this must be acquired through formal learning. Although many people have graduate degrees and may even have written scholarly research articles and books, this does not mean they have mastered and perfected the English language. I have known many English-speaking graduate students who had problems producing papers with high-level English. This is because the language has rules and forms that must be understood and carefully practiced before mastery can be attained. So then, merely having the ability to speak the language in everyday situations does not mean that one has mastery of it.

No one needs to teach a child to speak the everyday language into which he or she is born. As the child develops in the environment in which the language is spoken, he or she develops the natural ability to speak it in the same way others speak it. Interestingly, the child's usage of the language tends to follow the same pattern in which others speak. This means if people in the child's environment speak broken English, that is how the child will speak.

Learning to think effectively and skillfully is like learning and mastering one's native language. As humans we have been born with the natural ability to think. Regular everyday thinking is like regular everyday usage of English. People can develop a normal everyday pattern of thinking like that of most people in the same environment. But there is much more to thinking than this everyday pattern. As we have noted earlier, there are operating principles and creative power in thinking. Unless these higher levels of thinking are acquired and mastered, our lives will never move beyond the mundane.

No great amount of effort is required to think about walking to the mall, saying hello to a friend, deciding what to wear to work, where to drive to work or what to buy for the home. Some of these occur almost automatically because they have become regular patterns of thinking. On the other hand, sitting down and carefully drafting up a plan for your future or trying to find a way to effectively manage your bills requires more complex and careful thinking.

You may have heard the saying "Talk is cheap." Talk is cheap because such talk flows from thoughts that are of poor quality. Merely thinking something great and speaking it does not mean your thoughts have lifting and soaring powers. Just about anyone can come up with thoughts of grandeur, but remember, not all thoughts are created equal. All birds have wings, but not all wings are designed to soar or even fly.

The types of thinking that generate great thoughts but have no soaring powers are those that have no connection to purpose. The kind of thinking that generates powerful soaring thoughts is produced through deliberate, purposeful, intentional and careful internal deliberation.

Your Thinking Is the Architect of Your Future

The activities and processes that take place in our minds involve two types of thought material, words and pictures. Remember we said that thinking is a process that creates, organizes and modifies thoughts. Well, embedded in this mental world is also the ability to design, create and manage images.

Stop reading for a while and think of someone you know or someplace you have been. Did you think only in words, or was a picture formed in your mind? Spell the name of a particular animal and see what picture is formed in your mind.

Let's take this a step farther. Think of your house or apartment and how you would change it if you had the cash right now. Right there in your own mind you created a representation of your home and generated ideas and reorganized the image of your home in all its details in your mind. This means that your thinking is the architect of your life.

You may rightly ask, isn't God the architect of our lives? God's task is not to design our lives; that is our responsibility. What God does is work in partnership with those who have submitted themselves to him. His Holy Spirit guides you as you learn his words and apply them to your decision-making and your life in general. You have been given thinking and volition, not to be a mental cripple but to be an active agent in the direction your life takes. With your volition you request the help and guidance of God as you navigate your journey through this world of uncertainty.

It is important to note that we have been given the ability not only to think but to produce strategic thoughts that are able to move our lives purposefully forward.

While it is true that because of our broken condition, our God-given ability to generate wholesome thinking and pure thoughts has become skewed, it does not mean that we have also lost our ability to generate creative and strategic thinking. A careful observation of the material accomplishments around us will attest to this. Every scientific and technological achievement you see around you was first a thought that was sketched into an image by thinking.

Though sin has definitely eroded our moral nature and corrupted our capacity for truth, humans still possess creative abilities. This means God has not cut off your ability to think in ways that create images of what your life can be or what you want to be doing five years in the future. Your imaginative ability is God-given and must be used to make you life as productive as you can. With your thoughts you can draft a mental image of how much money you would like to have in five years, what type of house you would love to live in, what type of career you would like to have, and so on. This is by no means limited to your personal life and dreams; it extends to ministry and the helping of others.

Just as we use our thinking to create possible future scenarios that we hope to transform into reality over time, we can think up and create new ways for ministry and for reaching the world with the gospel message. As the world becomes more and more technological, Christians need to think outside the box of creative ways of using such technology to promote the gospel. Most Christians have not come up short in this area. The message of the gospel is preached using every technological means available today. This is being accomplished through productive and creative thinking. Unfortunately, however, there are those who are still afraid of thinking big and continue to bury their talents in the sand, hoping for a miracle rain.

The designer of any architectural drawing or painting, although beginning his or her work with a single stroke of the brush or a single line, has a form of the final image in mind. In like manner, your image of the future will begin with a single thought and a single stroke of the imagination.

Let's go back to God for a bit. From the Bible we learned that God does not work by chance; every detail of his work throughout time was planned. How then do we suppose to go through life without a planned agenda, just hoping that somehow luck or some miracle will come our way?

People who fail to use their thinking to visualize and sketch an image of their possible future usually end up in situations and conditions of life they are far from happy with. No one should begin work on anything without a clear image of the final outcome as well as a detailed plan of how to arrive at such an outcome.

This is why so many people fail in business: they have no image of the future, and even if they do they have no plan to get there. What they have as a plan is usually a mental rough draft of the day-to-day operation and tasks of the business, which typically does not extend beyond a couple of weeks or months at the most. Consequently, they have a big start but eventually run out of steam a few weeks or months along the way. Frustrated and unhappy with the situation and not wanting to take the blame for lack of careful planning, they scapegoat others.

While no plan or thinking is perfect, it is our responsibility to think productively and draw up detailed plans for our lives. In Luke 14, Jesus compared counting the cost of following him to the careful and diligent planning of one's life tasks. He noted that to have success in the undertakings of life, planning must always be done with the end in mind.

Here you are challenged to begin using your thinking and imagination to create productive future situations and develop plans to help you reach them. Unless you think about it and see the image of it in your mind, you really have nothing to work with or attain. Conversely, it is important to note that not every vision or goal you create in your mind is attainable. Some visions are unrealistic and cannot be attained even if you live 1,000 years. The vision you create in your mind must have measurable short-term goals and a reasonable attainment time attached to it as well as doable action steps.

Time can always be adjusted and processes and plans altered as you move toward the attainment of the vision. Every designer or artist knows that the design being worked on may need to be modified and refined before the final product emerges. In writing this book, I have made revisions several times. Every time an artist revisits her work she will no doubt see parts that need extending or reworking. In a similar way, every time you revisit the image you create in your mind of your future you can modify, extend, erase and rework it so that the final product is more attainable and fits with your values and what you need.

As you will learn throughout the rest of this text, we create unnecessary limits for ourselves because we fail to take the first step and learn how to think in meaningful and productive ways. Your thoughts are the basic material used to create images and make changes in them. In your thought world you have an unlimited repertoire of creative skills and imaginative material. The only limits to your thinking and creative ability are you and your knowledge of how to use the tools provided by your mind to their utmost capacity.

Your Thoughts Provide You Gateways to Possibilities

Your thoughts are not limited to creating images; they provide you gateways to possibilities. By creating slight shifts or changes in your current thinking about a current problem, your own mind can create possibilities that a moment before did not exist or come to mind. One small shift in your thinking can become the basis for significant changes in the perception of your reality. In this way, your thoughts provide you with the gateway to possibilities that can move your life forward to productive and meaningful ends.

We usually think in terms of possibilities when something stops working or is no longer working at an acceptable level or some desire needs to be satisfied. Have you ever reached a point in life or in the performing of a task where you felt stuck, stagnated, frustrated or bored? If your answer is yes, you are not alone; most people have. It is a feeling that you have exhausted all the resources available to you without much success. What do you do in moments like these when life seems empty, boring and stagnant and nothing seems to be working for you?

Some people throw their hands in the air and give up and become frustrated with life itself. Others may seek the help and counsel of those they consider to be experts.

Let's examine this situation a bit closer. Most of us experience the feeling of being stagnant and bored at points in our lives. For some people the feeling is temporary and transient. For others the feelings may persists for long periods of time. People experiencing a consistent state of being stuck in a rut in life usually are not able to see life's possibilities, because the gateways to them appear closed.

Let's take the example of Susan, who has been working at the same job doing the same thing over and over, year after year. Susan has become bored and frustrated from repeating the same thing over so many years. Feelings of boredom and stagnation crept up on her. What do you think is now going through her mind, and what do you suppose is the real basis for such thoughts and feelings?

Why would you feel bored with something you've been doing for a while? Oftentimes it's not that you don't like your life; it's just that you suspect there's something more, a greater sense of meaning and purpose for you, something that you are not currently experiencing and just can't seem to bring to mind.

Your feelings of boredom and being stuck are not meant to depress you but are indications that you need to create shifts in your thinking and generate thoughts that will open your mind to new possibilities. The moment you feel stuck and bored, it is your cue to look for possibilities and opportunities for change. Remember, if you feel happy in what you are doing and you are solving all your problems, you are not prompted to think of new possibilities. These feelings usually come upon you when you begin sensing there is more that you are not achieving. Boredom, frustration and feelings of being stuck in the rut of life are indications that a shift in thinking is needed and that you have more in you to develop or give.

There is absolutely no way your life will change if your thinking remains the same. Whenever you feel that your life is not going in the right direction, you need not blame anyone but yourself. It is your own thinking that provides direction to your life, shows you possibilities and helps you discover opportunities.

Think of a time when you felt stuck in a particular situation. How did you become unstuck? It was the way you began thinking that allowed you to see new possibilities. While people's thinking may not provide them with the appropriate standards or values on which to live moral or even wholesome lives, it is nonetheless through their thinking that they become aware of the need and begin seeking for such standard and values. For example, when a person decides to accept Christ in his or her life it is by thinking about their need for wholeness and redemption. No one can truly repent and come to Christ without thinking about their moral condition and need for salvation.

Let us examine the nature of possibilities a bit closer.

Possibilities do not exist as objective realities in and by themselves. They are created from our own thoughts as we begin looking at things in particular ways. It is in this way that our thinking transforms external situations into possibilities. Yes! It is our own thoughts that create possibilities from existing reality.

To better understand this, let's consider the example of two teenage boys trapped in a burning apartment room on the 35th floor. Not being able to come up with any solution for escape, one of the boys decides it is useless and prepares himself for what he considers certain death. The other teen, refusing to give up on life, resolves that he must find a way of escape before the fire closes in on them. Looking around at what's in the room he comes up with a creative idea. They can make a rope from all the cloth in the room, including parts of their own clothing, and climb down. This they do, and both escape a fiery death.

While both boys saw the same stuff in the room, only one could conceptually transform those materials into a rope by which they could escape death. For one boy there was no possibility of escape; for the other escape lay in changing the way he thought about the ordinary everyday things around him. Why did the other boy not think of such a possibility? Simple: he did not know how to move his thinking out of the box. He saw things as they had always appeared to him in everyday life.

It is your thinking that changes the way things appear around you. The moment you shift your thinking you create possibilities and change your reality. This is because possibility is an inside job created by shifting the dynamics of your thoughts beyond the restraints created by the appearance of a current situation. You cannot think of possibilities without moving your thinking outside the box. The moment you think of possibilities within the context of a current situation you eliminate or modify a belief, either about yourself or about the situation.

It is not hard to see why some people are stuck in life with feelings of frustration and boredom, complaining about the same situation year after year. Here is the challenge: when you feel bored, frustrated and stuck, try changing the way you think about your situation. Try brainstorming. Write down your thoughts, even if they seem weird and unusual to you. Ask hypothetical questions of people who have situations that are similar to your own. Your unconscious mind has a way of sending suggestions to your consciousness at times when you do not expect it, so carry a writing pad and be ready to jot down these suggestions of possibilities. Finally, examine the current situation in which you feel stuck and bored, and challenge your beliefs about yourself and about the situation. Begin thinking outside the box.

Let's say you believe there is nothing you can do to change your current situation. Challenge this belief about what you can and cannot do. Ask yourself why you have come to hold this belief and what about you that is so weak. In addition, identify what being in this condition has taught you and how it has made you stronger. See how you can use these strengths to make different decisions and create new possibilities for your life. Remember, the young man in the burning apartment saw possibilities in the material in the burning room. Materials from which your mind creates possibilities are all around you, even in the situation you are experiencing boredom and frustration with. The truth is, possibilities are usually not far away; they are always within your mental reach.

Your Thoughts Are Seeds for the Harvest of Your Success

Like seeds that are carefully planted to produce fruitful trees, well-planted thoughts have the ability to produce great and fruitful lives. While thinking plays a critical role in managing our thought life, if we give unproductive and useless thoughts to thinking for processing the product will be useless junk. The saying "garbage in, garbage out" stands true not only for computers but also for thinking. Thoughts that take our lives to the sky must be strategically planted and carefully nurtured.

Not all of your thoughts have the ability to take your live toward positive outcomes. Remember that a greater part of your reality stems from how you process the thoughts you have in your mind. In his now classic work *As a Man Thinketh,* James Allen noted that "Every thought-seed sown or allowed to fall into the mind, and to take root there, produces its own, blossoming sooner or later into act, and bearing its own fruitage of opportunities and circumstance." These thoughts are seeds that send roots into your perceptive and emotional life as well as branches outward toward your future. This means they have the power to affect your motivation, perception, feelings, behaviour and ultimately your future. The deeper the roots, the stronger the plant will be and the higher the branches will go.

Although we cannot always tell what will or can grow from a single thought, we have the ability to nurture the roots of our thoughts, allowing them to go deeper while sending their branches toward greatness. The thoughts that send deep roots into our lives fall into several categories.

First, there is the category that I call *positioning thoughts.* These are thoughts that do not channel you toward any particular career or destiny. They work on providing the suitable environment and the base strength for other thoughts that need to send their roots deep into your life. It is your own thinking that provides the base strength for other thoughts that will take you to the sky.

Think of the thought "I believe I am capable enough to succeed at just about anything I do." Or "I know that if I work hard enough, even if I fail I can eventually succeed." These are thoughts that position a person's mind with power and energy to be successful. On the other hand, think of the thought "I am not sure I have the ability to do this." The problem with most people is that they generate thoughts that focus on their weaknesses and failures rather than on their strengths.

Your thoughts create your internal environment. If your thoughts are not conducive to growth or deep enough to support impressive visions, every vision seed you plant, no matter the degree of its potentiality, will eventually die from lack of good soil or depth.

The second category of seeding thoughts is that which I call *dream thoughts.* These are thoughts you generate about specific situations, goals or vision that are situated in the future. For example, you have a dream thought that you will earn a college or university degree, secure a profitable and meaningful career, enter a Christian ministry, own your own business, marry and have children or own your dream house. These thoughts are specific seeds but unless carefully nurtured and cultivated will produce nothing.

Consider how many people you know who have great thoughts about their future that never amount to anything but empty words. Your dream thoughts are limited only by your ability to generate them. Some people are afraid to generate these thoughts because they know the next thought in line would be one that demolishes the first. Here is an example: "One day I would love to own my own business with a capacity to generate millions of dollars." Here comes the next thought: "Who would support me anyway? Furthermore, I don't even have enough to pay my mortgage, much less invest in the start-up of a business." The second thought is intended to totally destroy the existence of the first. Here it is clear that while dream thoughts are great they may not be able to take root and thrive because of parasitic thoughts that reside in the soil of your mind. Once a dream thought is planted, it is not allowed to grow roots due to these parasitic thoughts that live in your mind and eat away at the root of any potential fruit-bearing thought. Parasitic thoughts are similar to a vision virus in that they disable and cripple your potential to succeed.

The third category is *nurturing thoughts.* Merely planting a seed does not guarantee that it will germinate and grow. This is because most seeds require water to germinate and grow, even if the soil is good. Also, plant parasites may eat away at your plant, destroying its potential for producing. In this sense, merely having a great thought in one's mind does not mean that it will take root and bear some great harvest. To ensure such an outcome you must produce nurturing thoughts. Thoughts that work to challenge your self-defeating thoughts and build your self-confidence are called *nurturing, watering, protective* or *motivating thoughts.*

Nurturing thoughts produce watering and protective effects on your thinking. These are self-motivating thoughts that are able to challenge and invalidate those parasitic thoughts that work against you and your dream. Nurturing and protective thoughts are thoughts that should follow your dream thoughts. Consider the following example: "One day I would love to own my own home." Usually, following such a thought would be thoughts that give you every reason why you will not be able to succeed. However, you can stop these thoughts in their tracks by generating nurturing thoughts.

Here is an example of a nurturing thought: "I believe it is the will of God for his people to prosper and succeed; therefore, I don't see why I will not succeed if I carefully and strategically plan my action steps." Another example is "I really believe I have what it takes to succeed at this venture."

Always waiting for others to motivate you is a bad idea. It may never happen; then what? You have the capacity to generate your own self-motivating and self-inspiring thoughts that can lift your level of confidence and carry you toward your goals. Furthermore, if you have the Lord as your guide, he will impress thoughts from his Word to motivate and inspire you when you cannot seem to find any of your own.

The fourth and final category is *action thoughts*. These are thoughts that produce goal-oriented actions. Although all thoughts have potential, not all thoughts will produce work. Thoughts that produce action are those that are linked with purpose. Purpose-driven thoughts are thoughts that produce actions that are in line with your goal. This means not just any action or behaviour will get you to your dream.

Goal acquisition requires goal-oriented or purpose-driven thought. Having a vision or a dream in your mind is just the first step toward its acquisition. You must now take the next step and transform your thoughts into meaningful and intentional actions. Whatever is expressed in your external behaviour is a revelation of your internal world of thoughts and feelings. Because thoughts influence the generation of other thoughts and because actions are influence by thoughts, behaviours can always be modified given the influence of our own thinking.

Earlier it was noted that external events and situations cannot directly cause specific thoughts; rather, they exert influence on them, leading us to behave in certain expected ways. It is important to note here that purpose-driven thoughts that in turn produce goal-oriented actions can be influenced by external situations. People or situations in your life can influence your behaviour by influencing the thoughts that are generated in your mind.

This can be a negative thing or a positive thing. It is positive in the sense that because some people have very low internal power to generate purpose-driven thoughts, they can be influenced by external situations to do so. It can be negative in the sense that external situations and people can influence us to produce negative and discouraging thoughts about our ability to be successful. Being around positive people can work to influence positive thoughts in our mind. To this we will return later.

Conclusion

It is clear that we have been invested with profound thinking ability. Thinking, which appears to come to us naturally, can be cultivated and mastered to produce greater effects in our lives. Most of what we have experienced and are experiencing in our lives has associations with our own thoughts and particularly the way we organize them to form perceptions and interpretations of our experiences. That our thoughts have utility and efficacy that extend beyond our internal world of perceptions has profound implications. In the next chapter you will be introduced to the dynamic nature of change and the particular part thinking plays in its attainment.

chapter ten

THINKING FOR
Change

The thing to know about change is that it is inevitable;
it occurs whether you like it or are prepared for it.
But the most important thing you need to understand
about change is that you can also make it happen.

The chapter is labeled "Thinking for Change" because for change to be initiated and sustained it must have its roots and existence in your own awareness and thinking. Who you are on the inside and who you can be in the future are embedded in how you think in the present, not how you thought in the past. You cannot change, move forward toward success in your life or even believe in yourself unless you change your thinking in the present. It is your thinking that leads the way for meaningful change in your life.

It is also important to note that even spiritual change, which can only be generated through the Holy Spirit, must begin in our thinking. Such change cannot occur if we are not willing to co-operate with the Spirit and break with old patterns. Any change initiated in us must begin within our own thinking. Thinking for change then is critical, not only for success in our natural and social life but more so in our moral and spiritual life.

Although change is all around us, meaningful change only occurs when certain conditions are met and particular forces in us are activated. Because change has a lot to do with how we think, in this chapter we explore the relationship between thinking and change.

Understanding Change

Change is a real phenomenon. It is something that can be seen or observed through various processes, steps and phases. When we alter or modify something, we change it. When something changes it makes a transition from one form to another or from one phase to another. If something is left alone, it may undergo change, but such change is due to unguided, uncontrolled and unintentional forces operating within the environment. More times than not, when these unguided and unintentional changes occur they do not carry us in directions we desire.

One cannot discuss the concept of change without some reference to the change theory of Kurt Lewin (1890–1947). Kurt Lewin was a social scientist who introduced a three-step change model, known as *Unfreeze—Change—Refreeze*. Lewin proposed that behaviour is a "dynamic balance of forces working in opposing directions" (Lewin 1951). These forces, according to Lewin, are what facilitate change because they push people in a direction that causes change to happen. According to this model, one is said to be in the unfreezing process when he or she is able to move away from old patterns that are working against productive change. One is said to be in the change process when he or she is moving toward a new way of being. One is said to be in the refreezing process when he or she is establishing a new behaviour. According to Lewin, forces that work against the forward pushing forces in the "unfreezing" process are refraining forces that work to oppose change.

From Lewin's change theory we gather that meaningful change is not an automatic process but an intentional course of action that includes personal reflections and decisions. In the first stage of Lewin's theory, for example, change begins to occur when one first recognizes the need for change and prepares oneself for change. In fact, all three phases of his model require awareness of the need for change and decision-making toward change.

How does Lewin's model of change fit within the biblical model? While there are some specific differences between the two there are also profound similarities. For example, both approaches suggest that change has to do with one's awareness of the need for change; a desire to break from attitudes, patterns and behaviours that do not move one's life in a profitable direction; a move toward the desired behaviour, attitude or pattern; and an attempt to maintain such change. The difference between the two is what is emphasized as the primary mechanism of change. While both see change as rooted in the individual's awareness of the need for change, the biblical perspective acknowledges the Holy Spirit as the guiding agent in the process of change. This been said, it is important to note that the biblical model of change focuses primarily on spiritual change, which is able to produce changes in all other areas of the person's life and which is not possible without the work of the Holy Spirit. The model of change proposed by Lewin is for changes that, while not intended to transform our human sinful nature, move us beyond a particular outmoded lifestyle, pattern, attitude and behaviour toward success in our human undertakings.

Necessary Conditions for Change

If meaningful change cannot occur automatically, what are the conditions that must exist to facilitate its occurrence? The question could well be stated as "What does it take to transform ourselves from what we are to what we would like to become?"

For example, imagine where you are in your professional, occupational or personal life this very moment. Now consider the following questions: What would it take for you to change from your present profession to another? What would it take for you to improve your relationship with others? What would it take for you to improve your salary range in the industry in which you work?

No doubt several things are running through your mind. Some of these may include having a desire for change, thinking of going back to school and learning new skills, gaining new knowledge, becoming more motivated, believing in yourself more, having a desire for new meaning in your life, having a definite goal for which to strive, or just thinking differently about your life. If thoughts like these are going through your mind then you have just established some conditions for change. What you are in fact saying is that for meaningful change to occur some conditions must be met.

In thinking about these conditions for change, do you believe that each of them falls within your capability to initiate? If your answer is yes, you have just confirmed that you are your own agent of change.

From our discussion here two things have become clear. First, for meaningful change to occur, particular conditions must be in place through which change can be facilitated. Second, these conditions cannot exist without an agent that initiates them. Both the conditions for change and the agent of change become necessary conditions for change.

Figure 10.1 illustrates six necessary conditions for change. Let us examine each of these.

Figure 10:1. Necessary Conditions for Change

NECESSARY
CONDITIONS
FOR CHANGE

1
A CHANGE
AGAENT

2
NEW
MEANING

3
A SENSE
OF URGENCY

4
NEW
KNOWLEDGE

5
A PLAN
OF ACTION

6
IMPLEMENTATION
OF THE PLAN

Necessary Condition 1: A Change Agent

From the moment we were born we were thrust into a world in which we learned to be dependent on others. During these formative years of development, changes in our external environment were mostly under the control of those we depended on. While this is the natural course of human development, we were not meant to remain in that state forever. Our human developmental process requires us to move from total dependence toward maturity.

While maturity does not mean a total disconnection from relationships with others, it nonetheless requires us to develop a productive life course rooted in our own volition and thinking. This means as we become more mature we become more responsible for the choices we make, the directions we take in life and the actions we initiate.

As mature adults we are also able to become more attuned to the forces operating in our environment and our lives. While a young child can blame a caregiver for not providing certain necessities of life, a healthy and functioning adult cannot sit around and wait for someone to come to his or her aid with handouts. He or she has to find a way to bring these necessary elements into his or her own life. In other words, while we all live in dependence on some actions from others, a healthy and functioning mature person makes decisions and produce actions that facilitate personal survival and productivity. This is referred to as taking personal responsibility or having personal agency over one's life.

The fact that we have been given personal agency by God himself and have our own volition means that we are responsible for making certain changes in our lives, and unless we embrace that responsibility our lives will become dormant and unproductive.

Why do we need to become agents of change? The answer is, unless as persons we change and initiate change, both we and the process or organization we lead become stagnant and redundant. The question that we need to answer is, how do we take control over our lives and become our own agents of change? To answer this question we will examine several things about a change agent.

First and foremost, a change agent is one who *initiates change* by altering, modifying or replacing elements of a system or process so that it works better or produces more in the future. This system or process could be a company, organization, administration, church or one's present life conditions. Without a change agent, meaningful and guided change will not occur. Although things and processes can change as a result of forces operating in the environment, these are usually not changes that are desired or directional. It is the change agent who gives direction and meaning to change. Conditions will not change in your life and things will not move in desired directions unless conscious and intentional steps are taken by you to initiate and direct such change.

Second, a change agent *makes decisions* in the present that define and shape conditions in the future. Most people are not cognizant of the fact that the decisions they make in the present have significant bearing on future situations. The change agent is fully aware of this and makes decisions that he or she knows will influence future situations. In fact, to be a change agent you must become dissatisfied with outmoded and unproductive processes and situations you see around you and conceptualize how they can be changed to work better in the future. Regardless of what is happening in your situation, your organization, your church or your life, as a change agent you will have a vision of what could or should be. It is this vision that drives your governing sense of action.

A change agent has the ability to step back and look at the current situation in order to see clearly what is happening and what needs changing. If you cannot detach yourself from a situation in order to have a clearer view of the forces that are working against productivity and purpose, you will not be able to initiate or lead desired change.

Third, a change agent *has a high degree of self-efficacy.* This is the degree to which one believes he or she can be effective in what he or she does. You cannot initiate and bring about change without believing in your own God-given ability to be effective in the endeavour. Furthermore, you must believe that there is some benefit in the outcomes of what you do. A change agent doesn't pass off the buck of responsibility for change to someone else.

When you look into your life and realize that you are not progressing as you should or the organization you lead is stagnant and ineffective, what do you do? Do you pass the blame on to someone else? Do you sit back and hope things work themselves out? Do you hope that God will intervene by some divine miracle? Do you wait in hope for someone to come along and initiate the changes you wish for? Do you hope the stars and planetary systems will arrange themselves in your favour? Or do you roll up your sleeves and get to work, thinking and initiating needed steps toward desired change?

Fourth, to be a change agent you must *be aware of the need for change*. You cannot initiate meaningful and productive change unless you recognize that change is needed. Before an action can be taken toward change, it is important to determine why the change is needed in the first place.

The change agent is moved to action when changing conditions from without trigger the need to remain effective and relevant. The desire and urgency for change does not comes from within but is activated by situations from without. It is when something is not working or will not work well in the future that a trigger is pulled on the inside of the agent of change.

While the need for change may be quite apparent, not many people are attuned to it. If you are living from paycheque to paycheque year after year and you cannot see the need to improve your condition and begin taking steps toward such change, it means you lack what it takes to be a change agent. When something external triggers something internal, the change agent explodes into action.

Fifth, the *need to be relevant* in a changing environment fuels the energy and motivation for change in a change agent. No one wants to feel useless or ineffective. Yet many people live out their lives being ineffective in what they do. The change agent knows that if necessary and directional change does not occur, one's present life or performance or the process or organization one leads will become redundant and ineffective.

When relevance is applied to your personal life, it means you are effective in what you do because your skills and knowledge are reflective of conditions and changes around you. When relevance is applied to the process or organization you lead, it means these are in step with the times without compromising core values. Alternatively, if your skills and knowledge or the process or organization you lead are not in appropriate step with the changes around you, then you are said to be out of touch or out of step with the times and will be ineffective in what you do and redundant in what you have to offer.

The need to be relevant stimulates the desire and motivation for change. Desire drives self-motivation and action. Motivation does not usually occur without desire. People can be aware that they need to improve themselves to become more effective and competent but at the same time their desire is not strong enough to arouse their motivation and drive action. This results in inaction and stagnation. People move into action when they become strongly motivated by some desire to fulfill a need.

The ability to self-motivate is a critical attribute of being a change agent. There will be days when no one understands and may not even want to encourage you toward change and productivity. The change agent needs to find the desire and drive from within to make change happen. It is important that as a change agent you are able to validate your own thinking and actions. You must know if the change you are trying to make is important and necessary. When you feel that what you do and how you do it need to be more relevant, what you are actually feeling is a need to survive amidst change. In other words, when the forces that are driving the change have stabilized, what you do will still be necessary and relevant.

For example, if the company for which you work is changing all its computer systems and software and you decide that what you know and the computer and software skills you learned fifteen years ago will still be adequate in the face of such change, you will not survive in that company for long. On the other hand, if you decide to upgrade your skills and knowledge you will probable ride with the changes in the company. To be relevant then means to survive well and ride comfortably with change without compromising your core values.

Finally, to be a change agent, you must *take leadership responsibility to initiate and implement change*. It is always good to talk about what needs to change, but it is also important to initiate and implement it. You may have met many people who for years talk about what they need to do with their lives but never reach the point where they initiate any change. Taking responsibility for change takes you beyond just seeing, sensing or having a desire for it. Only when you take ownership and feel responsible for the change can you effectively implement it.

Sitting around and waiting for people to help you will not move you toward necessary and important changes in your life. You must arise when triggered by changing conditions and ignite the passion for change within your own self. It is the change you initiate that will often attract people toward you.

Necessary Condition 2: New Meaning

There are times when conditions around you are stagnant and you sense the need for new meaning for your life or the process and organization you lead. Desiring new meaning for your life means you have become dissatisfied with the outmoded and status quo situations around you and know there is more you can achieve.

The desire for new meaning is a necessary condition for change. In fact, it is individuals who are able to sense the need for new meaning that are often prepared to lead change for self, society and organizations. Being bored is a prompt that alerts you that new meaning must be sought and outmoded situations changed. Boredom is bad only when it incapacitates your thinking.

A change agent does not continue to live in boredom, because he or she knows that if change must happen it must be initiated by the change agent. No one else can bring new meaning to your life; it is you who must recognize the opportunities and desire and initiate steps toward its acquisition.

New meaning can mean a number of things. For example, it might mean redefining your goals and repositioning your thinking to be the most effective you can be. It might mean that your life can produce more and that you have the capacity to reach new levels of being. It can mean spiritual awareness beyond the everyday routines. It also means examining and re-examining why you do the things you do, why you lead the organization or process you lead. It may mean asking "What difference can I make or try to make as an individual?"

It is our end goals and visions that give meaning to what we do in the present. Consequently, if our vision or end goal is unclear and undefined, our sense of meaning will follow accordingly. It is in this sense that by creating a clear vision for our lives or for the organization or ministry we lead we are forced to desire and seek new meaning in the present that will lead to change in the future. New meaning means new thinking.

Although meaning and purpose comes from within, they are fueled by information from without. This information is then internalized and analyzed on the basis of your self-perception, self-efficacy, values and sense of purpose and vision. No one can make your life or what you do meaningful; this must be generated and flow from within you. Although initial ideas for meaning can be triggered from without, it is within you that the real work toward new meaning is worked out.

The moment people recognize that they need new meaning for life and truly believe they are their own change agent and as such responsible for the change is the moment things begin to change. For example, you cannot change spiritually or socially if you do not feel or recognize the need for it from within.

Necessary Condition 3: A Sense of Urgency for Change

A sense of urgency is a necessary condition for change. When there is no urgency for change complacency sets in, and over time the need for change diminishes and the status quo continues to be maintained. Individuals can sense the need for change and even know that they are responsible for making it happen but feel no urgency for it. The more we feel that change is necessary, the more urgent will be the desire for it.

How do you spur yourself or others on to overcome complacency? The need to survive and the need to be relevant, as noted earlier, are central factors that fuel the urgency for change. The next central factor that drives the urgency for change lies in one's sense of purpose and mission. If delaying change will lead to compromising the mission and purpose of being, then change must be urgent.

Earlier we discussed the questions that every change agent must confront. These include questions of identity and mission. These are the forces that drive the change agent to overcome complacency and move toward change. People who are complacent either are not aware of their mission or have lost sight of who they are and why they have been placed in certain positions. Serious researchers working toward a cure for cancer cannot delay in their task. They know that delay and complacency mean more lives will be lost to the deadly disease. Researchers working on strategies to enhance learning in the classroom also have a sense of urgency for their task. This is because every delay means some at-risk student will either drop out of school or fail school. Society is affected in some way when a student fails or drops out of school. In a similar way, a pastor or minister of the Word must feel a sense of urgency in not only preaching and teaching God's Word but also improving the efficiency of the operation of the ministry. To delay may lead to lack of effectiveness in his or her ministry in a changing world and compromise his or her ministry's ability to effectively reach the community with the Good News.

In respect to personal development, to delay improving your skills and knowledge for effectiveness may compromise your life or your company's effectiveness in the marketplace and therefore lead to the termination of your employment. Many years ago people used to work for the same company until they retired. Today this is no longer the case. Within a few years of beginning employment, your skills may become redundant and useless in a company that is trying to keep up with competitors in a fast-changing world. The world has become more of a competitive marketplace than ever before. There are global, technological, cultural, economic, political and social forces at work that are influencing change in just about every domain of human endeavour, affecting every area of everyday life. What does all this mean for the individual or the organization that is being led? It means developing a sense of urgency for change, for without such your life, your skills and knowledge or the organization you lead will become redundant and unproductive in a changing world.

Necessary Condition 4: New Knowledge for Change
Acquiring new knowledge is a critical component in the process of creating, adapting to or leading change. No one can initiate or lead change without new information. In fact, the very term itself suggests some form of transformation, modification or movement.

Let us take the example of a company (Company A) that is being challenged by a competitor company (Company B), which has begun using a new technology to effectively market a product they both provide. What would Company A need to do to keep up with Company B? To keep up with its competitor, Company A would need to know a few things, including customers' buying attitudes and current technology, in order to stay at least at the competitive level. Failure to acquire this knowledge might mean inability to attract new customers or even to maintain old ones. This is because people are not only influenced by changes around them but also more drawn to systems and organizations that understand their needs.

On a more personal level, to have relevant and market-specific skills or employability in a changing world means acquiring new knowledge. While skills such as interpersonal and communicative skills are critical in almost every segment of the workplace, market-specific skills are what will get you into a specific segment of the workforce. It is your market-specific skills that tilt your employability scale.

While your ability to communicate effectively might remain constant, your market-specific skills may not. For example, John is fifty-five years old. He has been a mechanic for thirty years and has worked on several models of cars. His past customers loved him and often talked about his pleasant attitude and ability to relate effectively to them. However, over the past five years fewer and fewer customers have brought their cars to his shop. He had to send some cars elsewhere for a particular service for which he had no knowledge or skills. Consequently, he has reached a point where he has to close down his shop because of a lack of customers. While John has excellent interpersonal skills, he has no specific knowledge or skills to work on newer models of cars. John has been accustomed to working on cars with minimum computerized technology. Now he's faced with cars that are completely computer-driven. Furthermore, he has not upgraded his knowledge and skills or learned how to use the latest computerized diagnostic tools. These new computerized models of cars do not fit with what John is comfortable working with, and as a result he has slowly become a dinosaur in his field and moved toward extinction. So while he has great communication and interpersonal skills, lack of market-specific skills make him ineffective and redundant in his field.

Where are you in your life right now? Are you aware of the changes occurring around you and how you are affected by them and what you need to do to remain relevant and effective? Or are you simply relying on the fact that you are a nice person and people love you because of your pleasant attitude and interpersonal skills? Are you a pastor and don't know how to keep your church relevant or how to move it through change? Are you a professional and feel redundant in the midst of change? Are you a teacher who no longer knows what strategy to use to enhance learning in the classroom? Are you a manager or owner of a small business and feel overwhelmed with the changes that are happening around you to the point where you feel you cannot keep up? Are you an entrepreneur who no longer feels motivated to take risks and initiatives because of overwhelming feelings of uncertainty in the marketplace?

If you answer yes to any of these, you need to acquire new knowledge. The moment you acquire new knowledge everything changes. Knowledge changes your view of things and helps you see through the uncertainties and complexities of life.

In 1956, Benjamin Bloom, an educator at the University of Chicago, developed what is called the cognitive taxonomy or cognitive domain of learning in which he identified six ascending levels of learning. These he referred to as knowledge, comprehension, application, analysis, synthesis and evaluation. Each of these domains takes the learner to a higher and more complex cognitive level of learning. Interestingly, in this taxonomy he placed knowledge as the first and most basic or fundamental component to the other components. In the cognitive domain of learning, knowledge is required before the acquisition or exercise of any other component of learning is possible.

The Bible also sees knowledge as a critical component for change. It refers to wisdom as *"the principal thing"* (Proverbs 4:7). What do you need to be a more effective pastor, leader, auto mechanic, engineer or administrator? Regardless of the position you hold, without knowledge you cannot effectively apply skills. If you have a skill to do something you have the knowledge of how to do it.

There are many ways to acquire new knowledge. Depending on the field you are in, it could be through extra training, school, reading, other people, seminars and workshops, or simple studying of trends and changes around you. The important thing is that for directional and meaningful change to happen, knowledge must be acquired. If it is not acquired, not only does what you do become redundant, but you and what you lead become dinosaurs.

Transformation occurs when one sees the world through the lens of new knowledge. In making relevant and needed change, you cannot just act arbitrarily; your thinking must change qualitatively as well as directionally. In fact, to make meaningful change, you must have a rationale for such change and also begin seeing things in the light of such change.

New knowledge not only challenges your thinking and gives you a rationale for change; it also aid your understanding of what the change will look like and what it will affect. The moment you acquire new knowledge, you become responsible for the change it necessitates.

This does not mean that every time you get new knowledge it must automatically lead to change. On the contrary. New knowledge must be tested against a number of things, including your core values, vision and goals, current trends, etc. Only when new knowledge is tested against some grid of value or truth should it be ready for implementation.

Necessary Condition 5: A Plan of Action for Change

A plan of action is a necessary condition for change. As a change agent you must bring forth and transform your knowledge into a plan of action. While knowledge is the fundamental and principal thing, if it is not applied nothing gets done. While knowledge can be motivating, by itself it does not produce work or change. While it challenges and exerts demands on you, it cannot make you do what you need to do. It is the need, urgency and desire for change that will activate your willpower.

Your willpower leads you not just to "I can do" but to "I will do." Your "I will do" is your resolve to do. It is this resolve that stands between your new knowledge and the change that must be carried out.

When you know exactly where you want to go and have a plan for getting there, you will be less anxious. Like vision, change must follow a conscious and deliberate plan of action. While you can have a goal without a plan, you cannot have a plan without a goal. The plan is the natural path to the goal.

For example, let's say your goal is to develop a new skill or improve on a current skill or knowledge. Your plan of action would include steps that must be accomplished as you move toward your goal. This may include allocating time and funds, setting priorities and timelines, and so on. You cannot set plans and establish timelines with no particular goal in mind.

Necessary Condition 6: Implementation of the Plan for Change

Once you have developed a plan for change, the final necessary condition is implementation of the plan. Change does not occur until plans for change find their way out of your mind, off the papers and into actual practice in the real world. Leading change for yourself, your family or your organization means making it happen in real life through carefully planned action steps.

Higher Order Thinking for Change

Why is it that some people know that change is necessary for them but live out their lives void of it? In this section we attempt to answer this question by discussing our higher order or second-order thinking ability. Understanding this aspect of your mental world will lead you to being better able to make the necessary changes in your life.

Let's begin with a question. Can we change our minds, and if so, are there different levels or degrees in thinking? The answer is yes. Higher order or second-order thinking involves the ability to think critically, logical, reflectively, evaluatively and creatively. Obviously, if there exists a higher order thinking ability, there is also a lower order or first order. Your first-order thinking is your everyday ordinary thinking, which comes to you easily, without much mental effort. It can be and usually is spontaneous, stereotypical, judgmental and nonreflective. While it can generate insight and truth, it is vulnerable to error, prejudice and bad reasoning.

In contrast to first-order thinking, your second or higher order thinking involves conscious realization. This means with this level of thinking you can analyze, assess and reconstruct your first-order thinking. At this level of thinking you can (1) evaluate and manage internal activities that do not support meaningful change, (2) impose meaning beyond the initial perception of things, (3) test initial assumptions and make decisions based on core values, strong evidence and truth.

Figure 10.2: *First-Order and Second-Order Thinking*

Imagine yourself on top of a roof looking down on your own self on the ground. From your position on the roof you can alter, direct and redirect any action initiated by you on the ground. Does this sound weird? Weird or not, this is the type of ability each person sets in motion when he or she initiates higher order thinking.

The ability to think about thinking is one of the defining factors that set humans apart from the animals. The ability to think about your own thinking allows you the mental capacity to see and hear clearly what is occurring within your own mind. Every thought, regardless of its nature, that appears on the screen of your awareness can be brought under supervisory control by the management level of your own thinking.

To understand this, stop reading this book for a moment and think of a thought that you would not otherwise entertain. Now, reflect on and scrutinize carefully the thought you have just generated and carefully evaluate its usefulness to you. Try modifying or replacing it with thoughts that you believe are more productive. When you subject the thought to careful evaluation, if you are successful in assessing its usefulness, you weaken its power to germinate and infect other parts of your mental world.

This had to do with thinking about thinking. You were able to look at and evaluate your own thinking and make changes to your initial thoughts as needed. You took the initial thought you believed was inappropriate or unproductive and made it obedient to the standard you imposed on it by your higher order thinking. You were meant to be in control of the conscious and mental activities of your own mind.

This exercise demonstrated several facts.

You Can Hear Your Own Thoughts

We have the ability to recognize that we are thinking about something. We can actually think about what we are thinking about. The thoughts and the thought-images our minds create are not hidden from our internal awareness but can be clearly heard and seen on the inside. The moment we hear them, they become our responsibility. Once they enter our awareness we can supervise and evaluate them.

Bear in mind that thoughts never act alone. They usually are accompanied by images, which serve to reinforce their purposes. Where do these thoughts and the images they generate come from?

They have two primary origins. Thoughts and thought-images, regardless of their nature, can be triggered from something in the external world or by our own thoughts from the inside, which include memories and perceptions. So then, whether we generate them or whether they simply appear by being triggered by some external or internal stimuli, once they enter the domain of awareness we have the ability to see and hear them.

It is like watching and hearing yourself from the inside. What do you suppose would happen if you became a mere internal onlooker of thoughts that are not in accordance with your own values or vision? The answer is, these thoughts could take up permanent residence and become your master. Thoughts, when left up to themselves, can bring your life into ruin. If you can hear them, you can manage them with your higher order thinking. Remember we alluded to this earlier when we noted that the Bible tells us that we possess the ability to bring thoughts into captivity and make them obedient to the standards of Christ.

Interrogate Your Thoughts Before You Believe Them

We have all been there, when we knew we needed to do something important but an internal voice convinced us not to and we followed like obedient children. We failed to accomplish what we desired because we believed what the voice told us about ourselves or about the task we wished to perform.

To hear a voice in your head does not mean you are psychologically unstable or crazy. On the contrary, the voice you hear is the voice of your own thoughts. These thoughts can either work for your growth and change or work to hold you back from growth and progress.

The challenge to most people is deciding which thought they should listen to and follow. Thinking for change requires us to be able to differentiate between the voices we hear and the images we see in our own minds and follow the voice or thought that moves our lives toward positive and meaningful change. Believe it or not, our thoughts can lie to us, and most times we are influenced to follow because we feel too helpless to confront them.

For example, after failing your driving test, you hear your own thought say, "I am just a failure." You have just failed at a task, so is your thought lying to you? A closer examination will reveal that your thought is a distortion of the truth. Failing in your attempt to pass your driving test does not make you a failure. All it means is that you failed at a particular aspect of driving that you need more practice at or knowledge of. With more practice and knowledge you will eventually succeed.

Because you have the ability to hear your thoughts you can interrogate them to determine their validity. Sometimes your thoughts do not directly lie to you. Rather, in order to convince you against growth and change, they take you through a series of what seems to be logical statements. As you approach a challenging task toward change, first a thought creates doubt in you by asking, "Are you sure you can do this?" Regardless of the motivation and enthusiasm that you have toward this task, hearing this immediately slows you down. Questions you may never have pondered before about your ability began popping up all over your mental world.

Second, before you have time to generate some positive response, it builds on the question by imposing suggestions like "Maybe you don't have what it takes to do this" or "Maybe this is not for you." Hearing this, you begin feeling a drop in momentum.

Third, while the momentum has slowed and before you have time to recuperate from the initial shock, you hear the voice ask, "If you fail, what will people say?" or "You will fail if you try, and then what?" Now your bubble is burst and your running momentum for the task has slowed to a mere walk.

Fourth, when you believe the thought is done with you it has something else to throw at you. You hear it say, "People will be disappointed in you if you fail, and some will even laugh at you for being so stupid." Hearing this and actually seeing images of the possibility in your head, you feel no more energy to move forward. You feel detained, defeated and discouraged and believe it no longer makes any sense to carry on. You have been brought to a complete stop, not by a bulldozer or a wall but by believing your own thoughts. The vision or goal you thought was close now appears unattainable.

At this point you feel there is nothing more you can say to yourself that will make a difference. Interestingly, you really have not said anything in response to your defeating thoughts; you did not even put up a fight. Finally, after what seems a long pause, you hear your thought, "You can save yourself all the embarrassment by just not attempting this thing; it is safer to remain in your present condition. Maybe you can try later." Following the deceptive counsel of your own mind you reluctantly decide to follow the instruction of your deceptive thoughts.

The truth is, you should not believe everything you hear in your head. Our thoughts are not infallible and often times work against our aspirations and dreams. As we have noted earlier, we not only have the ability to see and hear our own thoughts from the inside, we can also detain and take them in for questioning or examination. We can in reality stop the thought at any time we choose and subject it to careful interrogation. This means even before the thought has reached its complete state of being generated we can stop and question its right to exist in our mental life.

You can compare the thought against your vision or some internal reference of value or standard in order to test its authenticity and usefulness. Yes! You can actually test the truth claim of your own thoughts.

In order to convince you, your thought provides you with some truth claims and logic about your ability to initiate, adapt or lead change. You cannot challenge and change this thought unless you engage your higher order thinking. Your ability to interrogate such truth claims and mental logic resides only in your higher order thinking. This means if the thought or voice is against your vision or the particular value or standard you hold, you can bring the thought into subjection to that standard or dismiss it as unproductive. In other words, you can make your unsupportive and negative voice obedient.

There will be times when your own thoughts will not support your desire for meaningful change. They will challenge you to believe them and even coerce you if you try to put up resistance. Managing thoughts that are clearly against you is not an easy task. Many people have been brought to their knees and reduced to tears, having their energy drained out of them by trying to fight against unsupportive thinking. Unsupportive thinking can bring down your vision and keep your life in a status-quo rut. These thoughts must therefore be addressed early in their existence when they have not developed strong roots. Once they take up permanent residence they are more difficult to deal with. The longer they exist in our minds, the more subjected we become to them and the sooner we tend to obey them.

Even though more times than not we know that certain thoughts must not be believed, because they are working against our goals, we believe them anyway. This happens because we have not learned how to activate and effectively use the higher capacities of our minds.

In a previous chapter we noted that thoughts and beliefs tend to have the property of permanence; they tend to persist over time. In fact, when they are allowed to persist they will germinate and spread. They can even become stronger with every new experience. If your new experience is a positive one, they convince you to believe otherwise. On the other hand, if your new experience is a negative one, they convince you that it confirms what they have been telling you all along.

One thing to remember here is that logic does not always equal truth. Something can be logical but not true. One of the strategies of our thinking is to present us with convincingly logical arguments. The important question is, why do our own thoughts seem to work against us? Shouldn't they work to support our ideals and goals?

Not necessarily. Many of the negative and disabling thoughts we have are triggered by memories of past experiences or flawed perceptions developed over time. This is why we have been equipped with higher thinking capacities, so we can interrogate the claims these thoughts present and bring them under higher order mental supervision.

When we interrogate the directives imposed on us by our own minds we ask pertinent questions that can lead to change in the atmosphere and dynamics of our mind. Questions are the doorways to new knowledge. They are keys to understanding the unknown and unfamiliar. Questions are by far the most powerful mechanisms for understanding and change. The moment we ask a question we trigger a mechanism that can lead to change.

Where do you suppose motor vehicles, planes, ships, spacecraft, computers, the Internet, telephones, cellphones and televisions came from? These inventions and discoveries were born out of questions people somewhere in time asked or pondered over, which eventually led to these innovations and changes. Little children are always filled with questions about everything. The answers to these questions help them acquire knowledge about themselves and their external world. Most scientific research begins with a question, which leads to a new discovery and eventually to change in the way we understand and do things. Questions are not only avenues for gaining new knowledge about the world; they are also great channels for change of mind.

Your questions are keys in activating and employing the resources of your higher order capacities for change in the atmosphere of your mind. You are not limited to any one question but have a range of them at your disposal. They are more than just your defense against mind lockdown; they are your change tools. You will be surprised by the changes that will occur in the atmosphere of your mind when you begin to question thoughts that do not support your move toward opportunities and meaningful change.

Believe What You Think

The statement "Believe what you think" is not meant to confuse you. You were just told not to believe everything you hear and see in your mind. Here you are told to believe what you think. The truth is, to adapt to, initiate or lead change you must reach the place where you begin believing your own thoughts about the need for change. Although you have thoughts that are unsupportive, you also have thoughts that work to support your move for meaningful change. Although their voices are often softer than the other loudmouths in your mind, they still exist and can be accessed through your second-order thinking.

Let's take an example. You have the thought that, given the trends in your company, you should upgrade your skills. Immediately you are confronted with another thought telling you that you have been out of school for far too long to be successful in this endeavour. You counter that thought by thinking that you still have a working brain and can take up the challenge. Before you have time to even reflect on your last thought, a new thought, which seems to be logical comes into your mind. This thought reminds you of how terrible you did on the last job training your company sponsored, proof that going back to school to upgrade your skills is a bad idea. Now you are faced with two thoughts, and you have to make a choice to believe one.

Some people make the choice to believe those thoughts that seem to speak with more logic. Remember, as noted before, logic does not always equal truth. Furthermore, because negative thoughts appear to arouse your emotions faster and with higher intensity, their effects are usually more overpowering. In this case, some people will believe the thought that says they will not succeed rather than the thought that says they need to and can succeed. People who have been confronted with such opposing thoughts or voices know full well how hard it can be to make the right choice in situations in which negative thoughts bear down with strong logic and reason.

If you believe the thought that tells you that you will fail in your attempt to change, you will be held back, not by who you think you are but by who you think you are not. You believe you are not smart enough, not good enough or not intelligent enough. But if you believe in your ability to become, to change, to succeed, then you need to believe your thinking that tells you that you can and need to do so. Believing in yourself is choosing those thoughts that encourage you to move forward in spite of past failures and drawbacks.

Knowing that you can manage your own thoughts and make choices between them is the first step toward making productive changes and taking control of your life. Remember, the thought you select to believe will shape your emotional energy, drive your actions and ultimately define your future.

Impose a Different Perspective

Our perspective is the vantage point from which we see and interpret things from the inside of our minds. The perspective from which we view our experiences heavily influences the way we think, the conclusions we draw about ourselves, our future and approach to life. It is the perspective we hold that helps create the atmosphere of our thought world and gives rise to the type of thoughts that impose themselves on our desire to move our lives forward.

Oftentimes when we try to dismiss negative thoughts they come right back. In fact, sometimes our unsupportive thoughts are so deeply rooted that no measure of interrogation can shake them. They are like strongholds in our lives. Because we can hear our thoughts and see the images they create we can do more than question them; we can impose a different perspective than the ones they present. It is by imposing new and different perspectives on our mind that our thoughts are transformed and brought under mental and executive control.

In this case, changing your mind means changing your perspective. Changing your perspective means mentally stepping back and taking a fresh look at a situation or experience. For example, you were unjustly treated by someone in the past, you failed at something in the past or you were unable to measure up to yours or someone's expectations. How you view these outcomes now has significant influence on what you do and how far you go.

Changing your perspective requires you to mentally revisit these experiences and take a new and fresh look at them from a whole different vantage point. This can mean looking at the situation from the point of view that you lacked focus and maturity at the time when you failed. Your knowledge level did not provide you with the skills needed to perform at the task, but now you are more mature and focused. A new perspective on being unjustly treated—which has led you to be mistrustful of people—could be that not all people are the same and each person should be judged on their own merit and behaviour instead of being stereotyped. Instead of having this perpetual and enduring view of yourself as a victim, why not see yourself as a person who has had some failures and bad experiences but does not have to continue living a defeated life? Instead of seeing yourself as a failure, why not see yourself as a person who has failed at something in life but can still succeed at other things and with improved skills succeed at the same things? The moment you change your perspective, you not only change your mind; you change your life and start shaping your future.

The interesting thing about perspective is that it falls under your own control and is shaped by your own mind. It is your mind's way of interpreting and imposing meaning on something. Imagine that you took a picture of an accident scene. Looking at the picture you see one view of what might have happened. Imagine that you went back to the scene and took several more pictures. By comparing the pictures you might come to a different conclusion of what might have happened in the accident. The change in conclusion occurs because you have a change in perspective; you took a second look at the same situation from different vantage points. This is because many aspects of our reality are constructed and given meaning by us.

Extending the Limits of Your Thinking

While managing our thought life and bringing more productive perspectives to our mind is good, our mental ability allows us to do more than this. Not only can we evaluate, supervise and manage the internal dynamics of our mind, we can extend the limits of our current thinking.

Your current thinking was shaped and conditioned by many factors in your life. Some of these factors have already been discussed in previous chapters. Regardless of how your present mindset and range of thinking were shaped, these experiences set mental boundaries in your mind, allowing you only a certain range of thinking. This is one of the reasons why you feel you cannot attain certain heights, accomplish challenging goals or move your life beyond certain failures. Unknown to you, these experiences subtly established reference points and limits on your thinking. Although oftentimes you feel there is more you can do and greater heights you can achieve, you find that you cannot generate the type of thinking that will move your life beyond where and what it has come to be.

When you extend something you enlarge it beyond its normal restraints. What is your view of the future for yourself? Is it conservatively small and narrow or is it eccentrically large and inviting?

In the very first chapter we discussed the awesomeness and unlimited capacity of the human mind. Yet here we are suggesting an extension of its limits, a contradiction in terms. How can we extend the boundary of that which is so vast in capacity and potential? More importantly, how can we even think of expansion of something when its full capacity has not been used up or even utilized?

Although the capacity and potential of our mind are so great, we ourselves impose limits on them. Recall in earlier chapters we talked about the chicken and eagle mentality and the types of thinking that keep people in ruts like chickens and the type of thinking that takes them to soaring altitudes. By thinking like a chicken, not generating and cultivating thoughts that produce growth and productivity in your life, or living within the confines set by past experiences and people's expectations, you are imposing limits on your thinking. It is these limits that we hope to help you break through.

In these final pages of the book we will talk about opening the channels, removing the limits and enlarging the boundaries of our thinking. While we understand what is meant by enlarging a physical territory, what precisely do we mean by enlarging the limits of our mind?

Enlarging the limits of our mind follows the same principle of enlarging a physical territory. Whether it is a piece of land, an organization, a process, an industry or thinking, enlargement means to expand beyond the current space.

Remember, a limit by definition means the farthest operating point or the point at which you can go no farther.

Before turning our attention to the question of how to extend the limits of our thinking, it is important to briefly hear what the Bible has to say about the topic of enlargement of current operating boundaries:

- In Ephesians 3:20 the apostle Paul writing to the church said, "*To Him who is able to do exceedingly abundantly above all that we ask or think, according to the power that works in us.*"
- In Luke 5:4, Jesus instructed Peter to move from the shallow waters and launch into the deep, and there he should let down his fishing net for a great draw of fish.
- In Isaiah 54:2–3, God told the Israelites to "*Enlarge the place of your tent, stretch your tent curtains wide, do not hold back...For you will spread out to the right and to the left*" (NIV).
- In Daniel 11:32 we read, "*But the people who know their God shall be strong, and carry out great exploits.*"
- In 1 Chronicles 4:10, the young man Jabez prayed that God would bless him and enlarge his territory.

Is the God of the universe in favour of enlargement in our thinking and our lives? Absolutely! All the evidence, from the Scripture itself and the capacity and potential we have been endowed with, suggest that we can do more with our thinking and our lives than we have been led to believed. Let us now discuss how we can extend the limits of our thinking.

Manage Your Words About You; They Become Beliefs

Earlier in chapter 5 we introduced you to the power and function of belief. We discussed how some beliefs are formed and how they serve to limit our thinking. In this section we will extend our discussion about belief to show how the negative words we use when speaking about ourselves function as assumptions, leading not only to a belief system and limitations but total imprisonment of our potential and possibilities.

By definition, an assumption is a statement that is taken to be true without proof and from which a conclusion is drawn. Once a conclusion is drawn from an assumption over time it becomes a directive or governing principle that underlines and drives our patterns of thinking. The thing about holding a set of assumptions is that over time they evolve into not only a belief system but also theories of the self. Consequently, over the course of our lives we learn to speak in certain ways, particularly when we speak about ourselves. Unknown to us, the words we use when we speak about ourselves, whether to ourselves or to others, become statements of assumptions that we come to accept as statement of truth. The language we use can either set limits and restraints on our thinking or provide a wide range of possibilities for our minds and our lives.

Regardless of the particular nature of our assumptions, they are statements that over time become rules of thinking that determine the direction and quality of the decisions we make and the life we live. Assumptions can be positive and functional or maladaptive and dysfunctional. If your assumptions about yourself are positive and functional they will serve to give you an unlimited range of possibilities in thinking. If the assumptions you make about yourself are dysfunctional and maladaptive, they will work to limit your range of thoughts, holding your life in mental shackles. Generating thoughts that go beyond such restraints on thinking becomes almost impossible. This means such assumptions fail to serve any productive purpose. They limit growth and development and imprison your capacity, possibilities and potential.

Consider the following list of dysfunctional and functional statements of assumption people make about themselves.

Dysfunctional Statements
- If I fail at something, then I am a failure.
- If I cannot succeed at a present task, then I will not be able to succeed at similar tasks.
- I can do nothing to change the way things are; they are beyond my capability.
- If I ask her out she will only say no. I am just not the type of guy she is looking for.
- If I try and fail, people will see me as a failure.
- God will never grant me the favours he granted others; I am just not worth it.
- Failure is an experience that confirms I am a failure.

Functional Statements
- If I work hard enough, I will succeed.
- I can be creative if I put my mind to it.

- I can change things in my life because I can exercise at least some control over my life.
- I can do all things through Christ who empowers me.
- If others can do it, so can I.
- I am just as capable as others.
- Failure is an experience I can learn from to do things better.

When you compare the two groups of statements you will notice that the dysfunctional statements set limits on thinking while the functional statements open doors of opportunities. The dysfunctional statements bind you to the here and now. They allow you absolutely no opportunity to move from where you are in life. In other words, you are a prisoner to the words you use when speaking about yourself. The functional statements, on the other hand, set no limits on you. They are statements that give your thinking a range of possibilities. Functional assumptions remove restrictions on your thought world and ultimately your life.

Assumptions can and usually do lead to theories of the self. *Theories of the self* here means the enduring beliefs you hold about yourself and how you use these beliefs to predict future behaviour as well as to provide reasons for past actions.

People usually are not aware of their own language about themselves because these statements have been used for so long that they become not only automatic thoughts but also predictions and explanations about the self. Victims of such thinking may not be consciously aware that they are limiting themselves with their own statements and assumptions. Others may be aware but find that they are addicted to that type of thinking and don't know how to change it. When these assumptions become theories of the self they not only incarcerate your mind but hurt your life.

Let's take a closer look at what we mean by theories of the self. A theory can be a general proposition in which a logical connection is made between two or more changing situations. In the world of science, for example, researchers used theories to predict what can happen in a future situation given the existence of certain conditions. They also use theories to explain why things are the way they are or function the way they function. Researchers conduct experiments to either develop new theories or test whether or not current theories are valid. Consequently, theories are modified, proven to be false or confirm as valid, depending on the results of the researcher's findings. This means theories can be tested and changed.

Let's examine the predictive and explanatory nature of a theory as derived from the assumptions we make about ourselves. We will look at the logical connection between two situations. Consider the statement "I will not get the job, because I'm not smart enough." This statement has two parts. Is there a logical connection between these two parts? Absolutely! The first part (*I will not get the job*) is an assumption as well as a prediction (predictive assumption) of what will happen in a future situation. The second part is a statement of assumption about the self in the form of a reason why the job will not be acquired (explanatory). If this statement is limited to a single situation it cannot be considered a theory of the self. It becomes a theory of the self only when it is generalized to other areas of the person's life. For example, the person is afraid of initiating new things, extending himself or herself beyond the familiar or doing anything that is believed might show a perceived lack of smartness or incompetence.

When a theory of the self is established it is usually hard to break because it sets rigid boundary around the type of thoughts you can generate or entertain. The belief that you are a failure or you are not a smart person becomes your theory about yourself that predicts an outcome of failure across situations in your life. Your theory of the self is also used to explain why you failed at some tasks in the past.

Some theories we hold about ourselves are positive and useful in that they help us move with confidence towards change and development. On the other hand, there are theories we hold about ourselves that prevent us from moving forward in life. Even though our observational evidence contradicts some core aspects of our flawed theory of self, we continue to apply it to our lives. Extending the limits of our thinking means revisiting the assumptions we hold about ourselves and bravely eliminating or making necessary modifications to them. Only when our unfounded assumptions are challenged and changed can we think without negative restrictions and move our lives to new levels.

Speak to Yourself as a Second Person

Extending the limits of our thinking is not just changing the words we use when speaking to and about ourselves. It also includes how or in what voice we speak to ourselves. *Voice* here means speaking to ourselves as either the first or second person. Speaking to ourselves as the first person is the accepted and normal mode. In some cases, shifting this mode to the second person can remove limits set on our minds and thinking by our own perceptions and experiences. Here I am proposing that one way to open up the channels and remove unnecessary restrictions from your thinking is to speak to yourself as a second person, at least in times when it matters.

Although some people believe that talking to yourself is a sign that you are going crazy or is mentally unstable, most psychologists and researchers believe that exercising your inner voice can lead to improvement in self-control, increase in willpower and reduction in impulsive behaviours. In fact, the ability to talk to yourself is a major part of the human experience of consciousness. When you talk to yourself you activate neural circuitries in your brain and set in motion mechanisms that can work positively or negatively for you. You can talk to yourself through silent thoughts within your own mind or out loud with the use of actual statements. Sometimes it is more effective to use the audible than the silent voice. In either case, we hear ourselves.

Furthermore, because people always think faster than they speak, by speaking to yourself you turn on your internal mental control, which allows you more monitoring power over many of the thoughts that would otherwise slip through your conscious filter.

All our interpersonal relationships are based on another person talking with us. We began experiencing second person statements and interactions the moment we enter the world of people. This became the normal mode of interaction and expression between us and our parents and others.

The capacity for internal dialogue or self-talk is a natural ability of our minds and one that should be tapped into and use productively. People who suffer with mental issues in which they constantly hear voices are unable to turn off their internal dialogue and control the flow of information within their own minds. For example, they might find themselves hearing voices or having conversations with people who are not even in their external environment, suggesting that they have crossed the line of normality. We all hear our own thoughts in our heads, but they are usually not loud, uncontrollable or consistent enough to cause many problems. Learning to take control of this awesome internal ability for self-dialogue may very well work to safeguard our minds from potential mental issues. Learning how our minds work and using the capacity they allow us could be one of the greatest achievements of the ages.

People are accustomed to speaking to themselves in the first person voice. This is quite natural and usually occurs with ease and without much effort. As a result, in most cases we don't carefully process what we say to ourselves in the first person. Somehow, when we speak to ourselves in the first person the information does not always carry the effect we usually desire. What is the reason for this phenomenon, hearing but not processing what we say to ourselves? We hear what we say to ourselves but we do not listen and pay attention to our own voices, particularly when what we say is positive. We tend to listen to ourselves more attentively when the statements are negative.

Several reasons can be identified for this. First, we often take ourselves for granted. This means we often feel indifferent towards our own achievements and skills. We tend to believe we are good at something only when someone else tells us that we are.

For example, your boss says, "You did great on this project." Upon hearing this statement you feel happy. But you have been trying to tell yourself this very same thing and still ended up feeling incompetent. Here is what you have been saying to yourself: "I know I did well on this project, but I wonder…" Somehow you failed to convince yourself that you are that capable.

Second, when we speak to ourselves we tend to receive the message subjectively rather than objectively, meaning it is received as a conditional or provisional draft rather than an already verified message. On the other hand, when someone else tells us that what we did was great, unless we have good reason to believe otherwise we receive this message objectively, not as a conditional draft but as something authentic and verified.

Third, when we speak to ourselves in the first person, we allow our mind every opportunity to put up second person approach barriers, which is oftentimes extremely hard to break through.

For example, you say to yourself, "I think I am going to try every strategy to hold on to my marriage." The next voice you hear is your second person, which may say, "Why would you even think of such a thing when your spouse doesn't even show you the love you deserve?" Interestingly, there is a part of your mind (the second person approach) that will disagree with your first person's voice, and sometimes for good reasons. The issue here is not whether the voice is right or wrong; what is important here is that your opposing voice speaks to you as a second person. More importantly, it speaks to you more times than not with a more powerful and authoritative voice, which you tend to listen to and often obey.

Examine the following statements using the first person voice:
• I think I should finish this project in two days.
• I need to finish this project in two day.
• I think I should start studying for my exam early.
• I think I should consider going back to school to improve my competence.

- I think I have what it takes to complete the task.
- I think I am just as good as anyone.
- I think I did very well on that project.
- I think I should work harder on my marriage.

These are all positive statements pointing toward some intentional change. However, how many times do we really follow through with what we say to ourselves in the first person voice? Many times these statements do not give us the desired effects. The truth is, we often make positive statements about ourselves and what we need to do in our lives, but their influence on us is usually quite small and ineffective.

Examine the following statements:
- I don't think I have what it takes to complete this degree.
- I don't think I can do anything to make this marriage work.
- I don't think I can finish this project in two days.
- I don't think I have enough time to study for this exam.
- I don't think I am as good as students who are always getting over 90 percent in class.
- I am inclined to believe I did good on that project, but I don't think I am that good anyway.

Sometimes when we speak to ourselves in the first person voice we are ineffective in pushing our minds beyond certain restrictions imposed by our own negative thoughts. It is proposed here that at least some of these limitations on thinking can be removed by simply talking to yourself as a second person.

To start, when you speak to yourself as a second person you utilize the term *you*. For example, speaking to yourself about self-care you might say, "You will show more appreciation for yourself if you begin taking care of your physical appearance." It might be more effective if you include your own name before the term *you*. You can even challenge yourself. For example, "Mark, why do you always put yourself down? You have potential to do the job just like anyone else" not only challenges your restrictive assumption about you but affirms your ability to be successful.

Using the second person approach makes you the outside person. This allows you the ability to shift from the subjective "I-self" to the objective "you-self." By using the objective "you-self" you free your mind of many restraints and open up more possibilities for growth.

Let us look at some advantages of using the second person approach when speaking to ourselves. The list is by no means exhaustive; you may even think of more benefits than those discussed.

First, the second person approach allows us to think more *objectively* about ourselves. It allows us to detach ourselves (temporarily) from the subjective "I-self." In this, we see and speak to our own self as how someone else would. At the same time, although we are aware that we are speaking to our own self, the message is received as if coming from someone else and therefore as more objective and believable. As a result, we become more mindful of and listen more carefully to what is being said.

Think of my statement "I would definitely like to finish writing this book by the end of this month." The term *definitely* suggests some measure of urgency. However, although I know and tell myself how important it is to finish the book by the end of the month, did my mind received the message? Did I really listen carefully to and process what I said? Does this sound familiar? Now consider the same statement worded using the second person approach. "Clarence, you definitely need to finish writing this book by the end of this month." Which of the two statements do you think my mind will listen to more carefully and process with more of a sense of urgency?

The second advantage in using the second person approach is that you become the *subject of interest.* Consider the statement "I think I did a great job on that last project." Here you commend yourself for doing something well. How would the same message coming from a colleague be received by you? Consider this: "John, you did a great job on that last project!" Which of the two statements do you think would have more impact on your self-confidence? If you are like most people, your answer would be the statement from the colleague.

Let us replace your colleague with you, using the same statement as a second person. After reflecting on the job you did, you say to yourself, "You did a great job on that last project!" The impression created on you when you speak to yourself as a second person is not much different from when a colleague speaks to you. This is because in both cases, the statement "You did a great job on that last project!" puts you as the subject of interest. Being the subject of positive interest from others does something to you. It makes you become more aware of aspects of yourself and makes you feel important. When someone makes you feel important, you are more likely to believe what they say to you.

The third advantage of using the second person approach is that with it you create a *sense of urgency* about what you need to do. We often tell ourselves

"I need to get this done" but never get around to doing it. We just don't take ourselves as seriously as we would like to. Most times what we say to ourselves doesn't register with the same kind of urgency as when someone else speaks to us. Talking to yourself as a second person switches the dynamics of the dialogue and adds a measure of urgency to the message. You hear the degree of urgency in the message as if you heard it from another person.

Fourth, when you talk to yourself as a second person you *eliminate* a great deal of negative opposing thoughts. Consider the statement "I think I should tell Margaret how I really feel about her." Right after this first-person statement, you may begin hearing several opposing second-person statements, such as "Are you sure you want to do that? Remember what happen the last time you tried to tell a girl how you feel?" or "Are you so sure she feels the same way about you? What if she thinks you are a jerk?" Or "What if she doesn't find you attractive? How would that make you feel?" These is an arsenal of negative and confronting second-person thoughts that are likely to challenge your subjective "I-self" statement. The intent of these negative subject "I-self" statements is to demolish your self-confidence.

However, what if you use the second person approach in the first place? It would sound something like "Go over and tell Margaret how you really feel about her." There is no doubt that some negative thoughts will emerge, but nowhere as many or as convincing as when the first person approach is used. This is because when speaking to yourself as a second person your tone tends to be more instructional and commanding. In other words, when you speak to yourself as a second person you nullify many of your opposing negative second-person rebuttal voices.

The fifth advantage in using the second person approach is that you make yourself *accountable* to you. For example, consider the statement from a colleague that says "You need to complete this paper by tomorrow evening." This statement creates a sense of accountability in you to the person speaking to you. The statement "I need to finish this paper by tomorrow evening" does not carry the same weight of accountability as the first statement from someone else. The subjective "I-self" statement opens too many doors of excuses and diminishes the sense of accountability. On the other hand, the second-person approach makes you accountable to someone, and that person is you.

The sixth reason why using the second person approach is advantageous is that it provides both a *respected* and an *authoritative tone* to us. People do not generally want others to beat up on them or shout at them. Yet, even as adults, we at times do need to be spoken to with some measure of firmness. This firmness, however, must be tempered with respect and a tone that says we are valued regardless of what we have done or failed to do. When we speak to ourselves in the first person, sometimes we tend to devalue who we are. It becomes easy for us to beat up on ourselves. We usually do this less when we use the second person approach. We are more considerate with ourselves when we speak as a second person.

Let's try it. Go ahead and rebuke yourself in the first person for something you did that you are ashamed of. Now try using the second person approach to speak to yourself about the same thing.

Here is an example of the first person: "I am such an idiot for having done that." Here is an example of the second person voice: "Why did you do that? Could you not have made a better choice?" In both cases a rebuke was delivered, but the impact on the self was different.

In addition to been more respectful and considerate, the second person approach also provides an authoritative tone, making it easy to receive its message. Your authoritative tone is your leader as well as your supportive voice within. It is not usually demanding or devaluing. When called upon, it is a voice that can set clear and high expectations for you and at the same time give support for their attainment. The authoritative voice is particularly more effective in situations where you are uncertain or in doubt about your ability, when your self-confidence is low, or when you are challenged by your negative and unsupportive thoughts. When used as a second person, your authoritative voice can stimulate self-confidence, change the climate of your thought world and mobilize the energy of your mind.

The seventh benefit for using the second-person approach is that it can be more *affirmative and validating*. You can affirm and validate yourself much easier and more meaningfully when you use the second-person approach. For example, which of the following statements do you believe would be received as more affirming and validating? "Johnny, you did really well on that last exam; you are a pretty smart guy" or "I did really well on that last exam; I am a pretty smart guy."

Let's examine these two statements carefully. Essentially, they are saying the same thing. However, although the second statement is a statement of affirmation and validation, it makes you feel like you are trying to convince yourself that you are smart. It also comes over as if you are trying to elevate yourself about something that may not really be so. When you use the second-person approach to affirm and validate yourself, because you are detached from the subjective

"I-self" the validation and affirmation is received as if coming from outside yourself and therefore as more objective.

Finally, the second-person approach works more effectively when we remind ourselves of our *past accomplishments*. There are times when we feel discouraged and think very little of ourselves, when our self-esteem dips below acceptable levels, dragging us down in an emotional dump. Trying to remind ourselves of past accomplishments oftentimes fails to lift our spirits or activate our motivation. Yet when someone else comes along and reminds us of the very same things, they often succeed where we failed. Encouragement and motivation from others seem to work better on us than when they come from our own mind. One of the reasons for this is because there is something about being spoken to in the second-person approach that is arousing and activating. Something happens in our minds when people put us down and demean us and when they confront us, challenge us, encourage us or remind us of past successes. The same effects can be felt when we speak to ourselves in the second-person approach.

Create Gatekeepers of the Mind

We can expand our thinking not only by speaking to ourselves in the second-person approach but also by creating dominant thoughts. Your mind is guarded by what here is termed *gatekeepers*. In an earlier chapter we discussed the idea that thoughts are the material of the mind from which ideas, beliefs and assumptions about us and the world are constructed. Here we expand on that idea by informing you that your thoughts, particularly those that have become dominant, also work as gatekeepers of your mind. Once they achieve mental dominance, they become the grid to which other thoughts are referenced and compared before being transformed into action.

When we think of a gatekeeper we think of one who basically keeps guard at a gate. The primary function of such a person is to monitor and determine who comes in and who goes out of the gate. Our thinking works much like a gate to our mental world. However, it is not just any type of thinking that determines what gets in and stays in and what goes out and stays out. Rather, it is our dominant thoughts that exercise this control over the gate of our minds. This means our dominant thoughts work to either safeguard our minds, open our minds to new possibilities, or block our minds from productive possibilities and rigidly exert dictatorial control over our thought world.

In fact, our dominant thoughts are primarily responsible for creating and directing the life we have lived so far and will create and direct the life we will live from this point forward. If we are predisposed to acting on our dominant thoughts, why don't we work to implant our own minds with the type of dominant thoughts that will serve us meaningfully and productively? Remember that whether our thoughts are positive and good or negative and bad, they predispose our minds to act on them. Extending the limits of thinking means creating new dominant thoughts that will work to unfreeze our minds from their status quo state and allow them the freedom to maximize their potential and utilize the range of possibilities they allow.

For many people, achieving a bit of mental flexibility in thinking is nearly impossible because of the gatekeepers they have guarding their thought life. If your mind will not allow you the opportunity to think beyond certain experiences or the traditional box, and when you do try you are beaten back into subjection, you have a dominant and abusive gatekeeper in your thought life. When this happens you feel you are in a mental prison or, more accurately, a mental lockdown. Releasing your mind to soar to new levels requires you to rid yourself of dominant thoughts that operate as authoritarian gatekeepers and work against your life and vision. Developing new dominant thoughts will create a new sphere of influence on your mind and extend the perimeter of your thought world.

A dominant thought is not just a pattern or group of thoughts. Rather, it is a model or blueprint that sets boundaries on thinking and facilitates the generation of types of thoughts towards particular outcomes. A dominant thought is a prevailing or governing belief, conviction, opinion or perspective you have about yourself, life or a goal. In other words, it's your statement of position about you or an attitude you are taking in respect to you, life or a goal. Once established, your dominant thought becomes your sphere of mental influence as well as the centre of mental gravity and activity. Your dominant thought sets the operating temperature of your mind and recalibrates the level of motivation necessary to move forward.

Keep in mind that dominant thoughts are not your everyday half-hearted or transient way of thinking, which cannot bring about intentional actions. Half-hearted thoughts are not powerful enough to dominate, consume or influence every area of your life. They are usually not at the level of strength where they transform into reality. These do not bring together the mental energy and awaken the willpower you need to execute plans. You will not experience passion, motivation or determination on the levels that is truly transformational until you have dominant thoughts that are productive and life-changing.

In the preface I noted that this book is not about replacing a negative thought with a positive one but rather about self-discovery. It's about knowing yourself from the inside, knowing what moves you and what keeps you back, and taking action to shift the balance of influence within your thought world. It's about taking an inward journey to the centre of your thought world. A few moments or days of positive thinking will not and cannot create dominant thoughts that will empower and move your life forward.

Creating dominant thoughts requires you to do several things. First it requires that you ask yourself *questions* regarding what you would truly love to do, what type of person you would truly love to be and what goals in life you think are truly worth pursuing. Although we live in a world that provides a myriad of distractions, making it often difficult to identify any one thing of profound interest, it is not impossible. Identifying things of importance activates something within you. Only when you have identified something of interest, something that will make your life meaningful, something that you believe will make your journey here on earth worth living, will you begin creating and nurturing dominant thoughts.

Second is the issue of *focus*. Focus is about giving up or letting go of other things and making sure that something very important gets attended to. When you focus you create a centre of mental gravity. It is from here that you provide the greatest influence on the type of thoughts you generate. Your focus or dominant thought is the centre around which your mental energy and activities converge.

When you bring your mind to focus you activate particular regions in your brain that in turn activate other mechanisms that provide you with the type of psychological resources needed to generate motivation. You can never really know what you can accomplish until you begin to focus on something you think is really important. It is here that you remove limits and begin expanding the boundaries of your mind.

Creating a dominant thought pattern requires that you bring your focus to bear on that which you have identified as seriously important. Here is what happens when you focus. Your mind generates more ideas and thoughts about the subject of focus. This works both ways though. If you focus your mind on unproductive things, you will see more negative things in almost everything you encounter in life. You don't attract them to you; it is your focus that is drawn to them. This is because the gatekeeper of your thought world is negative, which allows only the negative to pass and filters out or blocks the positive. On the other hand, if you focus on positive and productive things, your gatekeeper will be of such. It will become easier to see the positive in things instead of the negative. You will see possibilities and opportunities where otherwise you would have seen discouragement and failure.

Although negatives and positives exist in almost every situation around us, making it impossible to not bump into them, it is our dominant thought that determines their degree of influence on us. Do you believe Michael Jordon, who is considered one of the greatest basketball players, would have reached the height of his success without focusing on the game? The game was his focus and passion. What do you suppose was his dominant thought? What do you suppose he thought about more often than not? He came to be associated with the game of basketball in so much that it is difficult to think about basketball without thinking of Michael Jordon. You don't reach those levels of success without having a dominant thought that motivates and drives you.

Reverend Billy Graham is considered one of the greatest evangelists of our time. It is said that he has preached to more people than anyone else in the history of the Church. What do you believe consumed his thought world—sports, music or some other entertainment interest? He became a powerful preacher because he had dominant thoughts about reaching the world with the gospel, and that fueled his passion and held his focus. The apostle Paul himself said that because he was consumed with thoughts of the excellence of Christ, he pushed ahead toward this excellence, leaving unnecessary things behind (Philippians 3:8–14).

If people feel driven, they are driven by a dominant thought. People who are confused about what they really want to be or achieve in life do not have a central focus or dominant thoughts. These are the thoughts that will consume them, mobilize their internal energy, set them on fire and define both them and their mission in life.

Third is the issue of *consistent thinking*. The song "I Believe I Can Fly," by Robert Kelly, is fitting here. Merely believing something gets you nowhere; you have to internalize it into a dominant thought, meaning you constantly think about it every day and night until it consumes you and sets you ablaze. Until every string of thought in your mental world vibrates in harmony with your dominant thought you have not yet establish a true focus for thinking. Dominant thoughts give birth to zeal, and zeal leads to mobilization of energy for action. With zeal you break limits, extend yourself, cross boundaries, overcome obstacles and achieve challenging goals.

What are your dominant thoughts? What are the thoughts that consume you each day? Do you feel driven toward some goal by your thoughts? Do you feel that although you are living in the present, the eyes of your mind are beyond the here and the now and are focused on what you are moving toward accomplishing? More importantly, are your dominant thoughts moving you forward, or are they holding you in a crippling position? No one should live his or her life without the passion and zeal to move his or her life forward productively.

The moment you develop and cultivate a dominant thought pattern about something good and productive is the moment everything changes in your life. From that moment onward everything else in your life is influenced by your dominant thought pattern and is consequently drawn into the centre of your mental gravity. Remember, earlier we noted that one of the operating principles of the mind is that it operates effectively through dominant thought patterns. Knowing this allows us the opportunity to work along with our mind, not against it.

Conclusion

We are not helpless beings subjected to negative and limiting thoughts but can actually bring our thought world under supervisory and executive control. Not only can we interrogate and evaluate our own thinking; we have the ability to extend our thinking beyond limits imposed on our minds by unsupportive and redundant thinking. Change in our lives is contingent on our ability to supervise and direct our own thought world.

In the next chapter we take you to the final step of your journey in discovering the eagle within.

chapter eleven

WHERE EAGLES *Fly*

*Accepting ourselves for who we are in the present is
only the beginning of the story, not the end. We must cultivate attributes
and define ourselves in terms of what we can be and who we can become.*

This final chapter takes you through the final lap of your journey on discovering the eagle within. The fact that you have come this far in the book suggests that you are ready to go where eagles fly.

Create a Personal Brand Experience for You

Discovering the eagle within does not stop with expanding the limits of your mind; it involves creating a "brand experience" within you. This brand experience is not something you experience from without but something you intentionally and thoughtfully create and launch from within.

Throughout our lives we experience many things. Some of these experiences are good and others bad. For the most part, our experiences in the world are reactive. What we think we are experiencing is really our reaction to our own perceptions of the events in the world. Although these perceptions and reactions occur within the domain of our consciousness, most people don't realize they can actually manage them so that their experience of the world is less negative. We can channel the capacities within us to reshape our experiences, particularly our experience of ourselves.

For many people experiencing themselves is the last thing they would want to do. They believe there is nothing exciting or important about themselves to be experienced in any meaningful way. Consequently, unless they experience something from outside themselves they live lives without any meaningful experiences.

In this final section we invite you to experience yourself in a brand new way. We invite you to the "brand experience" of you.

The Purpose of Branding

Branding is not a new practice. Branding to show ownership of cattle has been around for centuries. Products used in trading were also branded or labeled to identify their sellers and to convey particular meanings to potential buyers or customers. Companies today have followed the same practice of creating brands so that their product is distinguished from other similar products as well as to create a particular impression on consumers.

The modern concept of branding goes further and does more than merely distinguish a particular product from other similar products on the market. It conveys a specific message as well as a brand experience to consumers. There are many products on the market that function almost the same way, making it hard for consumers to select one above the other. Furthermore, because some competing brands are so similar in terms of their functionality, it makes it hard for a company to communicate their product's unique benefits to potential customers. To overcome this challenge some companies have turned to creative strategies through which they carefully create a strong, memorable identity for their image and products. The purpose of this process is to communicate a brand image or "brand experience" to the mind of consumers.

When a company speaks of a "brand experience" it is usually referring to the customer's interactive experience with the brand. This means every time a customer interacts with the product his or her overall perception of it is pleasing and satisfying.

Why do people want to buy a brand name product when it is often more expensive than other similar products? The answer will no doubt include their particular experience with the product. While many aspects of a brand may not be unique to the brand itself, the particular way in which these features are brought together and integrated is unique, allowing for a particular customer experience.

When a company creates a brand and wants its customers to experience that brand in positive ways, it takes care in how the product is developed, packaged, marketed and sold. This means everything about the product, from its design, packaging, marketing, looks and feel to how it performs, presents the customer with an experience that imprints an impression of quality in his or her mind about this particular brand that is not easily shaken.

Every company knows that a brand is not an easy thing to build. First, the company needs to create appeal and interest in its product and attract the attention of people to its brand. Second, merely creating appeal and interest and attracting attention to its brand is not enough; these can easily diminish. A company needs to go further and hold the customers' attention and interest on the brand. This means the company needs to positively affect customers' perception and influence their opinions and beliefs about the product. To do this the brand needs to satisfy and meet every expectation of the consumer. Third, a company needs to have people believe and trust in the greatness of the brand. When compared to competing brands, in the mind of the customer, this brand communicates a sense of superiority and excellence. For a company, then, its brand is everything; it conveys to consumers the company's culture as well as what it aims to accomplish.

When a company creates and launches a brand, it not only strategically positions the brand in the market and in the customer's mind; it actually makes a promise to its customers. In this the brand represents the company's promise that tells consumers that the company is able to meet their needs as well as provide them with a high quality product that is hard to beat.

Several years ago a Kirby vacuum salesman came to our home. Although we had just bought a new vacuum and thought we did not need another, we courteously let him in with the intent to merely listen to him and then dismiss him. Once in he introduced us to the Kirby brand of vacuum and went on to demonstrate its features, effectiveness and superiority. He gave us an experience of the Kirby brand that clearly outshone all the features of the new vacuum we had. Interestingly, not once did the salesman communicate any indifference toward our vacuum; he simply demonstrated the functionality and superiority of his product. Although his vacuum was much more expensive than the one we had bought, we purchased it, because it gave us an experience that was worth investing in. It lasted for many years. Today we still talk about the quality of our Kirby vacuum.

Your Personal Branding

In much the same way that a company works hard to create a brand experience for its customers, people can create a personal brand experience for themselves. Once developed, a personal brand image creates your expectations of you. It defines who you are in the here and now as well as where you can go and what you can become and how to get there. It also communicates to you as well as to others your values, how you operate and how you are different from everyone else.

Your brand image is a promise to yourself that you must keep. Your personal brand experience is everything about you—spiritual, emotional, intellectual, volitional, social and physical—that you can experience and that converges in a way that makes you feel that you are here on earth for a divine purpose. Your personal brand integrates every dimension of who you are and desire to be into a coherent representation that you as well as others begin to experience. It is what you experience about being a unique creation of God.

This experience emerges not only from the integrative functioning of the various capacities within you but also from the perceptions, expectations, opinions and beliefs you are able to create about you. What's more, this "brand experience" goes beyond you to influence what people experience in their contact and interactions with you.

Consider these questions: What beneficial experience do people have when they interact with me? How would people describe their experience after interacting with me?

People do experience us in ways we wouldn't like them to. We also experience ourselves more times than not in ways we do not like. The good news is, we can do something about our experience of ourselves and the experience people have of us. If these experiences are positive and good, they can be improved to levels where, like a good brand, we move the masses and eliminate the competition.

Your personal branding experience is your opportunity to aspire and achieve. It is your personal authority to chart a new path for you. This is because you are able to see and experience yourself from the inside. When you know who you are and what you are capable of from the inside, you come to realize that setbacks and challenges are temporary events that serve as indicators of the journey you have been on and are not final destinations in and of themselves.

Remember that a brand experience both creates expectations and meets expectations. Here your expectations of you are rooted not so much in your past but in a new knowledge of who you are and what you are capable of as a human being. You can call your personal brand experience your true identity. In the same way that a company's brand is its identity, your personal brand experience is yours. With it you come to see yourself clearer and know yourself better.

It is practically impossible for anyone to arrive at such personal depth and experience of themselves without embracing the truth that they are created by a masterful Creator and invested with attributes and capacities for success and greatness.

Benefits of Branding

When a company works hard to create a brand experience for consumers, it does more than sell a product; it creates a reputation in the minds of consumers who like and enjoy its brand. Once created, this brand experience is not easily destroyed. If a defect is found in its product, for example, the company's reputation will not be easily destroyed; neither will the faith of its customers be quickly shaken. Because it has been consistent in the delivery of a brand experience, its customers will be willing to give the company reasonable time to resolve the problem.

An example of this is Toyota. In 2010 the company was plagued with several defects in particular models of its vehicles, which led to a massive recall. The company that had promised quality and excellence in its brand was failing to hold up its end of the bargain. However, the Toyota brand experience was so valued in the minds of consumers that customers considered these problems temporary setbacks and were willing to give Toyota the chance to fix what was wrong. Customers never lost their faith in the Toyota brand amidst these challenges. In fact, at the time of the writing of this book, Toyota's reputation as one of the world's most valued and trusted brand is unscarred.

Another example is the national scandal Johnson & Johnson and one of its subsidiary pharmaceutical companies faced in 1982 when several deaths were reported from poisoned Tylenol capsules. This resulted in a nationwide recall of millions of Tylenol products. Today the Tylenol brand is still with us and alive and is even more popular than it was in 1982. How do we explain this? Although this was a significant setback for Johnson & Johnson, had it not been for its strong brand value people would not have given the company another chance and the company would not have survived the crisis. This is why, as we noted earlier, for a company a brand is everything.

Now consider a less reputable company, a company that gave customers no particular brand experience or a lesser brand experience. If products from this company begin failing, what is the probability that customers will give it a second or third chance?

If you think this only applies to companies you are mistaken. The type of brand experience we create for ourselves determines whether or not we lose faith in ourselves and our ability when we have setbacks and failures in our lives. If we have created a good brand experience for ourselves—which means we are comfortable with our ability to accomplish the things we set our minds on, with our God-given potential for change and growth, and with our ability to relate to and positively impact others—then we will be more inclined to give ourselves a second chance when we fail at something. Setbacks and failures will be seen not as compatible with who we have become or are becoming but merely as bumps in the road resulting from our imperfection. We will be aware that we possess the ability to do better and go farther. For that reason, brief setbacks and failures will be perceived not as self-defining factors that tell us who we are but rather who we are not. When we fail at something and say to ourselves that we can do better, what we are actually telling ourselves is "This is not who I am. This failure does not demonstrate what I am truly capable of but merely what I need to do better."

Why do we need to create a personal brand experience? This question has been partially answered when we mentioned that having a brand experience safeguards our self-reputation. It makes it easier to trust our ability and forgive ourselves for mistakes and imperfections. There is another important benefit. Most marketing experts believe that when a company builds a brand they are actually building long-term sustainable growth within a segment of the market. By providing consumers with a brand experience, a company in effect strategically positions its product in the market and thus attains its sustainable long-term growth. With both companies and people, long-term sustainable growth and branding appear to be inherently linked together.

Some brands have survived many years, while others have been eliminated from the market. Pepsi and Coca Cola are soft drinks brands that have been around for many years, and their products continue to be drinks of choice for millions. There are also many soap and detergent brands that have survived the times. They survive and continue to do so because they have created long-term sustainable growth with their brand image and the experience this image communicates to consumers. The extent of the faithfulness of these consumers to these brands is what is referred to as "brand loyalty."

By the same token, people who have developed a personal brand image have a better chance of overcoming obstacles as well as setting and achieving challenging goals. They are able to do so amidst life's challenges, because that is what a good brand image does. It solicits and holds our loyalty.

While the possibility of giving up on the pursuit of a demanding goal is constantly before you, it is the knowledge that you have what it takes to attain it that helps you persevere toward its attainment. You have become loyal to your pursuit because you know you have been created for a purpose. In your mind you already have an imprint of your capability and have developed some level of trust in your own God-given ability to achieve something great. It is with these imprints or, more accurately, your inner personal brand experience of who you are and are capable of becoming that moves you forward in spite of overwhelming challenges in the present. In this, your growth toward greatness or an achievement is sustained because of your knowledge that you have a purpose along with your inner experience of what you are capable of doing.

Creating Your Branding Effect on You

In order to influence consumers' behaviour, a company needs to understand consumers on at least two different levels. The first level has to do with the consumer as an individual. On this level a company needs to understand how the consumer thinks, feels, reasons and makes choices between competing market alternatives. The second level has to do with the consumer as an individual who is part of an environmental context and as such is influenced by factors and dynamics within his or her environment. However, while these levels of consumer knowledge is important, a company must go farther and understand how the consumer processes marketing information and makes marketing decisions. If a company fails to understand these attributes and dynamics about consumers' behaviour, it will be ineffective in reaching potential customers with its products. Once a company understands the nature of the consumer, it can now develop and market a brand that will not only meet consumers' expectations but create a positive effect or experience on potential customers. This is what is referred to as the "consumer or branding effect."

The example of the branding effect fits well with discovering and launching you. It is not until you begin understanding yourself on multiple levels that you are ready to create a brand experience that is uniquely you that others can come to know and also positively experience. Creating a personal brand experience for you is one sure way you can position yourself in the midst of change and challenges.

Your personal brand challenges you to maintain consistent growth and development. People who feel they are stagnant in their lives and that life is boring and dull are those who are not growing or developing. Having a personal brand image suggests you are experiencing yourself at a new and higher level. This experience of yourself is linked to your experience of growing and becoming. It is associated with your belief in your capacity to accomplish something worthwhile.

The question to address now is "How do I experience who I am, what I am capable of and what I can become?" There are several things you will need to do. First you need to discover or create a personal *appeal*. If something is appealing it evokes or attracts your attention and interest.

Consider how you would answer the following questions:
• How interested do you feel about yourself?
(*How much interest do I have in me?*)
• What about you do you find most appealing, arousing and interesting?
(*Is there something about me that I find appealing, arousing and interesting?*)
• What about you attracts your interest to yourself?
(*Is there something about me that capture my interest?*)

Among the first things that influence our decision to buy a product is its appeal. The appealing features of a product attract consumers' attention to the product, therefore increasing its ability to be sold. The human brain is responsive to things that it finds attractive and appealing. Our emotions are very evaluative, and companies are very much aware of that and do everything they can to capture and hold our attention and interest by making their products appealing. In this, the appealing features of a product determine how long it sits in the seller's establishment.

In the same way there is an association between how you appeal to yourself and your ability to move your life forward effectively. People who don't like anything about themselves will have difficulty setting goals and reaching forward toward their attainment. The key to creating a personal brand experience is first to discover something about you that you find interesting and attractive. It does not matter where in life you are or how you have come to view yourself and your ability; there is definitely something about you that is attractive and appealing, and you need to put your finger on it. Keep in mind that you are not an accident but a creation with purpose. If you cannot find anything appealing and attractive about yourself, then you need to create it. This involves changing something about yourself that you feel could be more appealing to you.

Sometimes what blocks our vision of what is appealing about us is our own view of ourselves. We tend to focus on our weaknesses and failures rather that our strengths and successes. We often look down on our strengths as insignificant when compared with those of others. To create or uncover our personal appeal we will need to begin appreciating our own unique strengths and differences. These are what make us unique. It is when we are able to recognize these that our greatest potential will emerge.

The second thing you need to do is discover or create your personal *style*. Style means the distinct way something is done or expressed rather than what is done. We live in a society in which uniqueness is out of fashion and where people go to extreme lengths to conform to and be like others. We like to wear and be associated with other people's name brands, while at the same time our own uniqueness and style are buried in the sand. One of the mistakes people make is to look outside themselves for uniqueness and greatness when all the time these attributes are staring them in the face.

While there is nothing inherently wrong in wearing and using other people's brand, we must recognize that in this they are communicating their own personal styles as well as their personal brands. It is by discovering or creating and communicating their own style and brand that they move their lives forward toward financial success.

You are as unique and as great as they come, and recognizing this is your first step in creating a "you brand" experience. Going forward, then, begin changing the way you approach life. Change the way you think about your experiences. Instead of seeing the negative in your experiences, begin seeing the positive. If you did things carelessly, begin being more meticulous. If you were unorganized, try becoming more organized. If you were accustomed to putting things off until tomorrow, try doing what needs to be done today. If you never paid careful attention to how you appeared in public, try putting more detail and attention into your appearance. If you never paid attention to planning and details, try putting plans in place for projects and begin paying careful attention to details. If you were never committed to anything, begin showing commitment to the things you value. If you are accustomed to arriving late for appointments and tasks, start being more punctual. If you never paid attention to how you communicate with others, begin paying attention and make improvements where you see flaws.

Remember, style is not what you do but how you do what you do. More importantly, remember you are doing all this to create an appeal to yourself, not necessarily to others. Your impact on others will and should be a natural outcome of your own appeal to yourself. This is because your style is like something you wear. Others will see it and be drawn to or will be repelled by it.

The third thing you need to do is develop *persistence*. You need to remember that failure is a part of brand building. We are all plagued with imperfections and will fail several times before we succeed at the things we want to accomplish. Being resolute and determined are attributes that are critical to brand building. Without these you cannot hope to improve yourself and take your life to new heights. It is these attributes that keep you going in the face of challenges. Self-development and growth are not easy achievements and are not accomplished overnight. These are processes and lifelong pursuits.

One student, repeating a course after failing it three times, thought she was nothing but a failure. Smiling, her teacher told her, "My dear, you are not a failure; if you were you would not be still trying to succeed. In fact, this shows that you have tenacity, a strength that many people lack." Had it not been for this teacher this significant strength would have gone unnoticed by the student. The fourth time around, the student passed the course.

The fourth thing to do is develop the philosophy of mind that your personal branding is your *life investment.* Long before a company launches a brand it invests time and other resources into creating and perfecting all aspects of it. Companies do this because, as we have noted before, they are concerned about strategically positioning their product in the market for long-term and sustainable growth.

Investing in yourself means utilizing all resources necessary to develop your mind, refine your personality, reshape your thinking and develop your knowledge and skills. In addition, investing in yourself means becoming an expert in you. This means reflecting more on what you do and how well you do it. As you do this you will find that you will begin to gain more knowledge about yourself. As you begin gaining new knowledge about yourself you can begin making changes in those areas that you see need improvement and change.

Another way of gaining knowledge about yourself is to listen to what people are saying about you. Do not ignore the comments and statements others make about you, even in fun. Sometimes what people say about us and to us in jest emerges from a much deeper level of their consciousness. It is important to process and compare what is being said with what you are learning about yourself and again make positive changes where necessary. This in no way means you must go around analyzing everything and every joke others make about you. All that is being said here is that you must be reflective.

Remember that behaviours and perceptions are formed and can always be changed or modified; no one is doomed to any particular behaviour or perception for life. You are doomed to them only if you fail to recognize and make necessary changes. Everything you do to improve yourself for you is an investment. The degree of your investment in yourself determines your own branding experience as well as your growth sustainability.

The fifth and final thing you need to do in creating your personal brand experience is learn to *enjoy* you. On a scale of one to ten (ten being high and one being low), how much do you enjoy your own company? If you do not enjoy a product. what are the chances you will go out and purchase it or even sell it?

Does not the Bible tell us that we must love others as we love ourselves? Does it not say that we should do to others what we would really like them to do to us? Maybe you have read this many times and like others have missed the message. The premise for loving others is love for self. While there is dysfunctional self-love, this does not mean there is no authentic productive God-centred love for self.

Consider how you would answer the following questions:
- How much time do you spend with you away from others?
- Do you do things by yourself that you find interesting and enjoyable or do you always wish someone else was with you?
- Do you find your own company boring and uninteresting?
- Do you hate going places by yourself and always wish someone was with you?
- Do you always find it discomforting when you are by yourself?

When we enjoy something we get pleasure from it. People who cannot enjoy their own company or find pleasure in themselves will have difficulty sharing who they are with others or finding real pleasure in other people. It is who we are and have come to be acquainted with that we share with others. If we don't know who we are, have not had the privilege of actually meeting and being in and enjoying our own company, we really don't have much to share with others. Could this be one of the reasons why, after God created Adam, God allowed him some time to get acquainted with himself and his environment before creating the woman? Creating a brand experience requires that you first get to know and enjoy you. What would be your reaction if you learned that the product a salesman is trying to convince you to buy is not a favourite of his? In fact, instead of using the product he is selling, he privately uses a similar product from another company.

Learn to self-reflect. Spend some time by yourself away from the crowd and get to know who you really are and what about yourself you would love to build and grow into greatness. Begin identifying the little things about you that make you unique and different from others. Take a new and different look at yourself and begin thanking God for the small things that make you different and unique. Remember, every great and massive structure is built from small components. It is these small differences and unique features about yourself that when brought together move you toward greatness and success. In fact, as you begin learning and knowing more about yourself it becomes easier and more effective to share yourself with others. So then, instead of complaining about what you don't like about yourself, begin enjoying yourself in ways you have never done. You will find that your relationships and interactions with others will take on new meaning as you begin enjoying yourself.

Develop a Personal Philosophy of Life Statement

While creating a personal brand experience is a necessary component of the experience of change, we must go further and develop a personal philosophy of life. Initiating and making change is good, but change needs to be rooted in a philosophy of life.

A personal philosophy of life provides the rationale for change. It does this by helping you understand why you do the things you do. Why would you pick yourself up after failing at a task several times? Why would you set forth goals for your future that are bigger and more challenging than the way things are in the present and put plans in place to achieve them? The answer to each of these questions is rooted in your philosophy of life. For example, according to your philosophy of life you believe that your ability is not set in stone but can be improved upon; therefore, if you improve on your ability you will succeed at something you repeatedly failed at. Based on your philosophy of life, the future is not set or predetermined in any particular way; therefore you can always make goals, set plans in place and work toward their attainment.

Your philosophy of life also provides continual support for the changes you have made or will make. The changes you make will be challenged by either circumstances or your past experiences. Your personal philosophy of life will provide the road map through the maze of conflicting thoughts and feelings. When you fail, you will know that your failure is not self-defining. When you lose material possessions, you will know that these are mere life resources, not self-defining attributes. When you become sad, you will know that many of your feelings about the things in life are constructed from your perceptions and therefore can always be modified.

A personal philosophy of life comprises the core values and propositions for life that cut across the major areas of our life and personhood. Although a personal philosophy of life will vary from person to person due to different life experiences, there are core values and propositions that must be identified and use as guides for life. Your personal philosophy of life will include but not limited to the following items:

- Because you are created in the image of God you have a divine imperative to be productive and successful in the things you do and become.
- Your ability is not set but can be developed.
- Failure is not self-defining.
- Happiness is not something that happens to you but is derived from your own interpretation of events.
- Life has purpose and value.
- It is God's wish that you be successful.
- Your choices should be underlined by your core values.
- Your perceptions of your circumstances become your reality.
- Failures are not end goals, merely bumps on the journey.
- Meaning in life is constructed from within the mind.
- People really want to do good but often do evil.
- Possessing things is important but not self-defining.
- The future is not predetermined.
- People can change.

A philosophy of life statement should not be very long; a paragraph is appropriate. Furthermore, you do not need to include everything in the list given, only the ones that you feel are more self-defining for you. Write your personal philosophy of life statement in the present tense and in the first person voice. It is best to begin with the words *I believe*. The second part of each statement must begin with the word *therefore*. The adverb *therefore* is used here to introduce a logical conclusion following your statement of belief.

Here are examples of personal philosophy of life statements:

I believe the future is not set in any particular way; therefore I can move my life in the direction that seems more productive, meaningful and appealing to me. The things I possess are important to me, but they do not define who I am or what I can be; therefore if I should lose them I will not lose who I am or who I can become. My ability is not set; it can always be improved on. Therefore whatever I failed at now I can succeed at later.

I believe I am a unique person, created in the image of God; therefore my life must always move toward God and the things that bring glory to him. With God-given abilities invested in me I believe I can set and reach my goals and be successful in what I do.

Attract the Right People into Your Life

There is a saying "Show me your friends and I will tell you who you are." The people we hang out with and are closely associated with usually share some common attributes with us. In other words, we are like them in some ways.

Eagles are birds that do not have overwhelming need to hang out with other birds. There are birds that usually fly solo. This by no means suggests that you must be a loner. Rather, you must begin selecting who you hang out with and who you attract into your life. The people you are closely associated with and even like exert influence on you, what you become, what you do, how far in life you go and even how you think. Examine the association you have with others, the influence they have on your thinking and behaviour, and their contributions to your growth and growth potential.

Attracting the right people to your life is not an automatic process; neither is it some metaphysical exercise of mind power. It begins only when you are able to recognize your own characteristics, value and uniqueness and appreciate what you have to offer. Until then, you will attract people and create circumstances in your life that will reinforce the lowered value you've placed on yourself. As the cliché says, "Misery loves company." If you can see only failures in your life, you will always tend to be drawn to people who are failures.

How is it that some people seem to always meet the "right" people while others seem to only attract those who are more negative and unproductive? This happens because people tend to be more attracted to people who are like themselves.

How do you go about attracting the right people into your life? More importantly, what is meant by *the right people*? In this case, the right people are individuals who can contribute positively to the goals we have in life and the philosophy of life we embrace.

Human beings are social beings. The social aspect of who we are goes deeper than just merely desiring to be with others; we want to be with people who have similar attributes to us. People who lack ambition and determination to move their lives forward usually feel more comfortable with individuals with similar characteristics. This may be because they understand each other, can affirm and validate each other and can talk about similar things. They usually don't challenge each other to move forward or make each other feel uncomfortable for having no life goal or ambition. By the same token, those with ambition and desire to move their lives forward need to attract like-minded people into their lives.

Unfortunately, however, sometimes positive-minded and ambitious people find themselves in the wrong company, among people who lack ambition, motivation, and resolve to move their lives forward productively. The people they find themselves among are satisfied with what is, rather than with what can be. They think like chickens rather than like eagles and stay the course and maintain the status quo rather than charting new paths and challenging the unknown.

Let's do a brief exercise to determine who the right people are. Take a pen and notepad and write down at least seven characteristics you admire in people you consider productive and successful and who you would love to associate with.

Now be honest and real and ask yourself how many of these characteristics you possess.

Your next task is to write down the characteristics of the people you mostly hang around and are associated with.

Now ask yourself how many of their characteristics match your own. What you will begin to notice is that you are attracted to people who are like you.

It may be difficult to see the negative and unproductive characteristics of others in yourself, and you may even deny that you are like the people you attract. Therefore, to begin this process of self-change you must be honest and real with yourself. Ask yourself if you believe you possess the type of characteristics and attributes that successful and positive people would admire, value and be attracted to. Are you the type of person that people would like to work with and desire to emulate?

So then, to begin changing it is important that you do a bit of data collection on yourself. Find out how people see you and how they describe you to others. From this data you will know if people consider you negative or positive, open-minded or closed-minded, mature or immature, boring or interesting, intelligent or uninformed, confident or insecure, and so on. In order to begin attracting the right people into your life you need to start with you. This means begin changing yourself to be like the person you would like to attract into your life.

There are times when you really believe you can fly but the crowd you are in does not provide you with the momentum necessary for flight beyond a few feet off the ground. The characteristics they possess work to restrain your flight ability and cripple your growth potential. It is not that you don't possess flight and soaring abilities; it is just that the unproductive and limited conversations and perspectives you are surrounded with make it hard for you to recognize your true potential. When the crowd you associate with doesn't think like you do, their influence bears hard upon your capacity to move out of their confined and limited domesticated world. You can recognize this because they provide you with little or no growth stimulation. Their language and conversations are limited to the everyday routine issues they cannot see beyond. Because their characteristics do not match your own, more times than not you are left with feelings of confusion. Breaking from the influence of this company requires that you do several things.

Develop your own productive rituals or routines: It is easy to adapt to the attitudes of the people we hang out with. To break free and begin attracting the right people in our lives we need to develop productive routines or rituals. Remember. a ritual or routine is any prescribed pattern or practice of behaviour. They keep us on certain path and identify us with particular company.

If you want to attract ambitious, forward thinking and progressive people in your life, develop rituals and routines that demonstrate those qualities about you. For example, develop the habit of reading productive materials. Your knowledge base will begin to expand, and the content and nature of your conversation will begin changing. By reading you not only increase your knowledge base; you also learn new words which will expand your vocabulary. Consider joining a local library or buying books that will increase your knowledge and understanding on particular subjects that will work to increase your general and conversational intelligence. You can also develop the routine of listening to good speech to improve on your own speaking and communication ability. Another productive habit you can cultivate is thoughtful reflection about your life course. A habit of reflecting on your own behaviour and thinking increases self-knowledge and encourages change. In addition, consider becoming more acquainted with the Bible. It contains a wealth of knowledge about God, relationships, life and living. As your knowledge of Scriptures increase so will your knowledge of life.

Be growth-oriented: To be growth-oriented means having a forward-thinking mentality. Try to improve on everything you do. Embrace the belief that humans were created to grow Godward and upward, not backward or downward. Believe that frustration and boredom are signs that you need to develop and grow from where you are. Stop limiting your thinking to what is. Think of how you can turn what is, regardless of the state of affairs, into something better.

Do not be overly discouraged by present failures and mishaps but think of how you can learn from them to make better decisions in the future. See failures as an opportunity for change and growth. Begin seeing opportunity for change and growth in every negative situation. See yourself on a continuum of growth, destined to move your life from failures and disappointments to success and productivity. Always keep in mind that life is filled with disappointments and that these will always be present. Life's greatest accomplishments are usually those that are achieved in spite of the challenges encountered. It is the pain and hurts encountered along the journey that determine the level of joy associated with the accomplishment.

Start striving for excellence: Move your life beyond mediocrity. Stop being satisfied with less than excellence. Excellence is not perfection but is the closest we humans can come to it. Begin taking pride in what you do and begin doing what you do with a sense of excellence. The Scripture says, "*Whatever your hand finds to do, do it with your might*" (Ecclesiastes 9:10). This means to put effort and quality in your work.

Start identifying your skills and begin a course of self-improvement. If you speak in public, tell yourself that you need to develop and sharpen your speaking skills. If you play an instrument, tell yourself you need to master your playing skills. If you write, tell yourself you need to develop and improve your writing skills. Whatever your skills are and whatever level they are at, take the responsibility and the initiative to get them to the next level. Develop the mentality that you must always outdo your last performance, no matter how good it was. A great runner who sets a world record trains to beat his or her own record the next time. Your best is always in the past, not in the present or the future; excellence, on the other hand, is still ahead. Let this become your statement of the pursuit of excellence.

Be Open-Minded: To be open-minded is to be receptive to new and different ideas. This does not mean you must accept and embrace all new ideas as true. On the contrary, open-mindedness means that you are willing to listen, respect and evaluate the ideas of other people regardless of what their ideas might be. When you are open-minded you realize that not all people think like you, believe like you or hold the same worldview as you. But in spite of how weird their views

251

seem or how wrong you think they are, you are ready to listen to them and to give them an opportunity to share their opinions. By allowing them the opportunity to articulate their thoughts you open the channel for a mutual exchange of ideas. You cannot hope to convince anyone of your beliefs if you do not give them an opportunity and the respect to communicate theirs.

To be closed-minded is to be unreceptive and intolerant of the ideas of others. You are resistant to new ideas or ideas that challenge your own. You believe your ideas are absolutely correct and no one can teach you anything. Even though you might say others can teach you, because you are closed-minded you limit your own learning potential.

Closed-minded people only attract closed-minded people, and they never learn anything new. In addition, closed-minded people are usually redundant and in-the-box thinkers. They recycle the same old and often outmoded ideas. I think at the core they are resistant to new ideas because of the fear that they might be wrong or be unable to defend what they have so long believed. Even if a closed-minded person has truth, he or she will be unable to share it effectively with others simply because he or she has already locked others out.

Begin setting big but realistic goals: Stop thinking small and begin setting realistically big goals. To begin, your goal has to be clear and specific. Take a pen and paper or, better yet, your computer, tablet or smart phone and type in a goal you would love to achieve in two to five years. Remember from past discussions that the very thought of achieving the goal must infuse desire and passion in you. If this is not the case, you will lose your momentum on the path to your goal. Once you have launched your goal, think about it day and night. You will find that as you think about your goal in this manner your attitude, thinking and behaviour will begin taking new forms. It is when you are burning up on the inside for the achievement of the goal that like-minded people are drawn to you. They want to share their own passion with you because you will be able to identify with them.

Begin to engage yourself in productive conversations: Increase your level of communication skills and what you speak about by engaging in more productive conversations. Seek out people who you know speak productively and intelligently and start conversing with them. Most knowledgeable people really want to share their knowledge in conversations. At first you may feel foolish. but that is normal. Persist, and consider it a learning experience. Remember, though, to engage in high-level conversations you need to give yourself to reading and learning. Begin with reading material that will increase your knowledge about certain topics. For example, read the Bible if you intend to be able to converse about biblical topics. Read scientific material if you wish to increase your knowledge on related subjects. Read, read, read and read more. You can also improve your conversation range by watching documentary television programs.

Develop assertiveness skills: People who are shy and unassertive attract people who are shy and unassertive as well as those who love to control others. Assertiveness skills can be developed and mastered. There are many good books on assertiveness skills available. Here I will list a few guidelines to start you off.

People who are assertive do not talk as if they are in a hurry. Their conversation is unhurried and focused. They select their words with care and consideration. They communicate with clarity on issues, as well as with conviction. While they are sensitive to the feelings of others and take care not to embarrass or hurt others by what they say, they are not afraid to share their thoughts and opinions even if others do not agree with them.

To be assertive is different from being a loudmouth, a bully or aggressive. Loudmouths, bullies and aggressive people are so because they lack assertiveness skills. Assertive people do not have to shout at or put people down to get their point across or win an argument. They are usually composed, calm and not easily angered. They are also good listeners; they listen carefully before they respond. They are careful to ask for clarification if something is ambiguous before giving a response. While they can and do get upset and angry, they do not usually go around exploding on people. They do not fidget with or scratch parts of their body as if they are nervous while communicating with others. Neither do they appear uneasy or apprehensive when their opinions and perspectives are challenged in a conversation. This does not mean that they might not be nervous on the inside. Assertive people do become nervous and even afraid. It is important to remember that courage and assertiveness are exercised not in the absence of fear but in spite of it.

Be self-motivated and self-directed: Do no sit around waiting for people to come to your rescue or feel helpless and hopeless. People who lack motivation can only attract those of the same type. No matter how conditions appear or how meagre your resources, always remember that all it takes is motivation and, more specifically, self-motivation. People who are self-motivated and self-directed are easily recognized by like-minded others.

You know you are self-motivated and self-directed if you don't need people to constantly beg you to move your life forward or push you to be productive. If you have to be pushed and begged, dragged and pulled to initiate or do things for your own benefit, then you lack self-motivation and self-directedness. Consequently you will hate being around those who are self-driven.

To develop self-motivation, you need to start taking initiative and doing things because you have high interest in and love doing them. Let the reason for doing things that benefit you flow from within rather than from incentives people provide to motivate you. In other words, begin doing things because you are driven from the inside rather than being pushed and rewarded by people.

Be God-centred: While there is a drift away from the spiritual as it relates to God in our culture, there remains a deep yearning for something more meaningful. Understanding that we are unique, with capacities and potential beyond any animal, is to believe that we are beings of value, with values. The right people to attract into our lives then are those with values that reflect the true meaning of life and living.

Conclusion

As the apostle Paul tells us, you cannot run well with weights; you must leave them behind if you want to stretch yourself and reach to the goal ahead. This works for spiritual as well as other meaningful goals in life.

To take this seriously you must begin doing a number of things. First, you must start being your own consumer. This means to begin experiencing the best of who you are and can be. You cannot sell yourself to others if you can't appeal to yourself.

Second, you must begin examining the company you associate with and see if they are dragging you down or contributing to your growth potential. Third, cultivate character traits and attributes that define good, productive and successful people. Fourth, believe that you were created and given the greatest gift of all, your mind and its incredible thinking capacities. In fact, nothing I have written in this book about the awesomeness of the human mind would mean anything or make any sense if such a mind was not fashioned by a superior intelligent being.

The ultimate task of a functional mind is to come to know the true reason for which it exists. There is an eternal spark in each of us that can only be ignited by a divine touch. This is the ultimate eagle that resides in each of us, waiting to be discovered. Your fire will never burn and your passion will never be truly realized until you burn with zeal for that which is eternal and which transcends the material of the here and now.

REFERENCES

Allen, J. 2008. *As a Man Thinketh*. New York, NY: Penguin Books.

Bandura, A. 1986. *Social Foundations of Thought and Action: a Social Cognitive Theory*. Englewood Cliffs, NJ: Prentice-Hall.

Begley, S. 2008. *Train Your Mind, Change Your Brain*. New York, NY: Ballantine Books.

Belch, E. G., A. M. Belch, and A. M. Guolla. 2005. *Advertising and Promotion*. 2nd Canadian edition. Toronto, ON: McGraw-Hill Ryerson.

Berger, A. J. 1961. *Bird Study*. New York, NY: John Wiley and Sons.

Berk, L. E. 2007. *Development through the Lifespan*. 4th ed. Boston, MA: Allyn and Bacon.

Carlson, N. R. 2004. *Physiology of Behavior*. 8th ed. Boston, MA: Pearson.

Byrne, R. 2006. *The Secret*. New York, NY: Beyond Words Publishing.

Doidge, N. 2007. *The Brain That Changes Itself*. New York, NY: Penguin Group.

Duffy, K. G., and E. Atwater. 2005. *Psychology for Living, Adjustment Growth and Behavior Today*. 8th ed. Upper Saddler River, NJ: Pearson.

Festinger, L. 1954. "A Theory of Social Comparison Processes." *Human Relations* 7.

Goud, N. H. 2009. *Psychology and Personal Growth*. 8th ed. Boston, MA: Pearson.

Gooders, J. 1975. *The Great Book of Birds*. New York, NY: The Dial Press.

Harmon-Jones, E. S. and P. Winkielman, eds. 2007. *Social Neuroscience*. New York, NY: Guildford Press.

Krause, M., and D. Corts. 2012. *Psychological Science*. Boston, MA: Pearson.

Lewin, K. 1951. *Field Theory in Social Science: Selected Theoretical Papers*. Edited by D. Cartwright. New York, NY: Harper & Row.

Macionis, J. J., N. V. Benokraitis, and B. Ravelli. 2007. *Seeing Ourselves*. 2nd Canadian ed. Toronto, ON: Pearson.

Miller, L. 1990. *Inner Nature*. New York, NY: Ballantine Books.

Myers, D. J., and S. J. Spencer. 2006. *Social Psychology*. 3rd Canadian ed. Toronto, ON: McGraw-Hill/Ryerson.

Siegel, D. *The Developing Mind*. 1999. New York, NY: Guildford Press.

Solomon, R. C., and K. M. Higgins. 2010. *The Big Questions*. 8th ed. Belmont, CA: Wadsworth.

Solomon, M. R. 2013. *Consumer Behavior*. 10th ed. Toronto, ON: Pearson Education.

Thompson, R. F. 1993. *The Brain: A Neuroscience Primer*. 2nd ed. New York, NY: Freeman.

Wetmore, A. 1965. *Water, Prey and Game Birds of North America*. Washington, DC: National Geographic Society.

INDEX

M

Mental workspace 81, 82, 158
Multiple destinies 13, 29

N

Negative thinking 114, 127, 126, 137, 138
Nested destiny 30, 31
Neurological 3, 9, 10, 76, 169
Neuroplasticity 2, 4, 5

O

Operating principles 165, 168, 185, 233

P

Paddling thoughts 112, 113, 115
Paintbrush 81, 83, 85
Personal agency 13, 15, 17, 19, 21, 23, 24, 25, 27, 29, 31, 33, 35
Personal brand 237, 238, 241, 245, 246
Personal interest 20
Positive thinking 231
Potentiality 1, 2, 33, 34, 193

R

Recycle thinking 123, 124
Routine 38, 41, 48, 49, 93, 129, 128, 131, 158, 250

S

Sabotaging 103, 104, 105, 106, 107, 108, 109, 137
Scapegoat 125, 132, 134, 135, 136, 188
Self-fulfilling prophecy 53
Sense of purpose 33, 34, 35, 36, 204, 205
Sensory experience 77
Skill set 25, 26, 29
Social comparison 68, 70, 72, 257
Strategic thinking 129, 133, 134, 151, 152, 153, 154, 187

T

Talons of belief 40, 49, 97, 98, 99, 100, 111

U

Urgency 115, 202, 205, 208, 226, 227

V

Validation 36, 60, 64, 66, 67, 68, 228, 229
Vigilant 155, 157, 160, 161, 162
Vigilant thinking 155, 157, 160, 161, 162
Vision 4, 14, 40, 42, 44, 52, 55, 56, 67, 68, 69, 75, 76, 78, 80, 83, 87, 88, 89, 97, 99, 103, 111, 141, 143, 149, 154, 155, 160, 161, 168, 188, 197, 204, 242
Visionary thinking 141
Vision statement 90, 91, 93
Vision virus 155, 193
Volitional 7, 10, 11, 19, 32, 36, 165, 187, 200, 238

W

Wishful 116, 117, 118